BICENTENNIAL ABROAD

A DECLARATION OF INDEPENDENCE

Donald Moriarty O'Leary

outskirts
press

Outskirts Press, Inc.
http://www.outskirtspress.com

ISBN: 978-1-9772-1897-1

PRINTED IN THE UNITED STATES OF AMERICA

Table of Contents

(Photo) Spring 1973 My Freshman Year of College
With Tom Gibbons, Dave "Deacon" Favalo, and Kelley Corbett

Kingston, Toronto, Watkins Glen-(July 26-28,1973), Arizona State Univ. (Aug. 18-Dec. 20, 1974), SUNY Oswego, Daytona Beach, Cape Cod, N. Carolina (Outward Bound –Aug.8-30,1975)

FINALLY ABROAD!!

3. WINTER (FINAL) SEMESTER- January 25,1976 The College of Europe in Bruges, Belgium, Madame & Ridderstraat 12 (Hotel Europa), Grads & Undergrads, Classes, Town , Pubs, Basketball, Music ,Dance, & Road Trips(Brussels, Amsterdam, Paris, Cologne, Glasgow, Edinburgh, & London)

4. SPRING BREAK- InterRail Pass(March 27-April 26th)…Germany, France, Spain, Morocco (Africa), Monaco/ Monte Carlo, Italy, Switzerland-The Sights, Sounds and Smells………..

5. SEMESTER END- Classes, Final Exams, Visitors, Field Trips (Heidelberg…etc), Graduation, & Going in different directions

6. SUMMER- Germany, Austria, England, Ireland (June 24-August 17) BritRail Pass (August 18-August 25th) Knebworth Fair-All Day Concert…England, Wales, Scotland

7. FALL- InterRail Pass (September 17- October 16th) Denmark, Sweden, Norway, Germany (Oktoberfest-not all fun and beer), Austria, Greece -Athens, Crete, Island of Samos-(October 16-November 10th) to Turkey-Asia (November 10-November 30th)

8. HOMEWARD- Bulgaria, Germany, Belgium, England Bus, Hitch, Lorry, Ferry, Train, Plane and back to the U.S.A., (December 10, 1976) "Barely"….!

9. THE FUTURE- 1978 Trip, '78-'82 San Francisco-(Like Tripping), '82 Trip, '88 Trip, '89….,1990 onward The Family ☺

CHAPTER 1

Introduction

A TRAVEL JOURNAL, A Road or Path to Independence: With Hitching, Highways, Streets, Cobblestone, Autobahn, Ditching, Hiking, Trails, Ropes, Hills, Mountains, Cliffs, Beaches, Lakes/Lochs, Ponds, Seas, Oceans, Islands, Rivers, Canals, Channels, Straits, Customs, Currency, Languages, Trams, Trains, Tubes/ Metros/ Subways, Ships/ Boats/ Ferries/Canoes, Bus Stations, Planes(Parachutes), Airports, Runways, Delays, Detours, Crossroads, Pubs, Clubs, Disco, Hotels, B & B, Dorms, Hostels, Campgrounds, Family, Friends, Strangers, History, Art, Architecture, Windmills, Theatre, Museums ,Castles, Forts, Cathedrals, Temples, Mosques, Breweries, Winery, Ballet, Opera, Plays, Religion, Politics, Sports, Hornets, Bees, Ants, Midges, Mosquitoes, Roaches, Snakes, Slugs, Tents, Boots, Blisters, Backpacks, Sleeping Bags, Haggle, Drugs, Sex and Like Minded Acquaintances, etc.

MY YOUTH

A big part of my youth, I lived in the Tipperary Hill neighborhood of Syracuse, New York, where the main traffic light has the unique distinction of having the GREEN on Top! That's a significant fact of life that the area is quite proud of, going against the norm and all the conventional traffic laws. It signified the Irish Pride as the "IRISH" GREEN was above the "British" Red. Local teenage boys of Irish descent, threw stones at, and constantly broke the original traffic light installed about 1925, until the city allowed the green to be on top! They ultimately built a monument to the Stone Throwers at one of the corners just below the light, and it's become part of a pilgrimage of sorts to visit when one is the area....as it is supposedly the only one of its kind in the whole United States!

I went to elementary school at St. Patrick's ("The Irish"), and high school at Bishop Ludden ("The Gaelic Knights"). I was always proud of my Irish American heritage, where I grew up, and when: the 60's to early 70's. These were good but turbulent times. There were strong neighborhoods with very intense school sports rivalries, changing social values nationally with the civil rights movement, and global upheaval with the Vietnam War on the other side of the world.

ROOTS

Growing up listening to the strong Gaelic Brogues of my mother's family, while on visits to their homes, I wondered about my roots. My family was the O'leary's & Walsh's on my father's side and the Moriarty's & Kilcare's on my mother's side.

These Moriarty's (the local ones) were all from Ireland, they included my grandfather Michael, my aunt Nell, uncle Hugh, and Uncle Gene (a renowned boxer back in his day, who died when I was about six). The Moriarty's emigrated from Gortkelly in County Tipperary, Ireland, and on my mother's mothers side, the Kilcare's were from the neighboring Donaghmore in County Laois (Queens County until the Irish Independence in 1925).

After arriving in the United States, they first settled on Hamilton Street in Tipperary Hill, Syracuse in the early 1900's, very near to what is now known as the Blarney Stone (Pub). Later in life my grandfather, my mother, her two brothers lived near another one of the local establishments a few doors down on Wilbur Avenue, called Nibsy's Pub, named for Nibsy Ryan.

Our family visited these relatives in my youth in the late 1950's and throughout the 60's, and the adults spoke of things foreign yet somehow familiar. I longed then to travel to Ireland and elsewhere, as soon as I was in my late teens and onward. I would come into my own at another local establishment called Coleman's (Pub), as there seemed to be a recurring theme.

Pubs played a big part growing up, listening as a youth to our elders, and then telling our own tale as young adults.

There has always been a romanticized vision and memory of my family and our history, but way back in the late 1800's and early 1900's the world was a harder place. I had done some asking around, looked at old and tattered photos, and had conversations with family members over the years enough to know that our ancestors left their homeland for significant reasons, survival and just the opportunity for a better life. They left family, belongings, neighbors and friends of a lifetime, scraped together enough money to pay the passage to New York, from Queenstown (today's the city of Cobb) their port of departure from Ireland .

It seemed our whole family on my mother's side came over, from the very young siblings to the older parents, with the grown siblings leading the way, and a relative already settled in the States lending support and or place to stay, and a possible job.

ANCESTORS COMING TO AMERICA

After arriving in the USA in 1906, my grandfather worked, lived with the extended family, but something was missing. He went back to Ireland about 1913, on what a an older cousin said was an all American Irish hurling team. While there and visiting the area he grew up in, he looked up an old friend's sister from a neighboring town and county. He met and married her after a short courtship because he was longing for a woman with similar roots.

He went back to the States alone for work, and the bride (and now a mother with a ten month old baby daughter) joined him in 1914.

My mother was born in 1917, her brother John 1915, and younger brother Fergus in 1918. They grew up in that Irish household with my grandfather, and her older sister Kathleen, and her Irish mother Mary Kilcare Moriarty.

Kathleen got sick and died in 1920 at six years old, and in that same year her mother died giving birth to Edward, with the baby dying as well. From what I've heard, it could have been the Spanish Flu which caused their deaths as it did so many others in that era.

On a personal note- I think of my mother, only three years old when she lost her mother, older sister, and just born brother Edward, oh how traumatic and devastating to a three year old little girl, and her brothers only 5 and 2 themselves. It must have been very difficult for the remaining family- a father with three very young children, himself losing his wife and the children losing their mother. The father had to keep a household and his job, with some help from the extended "Irish" family and some neighbors from all over, and all mostly immigrants trying to make ends meet with their own families.

The children needed a full time mother, the father a wife, and apparently another family needed a home for their adult spinster daughter, another Irish immigrant. Within about a year's time they would have a step mother, and from what I have gathered, it was more for convenience than for love.

My mother and her brothers had each other, and focused on school work and I am sure housework as they got a little older. Their father was busy with his job at the local penitentiary as a prison guard, a hard man ultimately, who walked through the neighborhood with his gun which he brought home from his work.

These were very hard years from all I have been told, with the step mother being a very unloving person and probably even worse.

(Photo) 1929 The Michael Moriarty family with Mary Kilcare Moriarty (RIP 1920) image in front. My mother Ann Moriarty, Uncle John , Uncle Fergus, and himself, Michael Moriarty.

After her death, their father would marry again, this time to a neighbor with a son of her own, about the same age as my mother's younger brother.

My mother to get out on her own so to speak, entered the religious order of the Sisters of St. Joseph de Carondelet in Troy, New York. She started this new life to become a Catholic Nun in her young adult years, and was known then as Sister Mary Malachy Moriarty. It would help further her education during her four years in the convent (1938-1942, and ages 21-25), until she left-Thank God- for selfish reasons.

(Photo) Sister Mary Malachy Moriarty, my mother during her "Nun Years" 1938-1942

About three years later, she met and married my father, Arthur O'Leary, and raised her 3 boys, Daniel, Kevin, and myself. My mother went back for a College Degree at Syracuse University (1961) when we were 7,9,and 11 years old, my mother was 44. She started teaching in the Syracuse City School District after graduating, and ultimately became a social worker for the Onondaga County Department of Social Services. My mother was an inspiration, and taught us, by example and through education, that you can do anything, be anybody, and go anywhere!

My father, the classic Irish man, certainly came from a colorful family, especially aunt Loretta O'Leary Walsh's clan from Auburn, New York. There was my aunt Arlene, aunt Ann, uncle Don "Bunk" (I was named after him, as he got killed in a train accident the year before I was born), and my uncle Bill O'Leary. Uncle Bill and his lovely wife Lucille and their two children Billy and Catherine lived near us in Tipp Hill, and his son Billy (Willy) ran the local golf course at Burnet Park, where all of us kids would learn to golf...

These O'Leary's were not as recently from Ireland and didn't speak with a brogue or talk of the old country, as two generations earlier would have, like my great grandfather William O'Leary born approximately 1842 in Ireland and came over about 1870 (died 1913 RIP). Also, my father being 51 years older than myself, our O'Leary cousins were typically almost a full generation older and from a different era.

(Photo) 1905 The Daniel O'Leary family,
my father Arthur W. is front row bottom right.

(Photo) The O'Leary and Walsh clans in Auburn, with friends and family, my father lower left about 17.

My parents were always an inspiration for my search for adventure and education, especially my mother. As a young boy, they bought encyclopedias that I read from front to back, and in particular cherished stories about far off places, and adventures in history. I would relive adventure stories in the local woods, parks, forests, creeks, streams, swamp, lakes, hills, abandoned buildings or properties under construction in our area, both on the East Side of Syracuse where I was born, before moving to The West End of

Syracuse and Tipperary Hill in 1963 at the age of 9, where my mother had grown up!

(Photos) 1961-1975 coming of age with parents, with brothers, up to high school & college grad photos

Actually starting on my own adventures and travels was inspired by all of that....

JOURNALS

In 2011, my daughter Tess was applying for study abroad programs from her College at Hobart William Smith to go to Europe

(Wales)and South America (Argentina). That triggered me looking through some of my old travel memorabilia. And I found my journals from the 1970's, one from 1975 that I kept for an outdoor program called Outward Bound in North Carolina. This program immeasurably impacted how I handled myself and many of the experiences I would encounter. Also, I found a journal I kept for the following year in 1976 when I studied abroad in Bruges, Belgium and travelled extensively after. WOW, these were great finds!!!!!

As I started to read through them, I looked back and remembered with the eyes and mind of a very young man, and college kid again. It was the first time I read through them since I wrote in them, and it gave me some ideas to help inspire, and or caution Tess, who was going to study abroad in Carmarthen, Wales in January 2012, and to Mendoza, Argentina in the Fall of 2012. It would also hold true when her younger sister Zoe would go abroad via her Geology Department at Syracuse University to study for a semester in Dublin, Ireland starting in January 2015, and visit many other places, including Morocco, camel caravanning and snake charming!!!!

They both have had numerous adventures since, and continue to do so. I like to think in my own way, my adventures from the Seventies and after, added a spark or flame, and a strong desire to experience new cultures, people, and places!

The 1970's are more than a memory now after I found the journals that I wrote in while living and travelling in that era.

CHAPTER **2**

Backstory

AFTER A QUICK flashback, some of my more vivid memories were from my mid teens and on, in particular 1971-1976(Ages 16-22).

Getting our driver licenses at 16 and night license by 17, which created more opportunities for extracurricular activities, if you had access to wheels….With our coming of age came more responsibility to work, study (as college was not far away), and the selective service registration for the Vietnam War Draft.

Like all guys that turned 18 in this era, you had to register, which put you into a lottery for selection on who would go to war. Your birth date was randomly picked, and if you were in top 85-95 numbers (birthdays) drawn, there was a great likelihood you could be drafted in 1973-1974. Fortunately, they pulled the numbers, but didn't take the drafts from 1972 on from what we learned later!!!!

The Vietnam War officially ended in 1975, which was monumental during these times, especially for those involved or potentially, and of course their families.

The following year was 1976, an Olympic Year, a Presidential Election Year in the U.S.A., my brother Kevin is marrying Kathy, the New York Yankees look like a team again (sucked from '65 – '75, but still my favorite team, in all of sports), and by the way it's the 200th anniversary of our Country's Independence, "The Bicentennial"!

January 1976, more importantly it's the beginning of my final semester in college. It's not an ordinary semester either, as I am going to study abroad in Europe, and that would be just the beginning.

SUMMER OF 1971: First Real Road Trip

But, before my big trip abroad, in January of '76, I had to prepare and become aware, as well to reflect and contemplate some choices I made, and crossroads I would reach. Some roads we travel down, others we veer off and many we flip a coin, and just go for it!

Thinking of a significant choice I made with one of my best friends in high school, Deacon! We were friends since early in our freshman year of high school, Fall of 1968 when we met the first week of football practices. Deacon looked like a senior, or a coach, as he seemed and looked so mature.

What a bond we had, he was actually only a day older, but he looked about 5 years older. He had a full beard in his early teen years and me with my scraggly whiskers, to go with my pseudo long hair, ha ha. We explored many of the boundaries of the times, both socially and musically, concerts, parties, etc. Deacon, had the best collection of music and sound systems, and I learned more about both, because of him.

We could get beer at 14/15 years old and into bars as well, certain ones anyways. The legal age was 18 in New York back then. I was full grown at that earlier age, height wise anyways, and he was probably a couple years earlier. I was running keg parties by 16/17, and always had an older friend or two, to help with logistics (cars, for example).

I never forgot the time, Deacon and I went to explore New York City (via a ride to New Jersey with a classmate's family), late in summer before our senior year of high school, August 1971. It was also, a great opportunity to take a break from summer football work outs, and just to change the routine from the same old activities, ending my summer job a few days early as well.

Once on our own, by bus from nearby New Jersey into Manhattan, we hit the ground walking, looking at everything, larger than the life we were familiar with. We walked, and walked, stopped, looking around and up, and visiting the New York Public Library, Madison Square Garden, a very seedy and creepy Times Square, The Empire State Tower Building, and Central Park, all iconic images of New York City. That was pretty good start for day one, and we still haven't figured out a place to stay, you know it was getting late, why not save the money, and just hang out at the Port of Authority Bus Station for the night, all night!

It was dark, dirty, smelly, and cavernous, swelling with all walks of life. Those going places, short term, or long range, or waiting around for something to see, or do. It was not a place you could relax in, let's just say….

At about 2:30 a.m. we needed coffee, so we ventured out to an all night eatery. You had to order something to eat with the coffee, so I order a burger with it, and after spending $4.50 for a coffee and a burger, which shocked and pissed me off. It is 1971, and it was usually about $1.00 total, this must have been a late night premium. I went on a hunger strike for the rest of the trip to protest the high prices.

We walk back to the area in the station that we had staked out, and made sure one of us kept an eye open the rest of the night. The amount of characters we saw seemed endless and fluid. Nobody bothered us at all, except there were a lot of edgy stares.

We bounce up slowly, half dazed as the morning commute began in full swing. As we walked out the station, the first person we see, is all beaten up looking, as he had just gotten mugged at the Port Authority, after arriving from West Virginia! Wow, where we had just spent the night!

We were happy to be moving on, more walking and exploring NYC, we made our way to the United Nations building for a walk around tour of our own. After a while there, we start out walking towards a highway, and then hitching to Boston via Connecticut. It was like a puzzle, finding the directions, the correct highway entrances, exits, etc., out of the huge New York City metropolitan area. It was quite an endeavor to get on the correct roadways through the mass of Manhattan and onward.

It was hot and we were exhausted, but young and hopeful. We headed out and in three rides, starting with a short lift barely out of the metro area, to a longer one through Connecticut, with a final ride to the edge of downtown Boston.

We would get in to Boston by early evening/twilight, walking forever it seemed until we found a public phone and calling, until I reached the girl my older brother Dan knew from college at Bowling Green State University, in Ohio. I recall her name was Carol, and it blew her away, but she was not put out, it was so cool. She lived on the same street as, and same block as Fenway Park, home of the Red Sox baseball team.

We had a decent hike ahead of us, as we were on the Charles River, where the band shell is. This being a super hot summer day, and having been up for a day, and a half straight, and never having been to Boston, piece of cake to find her apartment, ha, ha! But, we had just maneuvered in and around New York City the previous day and a half, so it did not faze us at all….

She was very inviting, living with a guy, they were both cool, no other way to put it. We could crash, stay a couple days, "Far Out"! We got some much needed sleep, after getting caught up with our hosts, they made Deacon and I feel like family.

We got a fresh start in the morning, and we looked forward to exploring Boston now. It was much easier to get around, as the scale was not as monumental as NYC. We saw the Prudential Building and went up to the top, Boston Common, Beacon Hill, and of course Fenway Park, walk, walk, walk, and I am still not eating, crazy.

Deacon and I go to Walden Pond the following day, via Cambridge and Harvard, on to Concord, etc. via walking, bus, and hitching. You know I appreciated Thoreau more after visiting here, we walked around, swam in it (photos). We did not follow a guidebook, or a tour, just winging it, maybe one of our English classes finally paid off, or was it History class…

As we headed back to Boston, we got picked up by a "hippie" of sorts, a nice guy, in a VW van, who we got a little high with. I would finally break down and eat, as Deacon bought me an ice cream in the middle of Commonwealth Ave., after we got dropped off right in the heart of the city. Ice Cream was perfect for the day, the moment, and the place, as I was running on fumes. I felt so comfortable, it was a perfect summer day and night.

We would head back to Syracuse tomorrow, summer was winding down. We were again hitching, which was a big part of this adventure and the experience, the independence, low cost, and the freedom! What luck, as we got a ride from the outskirts of Boston, all the way to Syracuse (it must have been our sign: see photo). I remember upon arriving at my house, asking my mother to cook me this enormous meal, but my stomach had shrunk from not eating most of the time we were gone, and I ate about half.

*(Photos) New York City, Boston, Walden Pond
and hitching back to Syracuse 1971*

FALL 1971

Know what the crossroad was, I decided not to play football my senior season and my last year of high school. I was evolving of sorts, long hair, and scraggly beard, marching to my own beat, whatever that was. Deacon contemplated not playing as well, but had a lot of pressure, as he would end up being the team captain. You know the last three years I played, and my two older brothers before me. I would still check out some practices, and all my friends who were still on the team, for example Timmy P. who I had been very tight with since we started as freshman together three years earlier. We shared a lot together and knew each other's family like we were like cousins almost, in fact we called each other "Cuz"!

The tough, stubborn choice I made versus the gladiator type practices, there just had to be more I thought?

The school made me get a haircut, and shave two weeks later when classes started (Catholic school), then the head coach asked me out to the team, and I caved in. My own gut feeling was that I missed it, my friends, etc., but I was in for the worse three plus weeks of my life. I was being ridiculed at team meetings, "Jesus Christ, where's your purse", hippie BS, flower child comments, with the whole team laughing. The instigator was my specific position coach for linemen (wide receivers, tight ends included), who loved putting me through the most rigorous drills, against bigger, and fresher opponents.

I had to sit out the first two games as per league rules, for missing the first couple weeks of practice.

Homecoming was near, and I couldn't play yet, so I got together with few friends to guard the bonfire being prepared for the following day's events. It was a reason to stay out, and up all night, and we might as well enjoy ourselves. The local policeman came by to check on us much later, and even brought us some doughnuts. We (Danny D., myself, and a couple other friends) almost missed him, or him us, as our car windows were all clouded over "and smoke got in our eyes"… it must have been the dew in the air. What an all night event it turned into, a little party got bigger when other friends stopped by!

After being up all night, we strolled in to school the next morning, some other friends kept us away (hid us) from the teachers, administrators, coaches, etc., as we weren't in any shape to go to classes, or be in school.

Well, I had just worked a night shift!!!!!

MY LAST GAME....

I really looked forward to next week's game! I was two weeks behind, plus not much preseason conditioning, but I was still in great shape and ready to go, as my three previous years experience prepared me mentally.

The third game is upon us, I can finally play, and I go into the game in the second quarter, down a touchdown at Nottingham, and on their home field. A new quarterback goes in as well, interesting, but the coaches call the plays, no problem.

There was a running play called on the right side, where I was lined up, and I block down towards the middle. The ball is snapped, and I fire off the line to pick up and block their linebacker away from where our runner is going. Then something goes zinging over my head and OMFG (not a good catholic expression), it was a pass, which they intercepted, and ran it back against us for a touchdown!

All this happened in front of our bench, our fans, my parents, and my brother Kevin, who was home from College.

What The F… just happened, as I walked to the sidelines in disbelief, the assistant coach, my line coach gets in my face, and I told him what I knew. The quarterback comes by, and says it was an audible at the line, a pop pass to O'Leary! I'm O'Leary, and I never practiced that with him, or heard an audible, WTF…It was like the quarterback's first play in the game and he over rides the coach's call with an audible……

Well, the assistant coach blames it on my long hair for not hearing the audible (where the play changes at the line), and I get upset, so he told me sit on the bench, and we'd talk after the game. The head coach comes by, and asks (his turn), what happened, and the assistant, says it was a pass to O'Leary and he didn't hear the call, blah, blah, blah. I tried to explain again, but got interrupted by the assistant and flustered now, yelled to the assistant, "FUCK YOU"!

On the spot, I was kicked off the team and told to take my uniform off. There I am with no jersey on, or shoulder pads, with only my pants on, and I wasn't allowed on the bus after the game.

Fucking devastated, in shock, crying, I was so mad!!!

Probably two to three people besides me know what happened, the two coaches, and the backup quarterback knew what did or didn't happen. It was by the way, my one and only play of my whole senior football season!

Whatever, wherever, or what was the crossroads; not playing football, deciding to come back to the team, dealing every day with the harassment, or the culminating singular play season?

I guess I wanted to make big guy, "adult like" decisions in my life, and it came up to screw me.

FALL OUT

Within a week or two, not having football to go to, I chose other activities on a consistent basis. I remember a few of us talking about going to the Cornell campus in Ithaca, New York for a concert with Rare Earth at Barton Hall. I hitched down early in the late Fall afternoon, but the friends I was hooking up with that drove and had the tickets, got there later and never found me. I wandered the campus all night, in the rain, with no money, after looking for places to sneak in. Finally I crashed on the edge of the campus covered up with leaves, branches, as I felt a certain wastefulness in my mind and body.

As the sun was barely coming up the next morning, I wobbled

towards the road that led back to Syracuse, and started hitching. Thankfully I didn't wait long, as I really had paid my dues for naught, but the adventure...

Things seemed to be tail spinning a bit as it felt aimless for a while, a numbing feeling. It would be ok, hell I was still running the end of the football season keg party, as well as others to follow, since spring of '71, as a junior. Ok, I was not a saint, but I was entrepreneurial!

I had great intention for the future, as I did plan on going to college. I even borrowed my father's brand new "orange Ford Maverick" for a college tour at Niagara University. The first thing I saw was priest, then a nun, then my older brother Kevin...Well, I had just spent thirteen years of my life in religious institutions, and although I loved my brother, I needed my own campus....To follow that I spent the rest of the visit on the Canadian side, and I think I still have some of those fireworks!!!! To top it off, I got a speeding ticket (Almost) driving back, but because I did not have my license on me, the officer told me to mail it in....oops, I forgot, and I never got that ticket!!!! The lesson, no, just DUMB LUCK !!!

CONFESSION

I had a cleansing of sorts at the end of the school year, a confession, if you will, and it partly saved my rear end from not graduating. Some of the junior girls and myself, were off site during school hours, away from the school campus, and upon late return, they would be caught. I was mentioned also, and being the only senior, it was used to hold over my head by the administration, about a suspension, and not graduating.

I had to have the ultimate end of the year sit down with the vice principal. Not an official confessional (Catholic School), if you know what I mean, but anything and everything it seemed from my full four years was brought to bear (the bad stuff, that I had supposedly done).

I can never repeat it all in writing, though there were "RUMORS" of a Nun's Nervous Breakdown, Drugs, Keg Parties, AND OTHER ACTIVITIES!!!!

I had one last hurrah before my senior year ended, and it came out of the blue... A junior girl running for Student Council President for the next year, asked me to introduce her at the school wide assembly on "Ludden Day"! This was the end of the academic year, casual dress, wind down, and move forward day for the upcoming classes.

Thinking quickly and slyly, we snuck into the faculty lounge, grabbed an ashtray and some smokes. We returned towards the gymnasium entrance poised with lighter, ashtray and a cigarette. She lit me up and we casually walked through the length of the gymnasium in front of the whole school, students, faculty, and administrators. As I escorted her, she held the ashtray and we proceeded to the stage and I gave a brief introduction and endorsement of her candidacy, and she won!!!!!!!!!!!!!!!!!

I heard at a later date, some people thought I was smoking something else....had to be a liberal audience, and how "Rumors" get started ☺

I think I gained some clout from my earlier "Confession" that saved me from immediate suspension or expulsion! That and they just wanted me to move on.....

BECAUSE I did graduate on time, maybe a few minutes late ☺

SUMMER OF '72

High School behind me, crazy start to the summer. I was late applying to colleges, and still figuring it out through part of the summer. I hadn't taken my future, and my continuing academics too seriously for a while. I went through more social upheaval in the past school year than at any time cumulatively, not saying I wasn't partly to blame....

A number of friends, and I would take a couple camping trips in the Adirondacks. One in particular, with the greatest Northern Lights display I had ever seen, on the way to Indian Lake, near Malone, NY. I remember pulling over to the side of the road, and just mesmerized by the colorful radiating glows.

What a balls to the walls, blowout party at a friend's family's cabin when we get to our destination. Then we take a jaunt to the local town bar, looking for adventure, to the point where we were part of knockdown, drag out bar fight, which mostly went against us, and more harmlessly finished outside. We were more talk, but we survived, and a great story to re-tell.

On another camping trip, we were not far from where we were going to the Inlet and Old Forge area, in our dear friend Deacon's car, with Timmy P., and Frank L. and a tire flies by us going down a hill. It was our tire, and it wasn't waiting for us…. We luckily didn't crash, found the tire, and pulled one lug nut from each of the other tires to reattach the fourth tire.. Then in the next town, we borrowed some extra lug nuts, so to speak from a banged up car at a local garage. Sometimes, the camping is secondary to the road trip…. But, after we settled in at our campsite did we celebrate!!!!

Summer seemed endless, working outside with some mostly older characters.

In my crew at the County Park "Tree crew", which was an adventure itself. Having a tree cutting competition across from the boat house after a prolonged drinking man's lunch. We had other miscellaneous jobs, like rescuing picnic tables that floated out into the lake (Onondaga Lake),after major flooding of the area, and pulling boats from the bottom of the marina, after the same flood.

FALL '72- SPRING '74

Partying was reflective of my four years in high school up 'til and including my whole 1st year at Alfred State in "Happy Valley." ☺ Having many good friends probably saved me on a few occasions. Someone was always watching out for you and you for them. A few of us had gone from high school to college together, including Deacon, Vince, Dumbo, and I. We meet up with an old teammate from football, a year ahead of us, Tommy G.

Our dorm team, with Bob O', Myself, Deacon, Tommy G., Dumbo, Vince,etc. even won the college intramural football championship together, and shared many other amazing coming of age moments, at concerts, parties, road trips, etc.

Near the end of our freshman year of college we found out there would be no further draft to Vietnam for our age group, Fucking Fantastic, considering my roommates were #'s 3 & 5, and I was # 31. Back then they could still pick the lottery, and up to # 95 (out of the 365 potential birth dates), had a real chance of going from what we knew. The USA was withdrawing from Vietnam, after many years of an undeclared war, and TV coverage on a daily basis covering the atrocities on both sides it seemed. There were serious considerations of Canada and Sweden by me, as popular destinations of the times, as an alternative.

(Photos) Vince, Dumbo, Deacon & I in Buffalo, Syracuse crash bridal shower with Tim P. and Vince E., Va. Beach with Danny D. & Boris and Alfred St. dorm

THE SUMMER OF '73

We started off at a concert in Cornell's stadium, with Deep Purple and ZZ Top, that we snuck into. Deacon, Timmy P. and I with our cooler, saying the guy back in line had the tickets…the guy ends up bolting past at the entrance with security hot in pursuit.

The fun and misadventures would continue as we were up for anything! It would be a real wild time from my perspective, as it was a pretty mind blowing era, so to speak.

We had a great road trip to Virginia Beach for about a week, with seven of us friends camping outside , and a couple days at a motel, and of course the beach and partying. The freedom you feel when there's you and your friends, deciding behavior perhaps that is not the norm in your home setting. We were obviously not alone, as thousands of young people make these pilgrimages every, Spring, Summer, or Winter, it's what you can afford, and the time you make to do it.

The Summer Jam at Watkins Glen was a one day concert and the highlight of 1973, preceded by a couple days of all out partying at the race track, concert site, a proverbial "Lost Weekend". Supposedly 150,000 tickets were sold at $10.00 each, and we had our tickets, but supposedly up to 600,000 people ultimately were in attendance.

The concert itself featured, The Grateful Dead, The Allman Brothers Band, and The Band. My friends and myself, got there a day and a half earlier, and by the time the music started, so many people were literally fried, inside and out it seemed, as the temperature got to 90 degrees. I lost the people I was with and wandered towards the concert site the night before the concert, and rolled up and finally crashed on the edge of a drainage ditch, just outside the venue's entrance, with thousands of people all around me and I just crashed.

I would get a great start the following morning, the day of the music, and hence I got a great spot not far from the stage, near one of the medical tents. They were pretty busy, between the heat, and the excessive indulging, add to that limited access to food, water, etc. It was a survival of sorts, festival 101, but having been to other concerts, it was now all about the music, as I found my friends and enjoyed the day.....

The rest of the summer flew by, ramping up to my second year of college, and plans to take college more seriously after all, I was 19!

What a turn around, as I not only got my best grades in 5 years (high school and my 1st year of college), I applied and got in to Arizona State University, but also had a great time while here at Alfred State.

We would find many new friends off campus, at "The Trailers", where Deacon and I lived and the "The Cabins", and old friends still on campus. We had another, but more off beat intramural football team, while not winning it all, we were still competitive and didn't feel any pain. It brought together many of the off campus community, something to rally around in a fun, but competitive way.

Deacon and I, now roommates off campus, planned a trip at Thanksgiving break to Boston and Vermont. In Boston we visited an old classmate from high school, Patti C. and we went to see the play One Flew over the Cuckoo's Nest. The play was amazing and gut wrenching, and I remember saying they should make a movie about it, and who could play McMurphy? Thinking for a minute, "Jack Nicholson" I said...no lie! The movie would come out 2 years later.

Heading back to Syracuse, we visited a friend from college, Frank T. in St. Johnsbury, Vermont.. We stayed with his family, had dinner, and partied with him and his local friends, who had a particular way to indulge (codeine infused cough medicine-an opiate used to treat pain in the right dosage). It was a small town, and we got around quickly, made the rounds, so to speak. The next day we headed back to Syracuse with Frank joining us, as we would all be heading back to our college shortly.

A long weekend home to Syracuse from Alfred turned into a road trip to the north country at Potsdam State, where we were visiting a friend's girlfriend. It was on the way to Montreal we figured, and that sounded a little more exciting...so what the hell. Well were we sublimely naïve and extremely lucky as there were things in the car we ingested before crossing the border just to make our first visit to a French speaking area more colorful, as I made high school Spanish sound French, who would have thought?

We still had "Hot Dog Day", coming up in the 1 block long Commercial Section of town between the 2 colleges, Alfred University and Alfred State. Both colleges and the townspeople got involved with floats, vendors and a whole lot of all day partying for the annual celebration of the hot dog (who could have known I would quit eating meat in a few short months…Ha Ha)!

I would be moving on to Arizona State University in Tempe, AZ by the end of the Summer with Timmy P. who was transferring from Oswego State, and I would be transferring there as well after finishing the two year program here.

BUT, before that, we pulled off possibly the BIGGEST party of the year for the college at "The Trailers" in late Spring of '74! What an ending, or icing on the proverbial cake for our two year's here in college.

There was a bonfire, and a "shit load" of kegs (12 plus)which were all donated from the frat houses, the lake lodge, the college pub, other house parties ,and tons of food from people handing in their meal tickets at the campus dining hall.

There was Deacon and I, Vince & Mo, Kelley C., Frank T., and Dumbo, as the hosts of sorts. We built a dam in the creek nearby for people to wade in the water. The most beautiful girl I had ever known even showed up, Robin M., who left school after our freshman year. As I was walked through the bonfire to see her on the other side, I thought I died and gone to Heaven (or Hell ☺). Alas, she couldn't stay long, and the quick spark went out, as fast as it almost burned me up. Perhaps, I was dreaming or hallucinating….

We even had the local police directing traffic after a while, as word spread about the all day and into the evening party. It was easily the happening of that school year, and maybe the year before. It was the biggest party in our two years there at least.

Kelley C. and I spoke of travelling together some day, and Europe was the preferred destination at the time. I think we both had the will, but not the way, or the money at the time. Deacon and I, also talked about travelling since our junior year in high school, at least.

The one constant I had was my adventurous spirit, and zest for one's own freedom/independence.

SUMMER '74-FALL'74

I don't believe I was going to Arizona State University from Alfred State College. I think I was getting my shit together, instead of just going through the motions, but then I missed my graduation from Alfred to go to the REGATTA in Syracuse! PARTYING, ALMOST ALWAYS CAME FIRST." Back in the day, the IRA-Collegiate crew races on Onondaga Lake were EPIC PARTIES, with colleges from all over the country here to compete in crew... our Daytona Beach (Spring Break), Mardi Gras, New Year's Eve at Time Square, so to speak.

As an aside, I was almost knocked out by the local heavy weight golden gloves boxing champion, as a fight broke out with some acquaintances of mine, and these total strangers over emptying a cooler of ice, and accidently hitting one of their female friends. This big dude, knocked down one of my friends with one punch, and I went up to him to stop the fighting , as he reels around punches me in the face with a very solid punch, and knocks me back about ten feet. It must have looked like a cartoon, only for me to go up to him and shake his hand to congratulate him for the best punch I ever took. His friend stepped in out of respect or disbelief, and ended any further fighting shortly after.... We were overall feeling no pain today, I might add.

That Summer I worked at Rockwell Industrial Tool, an old multi floor factory, and had multiple jobs from the basement to the pent-house. I earned the best money that I had ever made, "piece work". The old timers were pretty cool, but appreciated us more if we didn't work too fast, even though we made more money, we understood.

The upcoming trip to Arizona for school would ultimately change my life forever, and I would never look back 'til now...

I barely remember the rest of the summer (except the redhead), until the night before leaving for Phoenix. What a party our friends Deacon, Matt, Marty, etc, had for Tim and I. I survived somehow to make it to the Airport, after being up basically, all night with the redhead.

ARIZONA

Never having flown before, my old friend Tim and I are off, and we actually end up in 1st Class after Chicago (thanks Denny, a friend's older brother who worked for American Airlines out of Chicago), "Free Scotch", felt no pain. Did you ever go to Phoenix or Tempe, Arizona in mid-August? It had to be about 118 degrees, dry heat, still heat, the life changes were starting, flying for the first time for example, and new climate adjustments.

Like 2 days later, after leaving a friend's frat house and eating pork chops, for me the 1st, and last time. We became vegetarians that day (and to this day, more a Pesceterian), as we felt the heat and the unusual meal, and it was a sign of the times as well.

Arizona was a polar opposite of Upstate New York, the weather, culture, terrain, and diversity. The campus itself was 10 times bigger than my previous school, and absolutely off a movie lot in appearance; palm trees, cactus, orange trees, and fantastic Southwestern Architecture.

Tim and I found an apartment close to campus which was very convenient, on E. Lemon Street. Not having a car, it was important to be within walking distance! It's funny, we all adapt in different ways, but we also find familiarity when possible. I loved the night Arizona State University (the Sun Devils) football games, as it was too hot in the daytime. I caught all the home games that fall, all night games of course as it was so hot…still in the 90's, and schnapps being the preferred refreshment. The year before they were 11-0 with Danny White at QB (future NFL QB with the Cowboys), but they were only 7-5 this season!

I also got into the basketball games for a while, in their brand new 14,000 seat arena. They were very good, with a star player named Lionel Hollins! The crowds were pretty small, as they were more of a baseball and football school up until now it seemed.

Tim and I caught great Jackson Browne and Bonnie Raitt concert with a couple of our new ASU friends, It was a small venue, more of a club and very intimate I recall.

It didn't take long to spread out, hitching in the desert for a trip to the Mexican Border, Town of Nogales, and to Tucson to visit a couple Syracuse friends, Martha W., and Kathy P., tubing on the Salt River, Horseback riding in the desert, hitching to LA for Thanksgiving and the ultimate was sky diving in the desert outside Phoenix.

The biggest experiences were:
1. Sky Diving in the Desert-watch out for the power lines.…
2. Vegetarian after 2 days, maybe it was the 118 degree heat
3. Hiking in Payson, N. Arizona-talked of Outward Bound the first time
4. Hitching to Nogales, Mexico-Indian blanket and sweater shopping, and eating

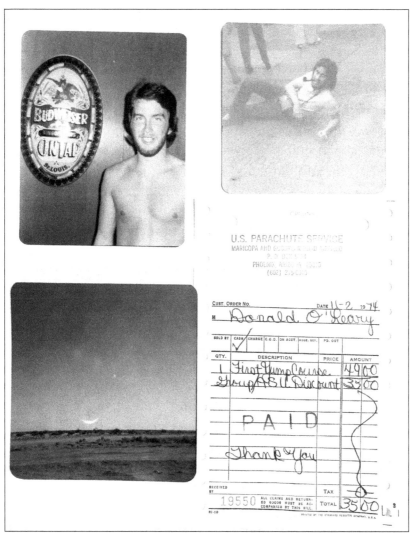

(Photos) Tempe,AZ- at apartment near ASU Campus,Skydive receipt and parachute pic , hamming up at MARX BROS name at Grauman's Chinese Theatre " Alter Egos" on LA trip with Tim Parry in Fall "74

THOUGHTS OF STUDY ABROAD

I started my interest in Study Abroad Programs, while at ASU. It was very competitive, being such a big school, and expensive, if going to Europe. The Asian and S. America study abroad programs were more convenient, and more common out of this area it seemed.

I still juggled decent grades, hell I wasn't going to waste my efforts from the previous year, I wanted to excel... What was a roadblock, was the lack of guidance at the school, I unfortunately was 2 credits shy of being a full junior (3rd year student) because my tri-mester courses transferred oddly and incompletely. As such I had a different advisor every time I went for counseling, starting at mid term, and preparing for the next semester. I just didn't ever get completely comfortable with the school regimen and their lack of structure for me.

I liked the Business program I was in though, the classes and the professors, especially my marketing class and an English elective about movies. That movie class had the history and contemporary view, foreign and domestic. Doing the reviews, and critiques on movies was very cool, and not so easy.....

The semester had many new experiences, and a very important mix of adventures. I flew for the 1st time, my 2nd time I jumped, as in skydiving, I became a vegetarian after 2 days in the heat 115-118 degrees, hitching to Mexico, Los Angeles, tubing, horseback riding in the desert,, hiking in the mountains... These were stepping-stones and that's what life is. I had no written process, even with the guidance counselors I was left to my own choices (NO WORRIES).

Thinking back about skydiving, I almost didn't do it, as the day we were scheduled to jump, right after our class training, the winds picked up, and they cancelled. The flight and the jump had to be rescheduled, and the training wouldn't be as fresh in our minds. My friend Tim, had something come up and couldn't do it, but I wasn't going backwards, so we were going the next weekend.

We were out in the desert, small single wing and propeller, with the four of us rookies packed in. I was going to be the last to jump out, and at the 3,000 feet mark, and waiting for your turn really had my juices bubbling. One, the next, another, my turn, and I go out the side door facing the wrong way, nope , then the wrong foot, again no, finally out the door correctly to a little platform, and hanging on to the strut, jump and release, the chute is connected and opens up, within about 3 seconds, about a 125'-0 free fall.

There's a pull at your crotch and chest from the chute's harness, absorbing immense pain ,and then enjoy the ride, but you still have to guide the chute with your toggles, direction, and ultimately the landing, at 40 +- miles per hour, depending on whether you were with the wind, or against it. Hit, and roll......

When all of us were done jumping and together on the ground, they said they almost called me back in the plane, as we were further off the jump area than they wanted. No way, was I going back in the plane, after climbing out of it fully....Then we turned around, and they showed us where the power lines were, wow I was close!!!!

Most adventures came with some degree of risk. It depended on other life experiences, previous adventures one had, and what the degree of difficulty it meant for each person.

I also learned a couple important things while in Arizona, that would help me set a course less travelled...Hitch hiking was a common theme, but I started that freshman year in high school on a smaller scale. Significant new inspirations, was learning about Outward Bound and Study Abroad Programs.

Looking at what lay ahead, I decided to transfer back East to SUNY Oswego (or Oswego State). My friend Tim had gone there, and was also going back East. We had a 46-hour road trip ahead of us, 3 of us in a VW Bug, and all our belongings. That was 46 hours straight, in a cooped up, no room to spare, stick shifting bug. We wanted to get home before Christmas... Our third roommate, John, was also leaving, heading back to Nebraska. Apparently we passed him in the night, his car broke down outside Flagstaff, AZ...dark, very late, he wrote us later...pissed off!

(Photos) ASU apt with Tim P. riding in desert, hiking in Payson, LA poses, & leaving with VW on 46 hr. road trip home

Experiences, were never far away that year, especially the adventures in the last 4 months. I had more life experiences in that time span than my previous 20 years combined, or so it seemed!

WINTER- SUMMER 1975

Who transfers from Arizona State University in December to start in January, at State University of New York in Oswego (on Lake Ontario, one of the "GREAT LAKES")? It was called the Snowbelt for good reason, ha, ha...

My experiences the past semester in Arizona would help me jumpstart my next stage. My first week of school I applied to Study Abroad in Europe, and I chose Bruges, Belgium at the College of Europe, as it had an undergrad program, which tied in with the Economics Program there, and the Business Administration Degree that I was working on. We would be taught in English but in a Flemish and French speaking city.

I was accepted, I was on a roll, finishing Alfred State, living in Syracuse, transferred to ASU, Oswego State, and now Bruges, Belgium, all in 6 months or so. When I looked back at finishing at Alfred State in June (went to the Syracuse Regatta on Graduation Day). I was at the time amazed, and genuinely pumped up to be going to ARIZONA, that seemed as much of a goal or destination. My imagination and efforts, bankroll or lack of, could also come in to play.

After settling in a bit, I had to make plans for Europe, and still handle my academics, get a summer job etc.

Also, I had to live in the moment, hence a spontaneous road trip to Kingston, Ontario with an old buddy from the CUSE. We hit the road and we end up in Canada, and it felt like we were in Europe, with a very cool fort, and colorful guard. It was the pub and club scene that was different and we felt adventurous meeting a couple lovely ladies who liked to dance and party…it was a great break from Oswego…

We had so much fun on that short visit, we went a little further to Toronto a couple weeks later, with a couple more friends. We were staying at a posh hotel, as these friends were working with a paycheck, not currently in college. You know we looked like something out of Saturday Night Fever after we changed, and again we danced and partied the night away.

But where's the agenda for every situation. I looked back and recalled hiking in Northern Arizona, near Payson, and a friend talked about Outward Bound, especially the one in North Carolina. Just like I learned about Study Abroad Programs while in Arizona, another piece of the puzzle would fall into place.

WHAT WAS OUTWARD BOUND & WHERE WAS IT?

It was backpacking, hiking, rock climbing, rappelling, white water canoeing, and camping in spectacular wilderness areas. This particular location was mostly in the Blue Ridge Mountains of North Carolina, and other nearby, mostly remote areas.

What did it mean for me, and what will I get out of it. I remember my mother was on board with every adventure I came up with, and even got me a Rotary Scholarship for the Outward Bound N. Carolina Program. It paid about one third of it as it cost $750 total, which was a lot of money in 1975, a semester's cost at ASU almost, a full year almost at Oswego, and I had to find a way to get there. Every penny mattered when I was growing up, if I saved by going to state colleges, or hitched, or greyhound bus, well it seemed natural.

This was a 23-day survival course with hiking, rock climbing, rappelling, zip line, solos, 3 day trek's in 3 different ways. All the time with 70+ people from all over, in 12 person groups, co-ed in our case, ages 18 to 25 in our crew.

This info was not that easily accessible, and communications were by word of mouth, library research, calling, and writing.

By January 1976, I will be going in the opposite direction, to Europe, which will also make 4 colleges in 4 years. It was really 4 in 2 years by the time I finish June 1974-January 1976, WTF!

In the meanwhile, here I am in snowdrifts 10-12 feet high. Oswego, NY made Syracuse look like an arid desert (Syracuse is one of the, and sometimes, "The Snowiest Large City" in the whole U.S.) with especially high winds off the lake in the Winter. I had heard of the ropes put up for students to hang on to, with the campus located right on the Lake, and from my own experience could see why!!!!.

I had a pretty good house off campus, three roommates including one, my friend Tim. We weren't too far from campus at Liberty & Cayuga, but it felt like the Iditarod on more than one occasion. Once in a while you give in to the elements, carve a seat out in a large snow bank, you wolf down a large delicious Oswego Subshop sub after a night of partying, and or 21 shots of Tequila at the Shacki Patch to toast my 21st birthday. Other amenities(pubs/bars) nearby were the Woodshed, Bucklands, Broadwells, all within a couple blocks or so.

We had some friends from Syracuse up for a party at our house (landlord was the Funeral Director next door) freaked a few people out, as caskets were stored there, and especially when someone passed out and was put in one of them.

I almost made it to Kentucky Derby that May, but my friend Larry's car windows were smashed the night before we were to leave. If I knew that night or earlier in the day I was ready to hitch….

We did make it to Daytona Beach for Spring Break in about 19 hours, staying with friends who rented a house (The Roach Inn, as big as mice, haha). A full day trip to Disney World was "Electric" under the right circumstances and the stimulation was felt in every bone in my body. Any adventure seemed feasible, only limited by your imagination, time, and money.

Oswego was a great place in the Spring, really could enjoy the Lake, and the City had a great PUB CRAWL, my favorite haunt being the Ferris Wheel. I would make it across the River to the Great Laker Inn on occasion as well.

The Summer of 1975 would fly by, with work, a nice long weekend in Cape Cod, horseback riding in the sand dunes along the beach and scuba diving (even speared a fish in one shot).

Summer School in Oswego was only 3 weeks every day and voluntary for me so I didn't have to take a Statistics class in The Fall semester. What a great time to be in Oswego when you really could appreciate the beauty of being on the Lake

With any spare time, I was constantly running and working out to prepare for the Outward Bound Program later in the Summer.

Journal, Pack, Boots, and Sleeping Bag (OUTWARD BOUND)

After 35 hours of driving by bus with many stops and changes from Syracuse, NY to Asheville, North Carolina, I arrive. I was running behind slightly, and I was directed to the wrong camp bus, and hence to the wrong camp for the younger crews, under 18's.

My first North Carolina adventure has started!

Because I am directed to the wrong bus and camp, I do get to meet the Director of the whole program, Dan Meyer, and hang with his family for dinner, and learned a lot about his background and dedication to this program. After dinner they get me to the right camp, as he brought along a couple of his kids for the ride to, and up the mountain! It was not a simple journey, especially at night, as you couldn't drive in all the way, and had to hike in the dark, shouting up ahead that we were coming up.

There is a 3-day expedition when I wake up, and hadn't even met the other people in my crew yet!

There are 12 of us in our co-ed crew, and 2 instructors: Me, Margie, Sharon, Craig, Larry, Bill, Sue, Andy, Gene, Chris, Scott, Sally, and Bob and Tomas our instructors. A new destination each day, and a group of three took turns leading each day.

We come across a Rattlesnake and Copperhead within a few hours, good thing they advised us of some precautions, stay away and or how to defend one self. We were very comfortable in just giving them the trail and walking out of the way and around.

I become pals with Margie pretty quickly, a fun loving, hardy girl from Brooklyn. The others in the crew, I will find out more as we got deeper into the program. My group, including Margie will lead the second day, using compasses along with the maps, and shooting an azimuth (direction of an object in the sky measured in degrees) to Table Rock Mt. and Hawksville Mt.

My feet start blistering within the second day! You can't prepare enough physically, mentally or equipment wise for what they are putting us through. I worked out all Summer running, playing basketball, and tennis, but not for 10-14 hours per day. Also, my boots needed more breaking in for the same reason, like they are getting now, but I couldn't have duplicated this experience....

We wake up in darkness, go for a run, and on the 3rd day they have us jump in to what felt like an almost freezing pond.

We are left up to our own ways and direction on certain stretches of the hikes, how to cross a creek or hike along side it. It's challenging either way, as I slip in, and myself and full backpack gets soaked.

The last half of the 3rd and final day of this expedition the instructors left us, and for us to find our own way back to base camp. And darkness was fast approaching.

All of a sudden, Margie gets stung by a bee or bees, and starts freaking out, then Sue also gets stung, but it's worse, as she is very allergic! We have to trouble shoot the emergency and it is getting darker and darker so we decide to push on because we don't have medical kits, and it is getting darker by the minute!

We have to cross ledges, traversing up the mountain, and then down. The girls are afraid, in shock possibly, and not so sure footed now. We send a few of us as scouts, sprinting ahead with flashlights to make sure we don't get lost and to find the main base camp quicker.

We are in an uncharted area for ourselves, it is rough terrain, darkness, and not knowing how bad the allergic reaction was, and how much time we had to deal with it. Gene is doing an excellent job leading, and we finally find the trail and our way to the main camp, and to help.

We still had to run back to the others and guide them down. It was a great team effort under duress, in a real rescue situation. Who knows what would have happened, especially with the allergic reaction of Sue to consider.

We settle down after Sue and Margie are looked at and taken care of.. We all head to the cabins, the 12 of us in the co-ed crew. After a bit, Margie is feeling better and secure, so her and I go off and have a smoke, get very high, snuggle up and relax.

PRETTY WILD ENDING TO OUR 1ST EXPEDITION!!!

Special skill training is coming up next. On Day 5 which consisted of the ropes, trees, high wire, balance beam, rope ladder, & boatswain chair, belaying signals for climbing, etc. and the Burma Bridge to zip line, and jump off............!

We go to the rocks, climbing with spotters, in a few different ways. After dinner, I have a very tough time, as I can't do the second climb on belay, missing holds, etc. It is so frustrating, I go blank, almost numb, and can't gather myself. My ego got the better of me, and I give up, and did something different. Switching it up, helped me... and I gain a little confidence back. I am beat mentally, and physically, as it was my first failure, very real, and humbling. Part of the challenge and the balance you keep within the coed interaction of the program, sort of role playing, alpha dog, etc. Not a day went by up to now, that you didn't notice the female and male interactions...

Today we do 3 climbs at the "Chimneys" of Linville Gorge and rappel as well. The climbs were especially good today since I had lost my confidence 2 days earlier. I had only 1 slip today on a tough 60-foot climb. The rappel was about 90 feet down the cliff versus up on a climb. I went last, and I belay (the ropes to anchor)for Sharon. We used double fisherman's knot for the harness, and we used the carabiners. We hoisted ourselves down with one hand (right), keep left hand free. I got my shirt twisted in the line (uncomfortable), but still made it down. It was a very free, a floating feeling, gliding down on the rappel.

Went down to Dangle Rock and practiced with 2 lines for rescues up mountains. We then simulated one, with Sue being hurt, and helping her down the cliff, took a long time, we then carried her on a litter.

Later Bob and Tomas come down after dinner and discuss the rescue and other attributes… I let out some feeling of inadequacies from climbing, from a couple days earlier, and others followed, and it felt great to talk about it, and with others opening up too.

Awareness enhanced, I actually wrote out a short will (see pp 49-50 area), and had it signed by a couple of the other crew members. "Who knows", be prepared, as I felt on the edge!

Tomorrow's another day, another expedition…….

The leaders get us lost on top of mountain, can't find trail, a lot of bushwhacking to cut some time. We're 5 hours off schedule, take lunch next to bee's nest and Chris gets stung and we all scatter. Earlier, Andy, Craig, and I got stung by hornets. They don't let go easy, bad sting in leg at back of calf. Some of the crew were exhausted and complaining, as it had been a 14 hour hike day until 10:30 pm.

Margie, Sharon, Craig and I lead today. We are going to the Blue Ridge Mt. Highway, towards Busick and on to Mt. Mitchell, the highest peak east of the Mississippi River, at 6,688 ft.

We go through Pisgah National Forest, up the road to Mt. Mitchell, Black Mt. Campground at the bottom. It usually takes 4 ½ hours to the top we are advised, and with Sue usually not feeling too good, and can't carry her whole pack, probably longer. We split up some of her things and still make it about the average time. Ironically after all this, we get to the top and it is all tourists, packed with the Sunday church goers, staring at us constantly. It was not what we expected at all, as we did not know there was a road to the top, and actually they were the first people we'd seen outside of crew people in a week or so.

After a lunch break, and the clouds coming in, we have to move on. We take off for our next destination, a shelter on the ridge about

4 miles along the ridgeline. It starts raining, lightning and thunder, so we can't afford to stay on top. We really hustle through the terrain, which has a lot of burned out, lightning struck trees, and we actually hike past a downed smaller aircraft that looked like it had crashed not long ago.

We get there in 3 hours, making it a 12 hours total hike. As leaders, we really had to be tough, no lagging behind, front, middle, and rear, setting the pace. The site itself was tight but protected, clean too, after what we hiked through, and it's still cold, dark and damp, as the torrential rain cooled the air. We didn't make any friends pushing the pace, but the instructors understood, and respected our judgement.

The morning was freezing and wet, and we have to hurry up and get going. We hike, and hike, and everyone is sore as hell.

Bob the instructor tells everyone, Don has a broken leg and everyone has to take care of me, and carry me down the Mountain. They make a splint and stretcher, and carry me down the mountain. Later we rap about how we handled the situation, as the others resented me getting off easy, and being carried, etc....(I, as well didn't appreciate the role, but none of us would have)!

WHITE WATER

The white water canoeing is next, and down to the South Toe River, at Green Mountain. We'll split into two's, then we go over paddle strokes and signals, Sharon and I are partners, this will be good, as we are both free spirited. We practice self-rescue, landing at an eddy, and eddy to eddy.

The bugs were out all night keeping me up, as Sharon and I both wake up about 11:30 pm, thinking it was 6 a.m., and time to wake up. We have a very good run the next morning. It's freezing out with no sun, and because we had to take a dip in river, before we left camp, ooh COLD!

Another day of white water canoeing, Larry and I are a team with me at stern, and him at bow, with more rapids ahead, as we dumped 2 or 3 times at some tough spots. After lunch we switch partners, Sue and I, with me at bow and Sue at stern, new for both of us. It's a lot easier at bow, there's a tough rapid ahead and we take some bad dumps. Sue loses her paddle often, but we find it, but 2 of the 3 times we really take on water. The last time, Larry and Sally rammed us on a rapid into a rock, but we're all okay.

We break about 5 p.m., and I catch up with everyone's bio's and we all share addresses, information, etc., but Bob. We practice mouth to mouth and I am with Sharon who was my partner of choice, as coed rescue practices have some benefits. Later, we rap around campfire, air some problems out.

We have a longer run the next morning, 5 miles or so, and I feel great, but then I stay back with Sue as she can't keep up. It's the last day of canoeing, and I have another partner in Andy, with me at bow. I have to work on my draw right, and cross draw for left. The best rapids today, a bit shallow or they'd be a 5 (the highest degree of difficulty).

Andy and I dump our canoe in a really fast rapid at a bend in the river between some large boulders! We get stuck beneath the water and our canoe overhead, as my foot was jammed between some rocks underneath. My foot was really stuck and I had to reach down, and taking some time and effort and with all my strength pull it loose and then free!! We were submerged totally with the water moving rapidly around us, and by freeing my foot finally, we took off down river, and we could then finally turn the canoe over to the right side after a while. The others couldn't tell what had happened to us at first, as we were hidden beneath the canoe.

What a recovery, what's one foot anyway, just kidding, but it was completely stuck, like in a vise!!!!!

Later, we eddied really well, and ferried across the eddy, also from a calm spot behind a rock to another calm spot. Stroking so hard, my arms and shoulders get really sore, as it is so shallow in spots, and the back of my neck is killing me.

We finish up and get ready to leave the South Toe River, to head back to base camp.

ANOTHER TOUGH AND STRESSED MOMENT DEALT WITH and MOVE ON!!!!

ROCKS

When we get back after supper, we do some rock climbing at the boulders with belay lines. I actually do okay on 3 ropes (easiest), used my legs instead of arm strength… much easier. Might do Table Rock, our final rock climbing destination, tomorrow?

Wake up to run as usual, take a wrong turn as I take lead, and I just know it's going to be a weird day.

We go to climbing hut, and find out we're doing Table Rock Mountain this morning, it's about a 400'- vertical climb in four sections, and scaling with Sue and I as partners, and Tomas as lead.

The first leg and we're first to go up, sunny and hot out. I follow Tomas a little nervous, but only one tense moment, it's about finding decent hand and foot holds, which I handled ok. It's like a final exam today, putting it all together, and most importantly is keeping your composure. That was a 100 foot section, I then belay for Sue, while I am sitting right on the incline of the cliff. Sue has trouble at the beginning, but proceeds fantastically after that.

The second leg is 90 feet for our next climb, and up to Lunch Rock for lunch afterwards. Meanwhile Tomas leads again around overhang at top of a cave, traversing to the left and I lose sight of him. He reaches top and I'm next, as I unhook from there and get the carabiners that Tomas hooked up to, in case he fell, then hook up the trailing rope which Sue will use.

The third leg is over 100 feet, and doesn't look very easy. I traverse left, then right, left, then straight up over the rock jutting out, and use a lot of upper body strength, instead of legs, but no real problem. It was more bothersome near the top, as it was all foot and hand holds, and they were dirty and covered with a moss like growth, which I had to wipe off, and then finish up, whew!

The fourth leg , or one more climb to the ultimate top, another 100' +- section, with Tom (instructor), a nice guy that I did the rappel with, and that I trust. Tom leads, then Bill, Andy, with Sue and me to follow. It looked easy, but they both have a lot of trouble with a rock jutting out, and far to the left. I am no different as it's the toughest spot all day. We use all arm strength, foot holds are too far underneath as I swing over and barely catch my waist at the edge, and fit in nicely hanging on still by arms, swing up on legs and pull up. Sue has a real hammy photo of me , as I finish up and belay Sue, again tough for her too, but Bob at bottom coaching her on, she falls once, but not badly.

Cumulatively it was almost 400' vertical climbing, our biggest and by far, greatest challenge!

Everyone makes it up but Sally, who fell badly on her 2nd climb, and hurt her arm and back. Tomas and Larry helped her down from the ledge, and she had to go to the hospital. Later we realize Sally can rejoin us, but would not be fully capable.

SOLO

The SOLO is next, and it's for 3 days and nights. We are given a little bag with peanuts, raisins, and a packet of hot chocolate, that's all. We can bring all our personal gear, there's a stream nearby, can't walk further than 25 yards in either direction. I am so exhausted from our climbs that I can't look further, write or think, it's Z out time!

Damn HUGE Ants all over the place, in my bag, my clothes, my poncho, etc. I can manage though, as we are so use to sleeping outside at this point in the program. I hope I don't get out of shape by being here on solo, physically and mentally, as we still have the final expedition and the half marathon in a few days.

Breaking up the monotony, I do some whittling on a small tree I cut, but I cut 2 of my fingers with my knife when the blade buckles. It really starts gushing, and in a panic, I stumble down to the stream to clean it out, and immediately the cold water starts to put me in shock. I somehow calm down and walk out of camp, following the trail we came in on. As I pass Larry's solo site, I tell him about whittling and cutting my fingers, as I hike past him. Bob is at the head of the trail, and takes me back to the main base camp, where he and Arlene fix me up with butterfly bandages mostly.

Sure, it rains while I am off site and most of my stuff gets wet, as I left hurriedly. I overall kept surprisingly warm and dry with footholds at base of tree in otherwise damp and hilly terrain, when I settled back in, just dealing with the pain of my throbbing fingers.

I dig being alone, with my own thoughts, and actions. at this stage of the program, as there is a lot to reflect on. I do my 15 minute breathing and meditation. I read some of my book and write to Wendy back home who I met earlier this Summer and started going out with, and think of now and future events. My fingers are throbbing though, and it's hard to write, and no rummaging in the forest either.

It is the bluest sky yet, makes me think of good times past, present and future. It is the last day of Solo, and barely a raisin remaining, no big deal. The future and travelling sounds great!

When we are all finished, we catch up on everybody's mishaps. Larry's cut tendon in his hand, also from whittling, is worst than my cut, Andy has a bad infection, and Sally has the bad leg and shoulder from her fall at Table Rock. We are all light headed and exhausted from the last 3 days. We are given a large watermelon by Tomas after we hike out, umm good, then a full meal.

FINAL EXPEDITION

Now for our final expedition, and without instructors, as they leave us off near Old Grandfather's Mt. The stars and the moon are really out, beautiful, but don't sleep great, because I have an upset stomach, from eating too much after the solo.

Head out over the unfinished Blue Ridge Mt. Highway. My legs are rubbery and hurting. We get in big discussion about our goals and purpose of our final hike. Larry has a lot to say, and he lets his temper get the best of him. We listen though and end up getting more out of final, as we vote 11-1 to take it easier, talk more, an easier pace for ourselves, roads and trails. Solo was still wearing on us, Larry's fingers especially!

Day 20-I don't have much life to me, with little sleep, and diarrhea killing me.

We trudge along, stopping at a General Store that we happen upon, and pick up jelly beans and cookies, who thought we needed money (first, and only time). Stop later for our lunch at a nice park in Mortimer, but we've got to keep away from the town of Kawana, "Rednecks, shoot you, to protect their stills" we were warned!

We set up camp, getting our tarps out as well, as it could rain, and about 10:30 p.m. it starts raining and thundering like you wouldn't believe. Everybody wakes up, as the rain is pouring through the tops and sides of the tarps, and washing down the nearby hill. Only Chris, Sally, and I stay dry, as the others are getting cold and wet, and there's concern about a flash flood with the creek below us. Sharon is screaming about lightning, and Sue is very upset, about itching from her allergies. Larry's worried the most, as he and Andy are the wettest. We help out the others with dry clothes and help them move to drier areas, alas we all get wet, but less stress for the others.

We get through it, and get some sleep finally. Wake up early and wet, and my sleeping bag is damp like the air itself.

Back to hiking, another stream, so what the hell as Larry bombs through it already wet, but now soaked. I slip a bit, one leg up to my knee; otherwise good practice for flex hopping. Some took off boots, but risky for cuts, and slipping, etc..

45

We're heading up now, up 1,400 feet to Chestnut Mt., then another 600 feet to the Orchard (Final Destination). We spread out, those that want to B.S., enjoy scenery and trail. Up ahead at Lookout Tower we break for lunch, relax for a while, writing, talking, taking photos, drying gear, etc. I actually got a couple recipes, for granola and yoghurt.

We hike the rest of the way downhill to the Orchard, which is where all the crews are coming together. The half marathon starts from here in the morning, maybe?

Great supper, everybody including Dan Meyer, Arlene, Tom also… It's great up here, as I go to sleep under the stars.

HALF MARATHON (ALMOST)

Today is the half marathon and the last full day with all 5 crews, about 65-70 including Dan, Arlene and a few others. It is 11-12 miles up and down the mountain(s). What energy and excitement is in the mountain air….

Letterrock Ridge is a steep climb and I've got cramps, and I stopped a couple times with diarrhea. At the top is Table Rock, then Linville Gorge at about the 2 mile mark. Bob passes me with about ½ mile to go. I finish strong with a top 10 finish, in 1 hour 39 minutes, record is 1 hour 20, Tomas did 1:28 and I came in 2nd after Tomas, out of our crew and instructors. I finish 1st in my crew out of 11, not bad with diarrhea and a vegetarian diet… Sue didn't run because of her infection, and of course Sally was hobbled after her fall.

I had mail waiting from mom and my friend Marty. We have personal talks with Bob and Tomas, clean packs, canteen, cup and plate, also, our 1st shower in a week.

THE SEND OFF

I eat so much at the Going Away Dinner, 3 helpings, and I'm not alone. We watch a movie on Outward Bound, which was very good for the background.

We finish up with a Blue Grass Band from Morganton, who were excellent. With Bob shouting out some calls and we have a high old time, doing some square dancing and the "Virginia Reel" with a lot of kicking, and whooping it up….After all we had been through together, it was such a high and phenomenal release and so much fun swirling around for the purest pleasure. It seemed amazing the energy we all still had, the smiles, and laughter 'til 11:30 p.m. beat finally! What a GREAT TIME!!!!!

Later, sit under stars with Sally for a while, what a day, Great!

OB-THE LAST DAY

August 30th It is a Saturday and we wake up early, hanging around, bullshitting. The whole camp meets up, very emotional, there are group photos, and we all leave at 9:30 am.

Goodbye Outward Bound, and a 30 minute ride down the Mountain, Aloha! I was fortunate, that I could catch a ride with Larry to Binghamton, most of the way home.

Outward Bound North Carolina climbing, hiking, etc......

POST OUTWARD BOUND!

It was a huge letdown when it ended... back to a routine, some more than others. I'd be at college a day later with a full load of 21 credits, and 5 months until I go to Europe in January, 1976.

An afterthought I had that maintaining my conditioning would have been great, but working out from 5:30 a.m.-8:30 p.m. daily wasn't possible with my school load. Within those credits, were horseback riding 1 and 2, Tennis 2, for conditioning and I ran every day, plus lived about 3 plus miles away and usually walked, or hitched to campus!

Some additional basics that I have learned for the Study Abroad next semester have now increased exponentially. I would create my own manual, partly designed from my own dreams, recent adventure, and willingness to expand on them further, including journal writing.

Looking back at the 3 plus weeks I just spent, it added up to about 2 months of work, or work out, at least for a typical athlete. It was fifteen hours plus or minus per day, active and exerting mental, and physical strength. I remember on solo, that I was worried that I would lose some conditioning that I still needed for the final expedition, and mountain ½ Marathon.

I had been in the best shape of my life, and I went from weighing 165 pounds down to 138 pounds of lean muscle. I hadn't eaten meat in the past year, and meat was usually a staple in the program's daily meal, hence I usually managed quite a lot on less.

I was confident in trying new adventures and meeting new people!

DEDICATION IN MY OUTWARD BOUND JOURNAL

A SIGNIFICANT ASIDE, WAS THE WILL OR DEDICATION I WROTE AND HAD WITNESSED WITHIN THE 1ST WEEK OF THE PROGRAM! I HINTED AT IT TO MY FATHER UPON MY SAFE RETURN TO SYRACUSE. BUT I DID NOT FULLY EXPLAIN SO AS NOT TO UPSET ANYBODY!

"Dedicated to my Family: Not one member in particular because my love is spread out equally and abundantly. I hope if anything does happen now or at any future moment in my course here in North Carolina they know I was doing what I wanted to do, feeling every emotion and fulfilling my wildest dreams. I feel I've got to learn myself and what I am capable of physically and what strains my mind and heart can take.

"To be followed:
    I request if I should die that my body be cremated and my ashes distributed among my family members. I wish my body not to be viewed in pieces or remembered with a plastic face or body. This I do request.

                                    Donald O'Leary"

"Witnesses: 1. Signed by crew member (female)
                  2. Signed by crew member (male)
                  August 14, 1975 "

THIS WAS NOT VERY LEGAL PROBABLY, BUT MY HEARTFELT AND AT TIMES STRESSED FEELINGS AT THE MOMENT! (Also this is the first time that I read it since my return from North Carolina Outward Bound in August, 1975! Today's date: July 24, 2019)

FALL 1975

This current semester at Oswego State was my 4th different residence (apartment or house) in a row, at Alfred, Arizona State, Oswego (2 sides of town), not counting my family home in Syracuse. I was becoming a nomad with a purpose, hell next semester I would be in Europe or 5 semesters in a row in a different residence.

I met a few people that would influence me along the way, like Judy F. and Richie E., who were going to Bruges from Oswego State as well, and Professor Ghobrial in the Geography Department who had way of teaching that you embraced the subject with a passion.

I was signed up for 21 credits, including Horseback riding 1&2 which was a great exercise in working with an animal, respect and discipline. French class was fun and gave me some of the basics, and Tennis 2 got me past the backhand and a consistent serve. Of course my 15 credits in Business (5 courses) which was my major, steadied me and brought me back to earth. A culmination of my last 1½ years dreams, aspirations and efforts was taking me to the next level and beyond.

I had the equipment, tools (so to speak), timing was perfect (or so I thought). It is what it is, budget was there, as the round trip flight, room, board, and tuition were part of the package.

Travel/Checklist

Bring:

- Backpack
- Sleeping Bag
- Tent- small 2 person
- Hiking Boots
- Shoes (Earth Shoes)
- Sneakers
- CAMERA – Yashica TL Electro (Christmas)
- Passport
- Money Belt
- Traveller's Checks
- Travel and Language Books, Maps
- Student Discount Card
- Youth Hostel Card, Book & Map
- Tennis Racket

Fall 1975 was almost an end to an Era and the beginning of a new one! I really was putting a lot together as I prepared for my next and ultimate adventure. I met a wonderful girl in the summer, and we kept in touch during the fall semester. She was at school in NYC, but from Syracuse as well. New roommates in Oswego were Bill O, from Scranton, PA (I knew him at Alfred), and 2 of Larry H's (from

Alfred) friends from back home in Long Island. It was an interesting mix of roommates, but we all got along. It wasn't too long before I would go, but I wanted to live in the moment as well.

There were parties of course, I even became friends with a couple rugby guys, and they had some great parties after their games. I almost played for the sake of conditioning, but I was too busy or rational, ha,ha. A new late night TV show on Saturday nights (SNL) started this fall, and as people caught on, they would build a parties around it. They had some great concerts in the Fall as well, Herbie Hancock, and the absolutely best for last, a young Bruce Springsteen late in the semester, December '75 at Laker Hall and at $4 a ticket (Oh to be young and a college student "La Vida Loca")!

BRUGES ORIENTATION

There was an Orientation Session at Oswego State on the Saturday before Thanksgiving for the upcoming study abroad programs. Figures, I miss it...bad communication, or just something else going on. Anyways, it would have been a good opportunity to meet my future partners in study and adventure. Alas, I wasn't always so organized, especially on my weekends, ha ha ha!

I heard it was pretty good, as Sue M. from Boston University came in, and others from SUNY Albany, Stony Brook, and Binghamton, as well as the Buffalo folks. Sue was the only non –SUNY student... good for her, very cool! I know Sue felt like an outsider at first, and though she was a bit shy at first...she would blossom like a beautiful butterfly.

Especially good, was the follow up house party after the Orientation, with a "GIANT TRASH CAN" mixed with a variety of punch like liquids, and of course some strong booze!!!! This crazy weekend was the start of a fantastic, life altering journey for the overall group going abroad.

The next time, or for some that didn't make it to the orientation, the first time they would meet their fellow students studying abroad, would probably be at JFK International Airport , or on the plane bound for Brussels in January 1976.

The hardest thing was maintaining the edge I had physically, from the Outward Bound experience, which was to be expected… unless I went into Navy Seal training afterwards!!! There was only so much time, especially this semester…

Europe would be so Unique in a lifetime of experiences, and so were many of the other experiences that prepared me. Actually you should appreciate the journey, the hard work, mentally, physically, even financially (budgeting)… plus who, what, where, why, etc.

So many crossroads present themselves in life. I had established or developed personal behavior that over emphasized partying up 'til I was almost 20 years old, and self exploration under those circumstances contributed to much of the blur. When choosing between events and activities under such a cloud, it blurred many possibly completely different choices. It's easier to know what you did, then why sometimes, especially looking back…

DECISIONS

I'd say, the "Best" Decisions I made at this stage were:

1st "Best"- Going to New York City and Boston (Walden Pond, as well), with Deacon. August, 1971 (17years old)

2nd "Best" - Going to Arizona State University with Tim in August 1974 (20 years)

3rd "Best"- Going to Outward Bound in August 1975 (21 years)

4th "Best" -Going to Europe (21 years old), really THE BEST, as the others were stepping stones!!!!!! I mean applying and getting accepted at this point .....

These decisions range from 17 to 21 years old in age. There were smaller opportunities, and some were not as life changing, but also created decisions at crossroads, too! In 1973, a growth spurt of sorts with multiple adventures, for example a week long road trip with friends to Virginia Beach, the Cornell Concert, Summer Jam at Watkins Glen, and a fall trip with Deacon to Boston to see Patti C. from high school, and on to Vermont to see Frank T. from college, Daytona/Orlando, Cape Cod, a trip to Montreal (trip for sure), and Toronto clubbing (not really me, but WTF why not?)...

School, friends, family, and sports – always had opportunities to do one thing, and I did another or 2 others, or consistently put off more important decisions... Where's the Map? My social skills were maturing, and my academics would get another jump start ultimately.

I thought I would surprise my family when I hitch hiked home from Oswego in late Fall for the Syracuse University football game at old Archibold Stadium versus West Virginia, a rival. It was raining pretty good and it looked like it was heading towards Syracuse.

Nobody was home though when I arrived, until one of my brothers came in. My father had just had a stroke earlier in the week and everybody was at the hospital. They didn't want to tell me as I was studying for exams, and I was immediately sad and mad at the same time.

My father "Daddeo to me" was a unique guy, a character out of an old Damon Runyon story..."Guys and Dolls like", although nothing gangster, but a loveable character! He was also 51 years older than myself or 72 years "YOUNG", way more "Grandfatherish", but truly a loving dad. He could talk the talk with the lowest down and out street person to the head of a local hospital or the owner of a former department store, all within a 30 minute span of time....

Well I got up to see him as quickly as I could, and had to bring my best to brighten up the mood, my own and my family's. My abrupt homecoming was just the medicine, as my voice and vibe clicked with Daddeo enough for him to recognize the youngest son was there. After our family reunion and visiting time was up, we still made it to the big game, albeit in a funky mood. The rains came and so did the refreshments from the adjacent fans and plenty for all....

Daddeo was pretty stable in a few days, but with a slight stiffness of expression, but not of his heart or soul ☺

It ultimately is an anxious time, going in to the unknown! Hell, going to Europe, was a quest! It wasn't that common, I knew nobody who had been there on a Study Abroad Program, especially in a foreign language speaking country – Bruges, Belgium , where French and Flemish was spoken... that's good, because I audited a semester of French 1, last semester ha, ha!

Seriously, all through high school, 3 ½ years of college... it wasn't that typical going to Europe, it actually was exotic for these times. One thing or another, it was unique for me, my family, my circle of acquaintances, and what does that matter. I beefed up on "Cojones" in Outward Bound and traveling in the Southwest (AZ, CA etc.). It would after all be my fourth college in four years on top of it, starting at Alfred State College, Arizona State University, Oswego State University, with credits from Appalachian St. for the Outward Bound program, and now the College of Europe!

Just two years earlier I sucked it up, to not only stay in College, but to improve my grades dramatically, so I could transfer to a good four year university, such as Arizona State University.

Things were looking up, now... I got a new camera for Christmas, a Yashica TL Electro 35 MM… good in its day. It certainly was better than the instamatic I used up until now…..

1976-JANUARY, THE YEAR BEGINS

I was still going out with a beautiful girl whom I met last Summer, she was a year younger and from a different college, but both of us were on Christmas break and we were still close.

We went to a show, a Syracuse Stage production of An Evening with Chekhov, (January 1976), and it was the coldest day of the year, snow covered streets, and the car died on me 3 times, before I picked her up. It was dead after the show, and I got a jump start again (twice). I drove back to my house, turned the car off, and we made a deal, if it starts right up we'd go up to my house in Oswego, because I still had my house key, and wanted to grab a few belongings….. We ended up in Oswego, beautiful romantic Oswego, 10-12'-0" high snow banks, seriously.

When you're young, an adventure is a car starting right away… even in the "Arctic." The drive back to Syracuse with my belongings, early the next morning did not quite have the same intensity, as the effects of the stimulating "play" had worn off, perhaps!

This is just a couple days away from departing Syracuse, to New York City, and Flying over to Europe, for my "Biggest Adventure Ever"

LET THE BICENTENNIAL BEGIN….ABROAD!

THE BICENTENNIAL ABROAD (SO IT BEGINS)

I am finally a day away from leaving Syracuse, New York, and off to Europe. My backpack is full, and I have all the other important travel necessities, such as a passport, traveler's checks, money belt, etc. I am packed for the long haul, the semester and beyond. I will be travelling to some of the most beautiful cities, and places in the world, for a semester abroad in Bruges, Belgium, my final semester of my senior year of college!!!!

I was taking off from Syracuse to New York City with Beth , *a girl from Oswego State's Paris Program and from Syracuse (East side), and luckily her parents were kind enough to drive us to New York City.*

Beth's parents knew their way around New York City, and took us to a very nice restaurant in the garment district, near where her father did business, called Morgens. I ate probably, the best and most expensive meal that I had ever eaten in my life: red snapper, stuffed clams, Shrimp Mornay, salad, sesame sticks, spaghetti, coconut meringue pie, chocolate mousse, with tea, and a scotch (Johnny Walker Red) and water.

Beth's parents were so nice and I was very appreciative, the ride alone from Syracuse was so special. They reminded me of the nice family I stayed in Los Angeles with one and a half years earlier (1974), when Tim P. and I hitched there from Arizona State University.

We are departing from JFK Airport tomorrow evening for Brussels, Belgium. I still had to go to East Meadow, Long Island, to hook up with my friend Richie E., from Oswego State. I took a train out there, and Richie met me at the station! We had to hurry, as we were going to a Bat Mitzvah, for his little cousin. I was so welcomed by everybody, all of Richie's family. I was Richie's friend, and we were going to Europe together! This time in New York City, and Long Island, was a trip unto itself.

Richie and I get along really well, as we were already acquaintances from campus, and then we got to know each other better because of the study abroad trip we both signed up for. He was much quieter than I, until you got to know him, and just a very good guy.

We got up early to drive out to Stony Brook's campus further out on Long Island, to hook up with a friend of Richie's, and getting stoned there just loosened me up for the trip, as we were finally leaving tonight for Europe! Richie wanted to tie up all his loose ends, as my business, and last minute goodbyes, were tied up 2 days earlier when I left Syracuse.

We eventually meet up with our future study abroad classmates, house mates (hotel mates) and some others going on to Paris, after landing tomorrow. It was surreal… it was actually here…I really had only flown that one time to Arizona, not counting jumping out of the small plane, ha ha. That, was more of a jump (skydive), than a flight actually!

This was an International Flight, with Customs, passports, etc. Most of us had never seen each other nor known each other's names, except those that met and partied at the pre-Thanksgiving orientation. There are thirty of us to be exact… plus other passengers of course, including other student travelers, with other destinations. It seemed like it would never get here, or that it was going to happen… Shit, I had no point of reference, shooting from the hip, financially, academically, socially, culturally or even a historic context, nothing but "What the Hell, Bring on the Next Adventure."

This was not a sightseeing trip either! As my mother suggested, if I could stay focused and study for one more semester, as I was to graduate at the end of the semester (assuming good grades were forthcoming).

I needed the five courses and the credits, every one of them to graduate college. I would graduate while in Europe, how cool is that! This was an Economics and Political Science Program, at a graduate school called College of Europe (Europa College), for International students from all over the world, approximately one hundred of them in all. We were thirty American undergrads, mostly juniors, except I think myself, and seven others that were seniors!

I got to know Judy F. and Richie E. previously, and most of the others were basically strangers, quite a few from the different SUNY colleges, other than through Oswego. Judy and I met last spring, when

I heard she was in the group going to Bruges. She was at least a year younger, also excited about going, and we became pretty close. It was an Oswego Study Abroad Program, but open throughout the SUNY Colleges, and as I mentioned previously, a girl from the University of Boston, Sue M. was included (way to go Sue).

Funny, this was all new, and I was still impressionable enough, and that was alright....

Hard to hold that energy and excitement in a container, how about the anxiety... a flight, over an ocean, at night, to a foreign land, language, cultures and the expense...It was all about the moment(s) and living in it....wherever it may be!

From what I could gather, we were all spread out on the plane, hard to figure who was in our group... it was a big International Airport (JFK)... I remember five or six of us hooking up at a bar in the terminal... Some we would meet, like Reenie G., Pat Ma., Mike K. Sue S., Sue M. and they seem to know others that we would ultimately meet. We would have plenty of time later to meet the rest of the group... especially if you were up for anything, and everything.

CHAPTER 3

Winter (Final) Semester: Europe

JANUARY 25, 1976-WE fly over Ireland at sunrise, with so many reflections from below, what a thrill as we approach Europe and finally land in Brussels. We flew with a Belgian Airlines, Sabena….which I will never forget as I still have their bright plaid blanket, which will come in handy for future events.

We finally get together after landing, and also find out who's going on to Paris (also an Oswego Program), Beth was off to Paris…You get bussed in either case, Paris for them, Bruges for us.

More importantly, we are in Europe, WOW! The airport, the people, cars, streets, buildings, busses…within minutes you feel, and see a difference. The people seem to be from everywhere, all over the world, clothing, languages, etc.

I noticed it earlier on the flight over and at JFK, people departing and arriving from all parts of the globe… But now the main language was not English, and the architecture, the transportation, the laws, the cultures, currency, etc.!!!!! Overall, I am too exhausted to think or be concerned about it right now, ha ha!

You know I'm not a big group person, even though Outward Bound taught me a lot about group interaction and keeping a journal. We were going to be sharing this bus, a residence, classes, and probably some adventures…Memories may fade, but with my new camera and journal skills, I was going to live it and document it as best I could…..

BRUGES (BRUGGE) , BELGIUM

It was a long bus ride from Brussels to Bruges, or it seemed long after the flight over and through the night. We now know who is exactly in our group, and we now had an opportunity to talk, get to know one another or start to, and laugh together.... There is a lot of built up excitement, like that champagne bottle as the cork is being twisted!!!!!

Because there is a shortage of rooms, a few of us will double up. I guess they thought Richie and I would make good roommates, which was fine, and we got one of the bigger rooms. There were a few others together, also sharing a room, usually much bigger than the singles, but people do like their privacy. Sue M. roomed with Marcia, Judy F. with Diane for example, and those that had roommates would know that person better for the experience and vise versa, all the good, the bad, and the ugly...

Richie and I ended up with a huge room, with a mirror and sink, and windows to the enclosed porch, which ended up being a convenient shortcut to the showers. Did I mention how cold the showers were (the hot water heater wasn't working), and it is January...welcome to Europe!

Hey, it's college, I didn't expect luxury accommodations. You know, we were clueless... No process, or brochures in advance, no pictures, etc. I think we had one half - page of typed information about the College of Europe program (which I still have).

Running on fumes, three hours of sleep in the last three days... Syracuse, New York City, Long Island, Brussels, Bruges, EUROPE... Hotel/Dorm, new town, school "Overload, Over the Top"! This is what I've been looking forward to for over a year, but it seemed like a lifetime of expectations, dreams, or A FANTASY COMING TO LIFE.

Settle in for a minute with Bart, the teenage son of Madame Bloumarte, our "Proprietress" of our residence at Riddersstraat 12! Bart speaks very good English, and he's big enough to help most who needed it with their luggage and a guide to our rooms.

Madame Bloumarte, Bart's mother is stern looking at first, but motherly in her personal rapport. She will be our house mother, cook, and friend or confidante, if need be, etc. plus their dog Rocky. It's our residence for the semester, but it is their home.

It's also January, cold, dark, and wet, similar to home, but milder, "damp", as we do a quick little walk about after unloading our things in our rooms!

I feel like you don't want to miss anything, anybody, anyplace, and you want to take it all in!

Back at the hotel for dinner, and I end up chatting up everybody… really our First Supper, then almost everyone goes out, but I did not… this is almost unimaginable ….WHAT, THIS IS MONUMENTAL, but I am in it for the long haul! The flight did take way more out of me than the flight one and a half years ago to Arizona…Tomorrow is another day, the second day of this phase of my life. Really similar phases for many of the other students possibly, as some had previous international experiences under their belt, and or came from more sophisticated, upper middle class upbringings, but not all.

This is going to be amazing, having a home base, a place to eat and sleep, and a new group of "friends", or acquaintances so far. From the first night onward, we 30 lived in an exceptionally happy house at Riddersstraat 12, and we are in one of the most beautiful places in Europe, perhaps the World, and certainly the coolest place I've been, Yee Ha!

This will be like a canvas, painted with my own personal touch, and I will be transformed as well in the process. The twenty nine other people I am sharing this with, all seem a bit unique as well. Who picks this team, and what game is it, what does everyone want to get out of it. I don't have a clue yet… although some seem poised and sophisticated, and others not, we would find a blended or common ground, and actually we were the common ground for each other. We would bond very quickly, like an extended family it would seem.

Even our dinners would be together, with a couple different students helping each night. I will never forget learning to love spaghetti mixed with catsup and mayonnaise (more like Russian dressing) or with butter. I didn't eat meat, and it was that or I could go hungry on that particular night! It wasn't the first time I adjusted my eating habits for a group meal, like I did for Outward Bound(losing about 25 pounds in those three plus weeks), holiday family dinners, etc, over the last year and a half since I quit eating meat back at Arizona State in the heat of August, 1974.

I had plans to wing it as far as the overall routine of the program, how's that for having plans. The school, classes, teachers, graduate students, my fellow students, the town and townspeople, and this, our place in time you know, that is an amazing thing. We create history for ourselves in this place and time, so we become part of a greater and more dynamic history!

As a funny aside to our new surroundings, one of the women in our program mentioned to me one of their first shared experiences. Madame's hot water heater wasn't working and their first baths were frigid January dips into deep white tubs, accompanied by peals of laughter (her words), complaining while resolving to overcome all the rigors of travel. Just the thought of it made me laugh, and remember my own first shower there, also with "Ice Cold Water"!!!!!

THIS WAS GOING TO BE MAGICAL IN EVERY WAY POSSIBLE!

(I get pumped, goose bumps, adrenalin….just thinking back !!!!! !!!!!!!!!!!!!!!!!!!!!!!!!!)

I could see the course focus was international, and in particular European Economics and Political Science, and the studies would come. Just being abroad you would learn so much about the cultures, languages, cuisine, history, architecture, currencies, finances, and the different forms of transportation, without opening a book.

Did I mention, the wines, beers, whiskeys, exotic smokes, if one partook that is?

SETTING, TIME, PLAYERS

If one was casting a play, story, or movie we had the ingredients, the Setting (Medieval Bruges), Time (1976) the Bicentennial back home, the Players, ourselves 20-22 year olds, the international students, professors, towns people, and others we would come in contact with. Finally, the opportunity and the freedom, with sometimes complete abandon to be in the moment!

The City of Bruges (Brugge is the Flemish name), which is Flemish in heart, history, and blood, with the canals, cobblestone streets, medieval buildings, windmills, and the faces of the Dutch and Flemish Masters, who were our everyday neighbors.

Well I swear, there are probably 30 out of 30 of us that really seem unique and unique exponentially, like 30 times the Fun, Greatness, and the MAGIC!!!! We were going to seek the highest or ultimate level of adventure, or society, whatever would cross our path, or we would pass through, and feed off each other's energy, and pick each other up when one might be down.

Richie and Judy, I knew a bit, but who are the others? There are 15 guys, Myself, Richie, Andy, Mike, Danny, Larry, Mike K., Walter, Rob, Bob, Robert, Jim, Carl, Art, and Christian. There are 15 girls, Judy, Reenie, Sue M, Lisa, Debbie, Cheryl, Helen, Judy H., Sue S., Pat Ma., Beanie, Diane, Marcia, Patty M. and Katie. We will find out more about ourselves as the semester unfolds. So far, it didn't seem like anything I was ever familiar with, I can't wait!

Each minute, hour and day, was taking a life of its own. What I mean is, are we, our own selves, with our own routines and habits. Are we a group, and supposed to do things in a certain way? We are visitors, but we are residents, locals for a time!! Our range and territory is our hotel, town, region, country and or Mainland Europe, and nearby continents, the British Isles, and of course Ireland, where I actually speak the language... My French from the class that I audited of course will improve, and my high school Spanish, and maybe I'll pick up some Flemish (Dutch like) and German too...ha ha!

I didn't think about it as much as you hear about it, from the administrators and advisors, we are foreign students here to learn, and there is a certain protocol!

There are rules at the hotel/residence, the college, the graduate residence, town laws and customs, etc. You know I am twenty one, a young man feeling his oats, from my bastardized academic/hybrid of college's background. Not exactly a stable routine, like four years at the same school of higher education, but two years at Alfred State, half a year Arizona State, one year at Oswego (2 disjointed semesters), an Outward Bound Program in between with 4 credits in physical education from Appalachian State, and now a final semester in Bruges, Belgium. Five places of accumulated academic credit in three and a half years. I really felt as much a nomad, gypsy, and now a student traveler.

I wish we all had a biography, a snapshot of one another, to share looking back, as I had created one from my Outward Bound experience (personalities & backgrounds). It was great to meet blindly, and get to know one another as time evolved. One might have more in common though if we had more info about each other, and taken efforts to bond differently, with a little background information. Hell, it was, what it was, we were who we were, freckles, blemishes and all.

It was a bit like Outward Bound, where initial images and thoughts, usually grow, or spun off, the deeper you experienced your own adventures or shared adventures, and even, day in, day out stuff. School, home work, the group dinners together, laundry (a novelty), cafes, bars, relative to one's budget as well ,and what you could afford!

From the beginning, a lot of our free time was spent at the local pubs, cafes, restaurants, coffee houses, which were great ways to meet locals, immerse in the culture, enjoy the music, and participate in everyday life. Not every day was a weekend for the local person though, and on weekends a lot of us would head out to other cities and countries.

I meet a great guy from Scotland, who has been living in Bruges for a while, Tom P. from Glasgow. Tom is very friendly, liberal, and he knows his way around Bruges. We hang together at a local café in the daytime, where it's all locals but himself and I.

We went out in fact my first full day in Bruges to Stokus (bar), with fellow students, Richie (my roommate), Danny, Mike B., Carl and Andy. We try beer after beer, talking, listening, laughing, and it was a busy place, with many others having a similar great time.

EUROPA COLLEGE (COLLEGE OF EUROPE)

We start up today at the College, learning school routines, the meeting of the professors and grad students. We also have to register with the city (visa).

Later on there's a dinner at the grad residence and we meet many of the grad students from last night (Stokus), as well as Gabby (Austria), Estelle, Anders (Sweden), Hans (Switzerland), Chris (Bob's wife), Catherine (Switzerland). It was a very nice gathering with cocktails and dinner. Myself, being a quasi- vegetarian (eat seafood), my meals are always an adventure, not necessarily on the exciting side though, like eggs on rice, with wine, cake, and coffee.

We all go out to the De Goezeput after (which is a laid back bar with overstuffed chairs and couches), and I meet an American girl travelling through from California. She is taking some time off from work and touring, and it's nice to be a somewhat local to be able to talk about Bruges, and speak with pride about this wonderful place I live in!

We then take off to Terre Halle (bar) with Judy, Walter, and Dan, and to the bar next to it where Pat works (who I met last night at Stokus). I meet Ann and Corrin from Knokke, which is on the north coast, and we plan on hooking up tomorrow for skating. Early night for us, maybe I am settling down a bit, ha ha!

Classes begin tomorrow, History and Geography are the first two subjects.

I volunteer with Richie to do a presentation on the book "Population Bomb", the world's population growing exponentially from previous generations! In 1976, it was pretty forward thinking and eye opening. It would be an interesting topic, and a good challenge to jumpstart our academic involvement.

Later, at the skating rink in Beaudwin Park, Richie and Dan skate (not I, a long story from my early childhood), but a fun place still, if you aren't skating. It was filled with music, some rides and games, and a lot of people. Tom, Ulla (Finland), Lisa, Ann and Corrin from last night, and we all walk back, and stop at the Lochedizzy (bar, with nice overstuffed chairs), and after that to Terrehalle and Pils(bar), where we run into Professor C., and by 3 a.m. we've had a great time and are very rowdy walking back in the overall quiet of the night.

THE BIRDCAGE

On the way back to our residences we find an old Birdcage out in the street. We start an impromptu soccer match or keep away on the uneven cobblestone streets, with Professor C. (a very cool, dignified and seemingly proper graduate professor). We carried it on for a while, but the racket was real and we get stopped by the police after a while! They were very serious, but they let us go with a warning, as much as we could understand. I think our enthusiasm was curbed but not shuttered and we're home by 4 a.m. !

Ulla, Tom's dear friend from Finland heads to Greece with friends on Friday. I probably won't see her again, as I already am feeling attached to some new acquaintances.

I think every day there's a potential party, a gathering of enough of us to create an adventure! It seems like I've met more people in the past few days then in all of the last year combined. It really is a "HIGH," open to anything, was the "Mantra" (it's only January 28, and we got here the 25th).

History and Political Science today, the professors are for the most part aware that we are part student, part travelers. The experience of being here and travelling elsewhere in Europe, is a "CLASS unto itself". After all, we would have stayed home in the States, if we were just wanted to go to class!

Tonight, we have elections for our group representatives, Richie, and I put our hat in the ring, but Bob and Beenie win. We had good intentions, no hard feelings. We stay in tonight, Tom, Richie, Lisa, and myself and chat with Jeremy, who is our director (an Englishman, part dorm director, college liaison, and one of our professors).

In the morning, Richie and I take a walk through town, up to this point we mostly had seen it at night. It is freezing out when we go to the Post Office, Bank, Dept. Store (Intervacion), the Belfry (10F). The Belfry is beautiful… take some pictures, it is 366 steps to the top, and is definitely a landmark standing over the market place.

We have French class tonight with English Nuns for 600 Belgian Francs, and 100 BF for the book with Sister Lawrence. I think I have enough classes, and I need the money….

"It is Friday," and our 1st weekend (we arrived last Sunday). We head out to King's Disco where I dance a lot with Judy, covering a lot of area and using the whole floor and all my best moves… ha ha! The place is pretty loud and packed, definitely the go to dance venue!

We then take off to Cactus where other friends are and I meet Mary and Greet! We hit it off, and I get a date with Greet for Sunday night. Mary speaks a little English, and Greet can speak as much English, as I speak Flemish, ha ha! We go back to my place and stay up to 5:30 a.m. talking sort of…. It's very tricky to communicate to someone you like, through an interpreter, like dating 2 women, who get to communicate back and forth, a safety valve for them… OK though!

(Photos) Hostel Book & Map, Train info., Bruges/Brugge study abroad info, backpack-boots-invaluable airlines blanket, and almost lodging in Monte Carlo …Ha Ha☺

FIRST ROAD TRIP-BRUSSELS

It's Saturday, so it must be the 1st Road Trip. I am going to Brussels today with Larry and Beenie. We try hitching for a while, but there are three of us and it is slow going and freezing, so we take a train. I only had 3 hours sleep, woke up at 8:30 am, get a 11:07 train for 150 BF, and get there at 12:30 to the Centrum in Brussels.

We walk out straight ahead to the Plaz, take a bus to Larry's uncle's house, Charles and Svena K., and daughter Janet (17). Very nice American family, husband works for ITT and they have a beautiful flat. The aunt makes us a wonderful lunch, CHEESE FONDUE (2 cheeses), and white wine, dipped with French bread, yogurt, coconut cookies, and wine to drink.

Afterwards with Janet, we go downtown to the Galleries, like a mall built inside of, or between, big beautiful older buildings, very expensive (classy). We see the Plaz, Manneken Pis (little man piss), Palace, Ave Louise (5th Avenue).

We head back to Bruges by train at 5:57 p.m., with Janet, Larry's cousin. We arrive back in time for dinner, and off to the Grad Party. It is Reenie G.'s birthday today, and she's twenty one if I am correct…

At the Grad Party, I meet Claudia (Italy), and I dance with a couple ladies from Greece and England, and the Greek girl was very nice in particular. I think dancing is like a language too, fast or slow (formal), suggestive, funny and or wild. We partied a lot all day and I am the last one to leave the party, and get home at 4 a.m. Janet stops in to say good bye in the morning, alas she is a bit young, but very mature.

I have been a little sick, and of course running myself down further, late hours, partying a lot, and very damp, sometimes freezing temperatures.

It is time to take a step back a bit, as the "Population Bomb" project with Richie is due soon. Tuesday evening I might have a date with Greet at Cactus, but I am stood up, "language misunderstanding"? I meet Mark the bartender, and an American Phil C. from Cornell-who had been studying in India. Phil is heading back to States on Tuesday, with his brother Paul, who was in a Paris Program.

I really am feeling shitty, as sick as ever. I haven't finished the book report, which is due tomorrow! We have a group meeting about the long weekend coming up, and the Spring Break from April 9th-26th, a week of school, then 2 weeks off (for study) a week off for Field Trip to Luxembourg, Netherlands, Strasbourg and Brussels, and 4 day trips also. I think on the school trips, you learn the most, because they are part of the educational experience as well, and they go into detail with translators, etc.

We make our report for the "Population Bomb", and it wasn't bad! Richie and I worked well together, and we both thought the topic was interesting. There have been a lot of distractions, I would say, so it was great to move on…

Just staying in, especially when sick, is still part of being here. Tom and Lisa do drawings of me, which are pretty good, definitely my likeness. Judy stops over too, as we seem to look out for one another, and someone always has your back! Tom brought kippers and shellfish for us. We really have a good group coming together, as we all seem to care about one another.

We have a visiting lecturer, Ms. Iniger a Belgian... speaking about Belgian history, courts, laws, etc... she's quite nice. There's a reception at the Town Hall, which Richie and I are a bit late, because we had to pick some beer up for our guests tonight, Greet and Mary. We get some Kronenbourg Biere, which is very good, and has a great buzz... Greet wants to get married, not fool around... they stay over again, and we're up until 5 a.m.

(Photos) Belfry, View to Europa College, Cactus, Ridderstraat, My costume with airlines blanket "kilt" and bottle of Scotch, Ridderstraat, DeGueseput

ROAD TRIP- AMSTERDAM

I don't believe it, THE FIRST BIG TRIP… seems like I have been here a while, it's only February 5th, I am heading to Amsterdam and Madame even prepared lunches for the trip, with cheese, eggs, oranges, bananas and bread.

Come to find out, some of my mates got wine with their bread and cheese for their trips as well….sausage too, but that was ok… ha ha (they know who they are)!

I don't get on the road until 2 p.m., and made it in 5 rides and 6 hours of hitching along the canals and smaller roads which was very cool, more scenic than the major routes and the people seem friendlier and are less in a hurry.

By the time I make it to Amsterdam it is cold and dark, and I have to hook up with the others at the girl's dorm in Nieuwendam (suburb). I meet up with Sue, Lisa, Nancy, and Stacey, some of whom are from Stony Brook.

Great finally hooking up, and off to downtown. We go to the Milky Way, a club (Melkweg), crazy place that costs 8 guilders for a 3 month membership. The place was very trippy, multi floors with a bar, private rooms, smoking hash right at the bar, which seemed quite routine. Mike, Danny, Andy, Richie who came up by train, and then we rendezvous here with all the girls now. We blend in quickly, somewhat out of necessity… It's a Unique Place, keep your wits if you can… some rooms had movies, private parties, with an offbeat and mysterious vibe, bizarre, but ok!

Later we go back to their dorm pub and meet Rolandt, a nice Dutch student. I stay with Nancy on the 6th floor, as we seem to hit it off. Nancy reminds me of a mini Barbara Streisand, whom I didn't know I had a thing for….

Now for a full day in Amsterdam, and we start at the Heineken Brewery at 10 a.m. until noon. If you work it right, you can get extra samples, full beers… Afterward we go to Rembrandt Square to a café, then to the Picasso Exhibit, and take a break back to Nancy's dorm…

Nancy and I go to T'Oxhooft near the American Express office, and meet Allen from Taco Tree (California). It cost 6.5 guilders for 3 drinks and admission (ok) near the Central Station. Others went to the Red Light District, 50 guilders ($20.00) for a hooker, seemed to be the going rate one of my mates found out... It's a crazy place, porno film for 5 guilders ($2.00), one lady slapped a guy in the face for taking pictures of her in "her window" (display). Strolling around, it was like being on a midway. Later hitched back with Nancy to her dorm to be alone, after a day's worth of entertainment...

Today I take in some more art at the Van Gogh Museum, which is beautiful. I was crazy enough to think I could walk away with a painting, just feeling mischievous and carefree... it didn't look wired or alarmed. Crazy just for the moment, but I gained my senses...I think it was all the "It Takes a Thief" types of movies I grew up with....

I meet a couple girls from Heidelberg at the Museum. Then go back, drink, smoke hash, get buzzed, and go to Red Light District with Nancy.

On our last day here we are on the tram in town, a few of us Americans, which was otherwise packed. There were people on it from all over it seemed, when all of a sudden, someone yells "Someone took my wallet, my red wallet". I had just seen one guy pass a "red" wallet to another guy coming from that direction. I grabbed the guy nearest me, and opened up his jacket where I saw him put the wallet, and it wasn't there... I was surprised, then quick thinking, flipped the back of his jacket and "there it was" inside the lining, I grabbed it... passed it forward to these 2 American guys. I said, "No problem, no police", to the thieves. The thieves then pushed a stop button above the rear door... exited and like that they were gone! "Anything could have happened, no lie." It was very impulsive to do the right thing, watch out for one another! They were come to find out, probably Moluccans (Indonesian), as others on the tram stated.

My friend Andy said to me later on, that I sure had "BIG BALLS" to do what I did. Whoever they were, they were very comfortable on and getting off the trams. No harm no foul, move on to the next adventure!

I head back to Bruges on Sunday with a tram to the outskirts of Amsterdam, then hitch to Breda, Antwerp, Ghent… then train rest of way to Bruges 96 BF($1.92) get in about 7 p.m. (6 ½ hours) Madame again is marvelous, as she had food waiting on the table, stuff my face and crash about midnight.

Madame would sit down and listen to your stories from the different trips or about something new in town, school, etc. We would chat for what seemed like hours, sipping a tea and eating whatever she had leftover or what she would be preparing for the next meal. It always seemed she was like my mother and genuinely interested in anything, everything, and anybody we'd encounter. Madame would listen, never interrupting, only if I asked what she thought or her advice…so completely "nonjudgmental"!

Madame seemed to know so many things, and or have many experiences in life, perhaps from being such a good listener, and all the students that have passed through over the years. It was impossible not to respect her and all she did for all of us. If she needed something she didn't have to ask twice. Funny, with my first meals here and not being a meat eater, I would not complain as I learned it was my choice not to eat meat. Well, it was a compromise to blend the condiments to come up with a suitable topping to the spaghetti, or sauerkraut without the wurst, etc…I was not the type to whine, but to adjust, and she was more than willing to help me, if it didn't cost more from the budget, ha ha.

The next day upon our return from Amsterdam, the Canadian Ambassador was visiting Jacobstraat (Grad Residence). He gives a presentation, and I notice some of the French grads mocking his accent and or content, like snobs, but who am I to judge? It is a beautiful day over all, especially outside!!!

I really mean to do well in school, and everybody is overall very good to us, and it's truly a very great opportunity, almost "Ivy League" like. They (grads) are all older than us, more sophisticated by far, but none the less, very approachable…

We go out Wed. night for Judy H's birthday, and it's another nice day (Spring- like Feb 11th) Mike, Dan and Beanie give their expose in Kormos's class. We go to the De Goezeput, and Terrehalle late, to help celebrate her birthday.

Abe Lincoln's Birthday is next, and Sue and Nancy come in from Amsterdam. We party of course at our Residence with beer, wine and whiskey… then off to the PICK, and everyone sings me Happy Birthday @ midnight. We hang with a few Belgians as well, a lawyer, designer, and a drunk!!!

The next morning, and it's my birthday now February 13th!!!! It will probably be a long day, and I will savor every minute of it ☺ Nancy and I go for a walk to the College and to the Main Square, and she did some shopping. We get some Bordeaux wine and cheese, then dinner @ Jacobstraat, late of course where we have more wine and scotch. Later about 10 of us go to Cactus, drink Trappiste with its 7, 9,or 11% alcohol content if I recall, and of course have too much fun…

Today, it's Valentine's Day, Nancy and I go to the Market Place and walk all over Love Lake Park, and race back for lunch. Try my costume on, I am going dressed as a "Scotsman" for the costume party @ Jacobstraat!. My kilt was the Sabena Airlines blanket that came with me from the flight over…. I was actually in running for best costume, but great time, dancing etc. BUMPA (Kiss Dance), waltz, polka, etc. Meet a few more grad girls from Netherlands, and Mary (American friend of Bob and Kris) visiting from Australia… Stay out 'til 4 a.m.

Our visitors, stay until tomorrow, we get stoned in Mike's room, then go see "La Dent de la Mer" Teeth of the Sea, or JAWS. It's at a beautiful theatre, and we also have a couple beers @ Cactus before the movie… The movie had French subtitles, but in English… The wildest movie I had ever seen, buzzed and never want to go in the ocean again!!!

Today, I play a little basketball, one on one with Mike B., on his birthday. We had picked up a ball at the local sporting goods store and the court was a distance from our residence, but worth the hike, as we had discovered on another day. We all go out to De Goezeput for his birthday later, but I am pretty beat, not staying too long.

I have a long, heart to heart with Judy when I get back, talking about our childhoods, and get caught up with our lives over here, and our backgrounds...

We play some 3x3 basketball a couple days later, there's me, Mike B. Richie, Andy, Danny, and Jim. We're really getting in to it, the exercise, the bond, the thing we all knew and liked (were accustomed to). We have an actual game with the Grad students later that night. Very physical game, and we beat them 52-27, but it was rough. It seemed more like rugby, or football at times, they didn't have the finesse of the game down, but played hard, and we respected that. They had a party afterwards, but I was really beat!

Also, there was always something happening next or around the corner. Like going to Paris, as I was supposed to hitch in the a.m. but too tired, and sore to go (BB game). It's a beautiful day, sweater weather and I meet a guy from Minnesota from 1st Bruges Program, in 1968, from McAllister College. Also it's Helen's birthday, but I am going to Paris in the morning!!!!!

ROAD TRIP-PARIS

I am on my way to Paris from Bruges hitching, as I walk about 16 km out of 20 km to Torhout, then get a ride to Menen, then another 10 km or more walk at least to ¾ way to Lille in France. Get a great ride from a guy in the Record Industry, and he gives me a cassette "Jacque Brell," then a truck driver to Roye, for 5 hours. I bullshit in English and my "Merde" (Shit)French with the young truck driver then help him unload his truck at St. Quentin, then a ride right to the Eiffel Tower @ 7 p.m. (11 1'2 hours) and I'm late for rendezvous with Dan and Andy. I walk to the Arc de Triumphe, by Ave de Kleber, about 8 p.m. and by 9 meet up with them, Lynn and Gabby.

How amazing, look where we are....PARIS!!!!! We walk down the Champs Elysee, then to Place de Concord, Notre Dame, along the Quai of the Seine River to the Latin Quarter and to a café! We just saw the most wonderful sites in Paris, Iconic images and voila, "We are in like Flynn" (Expression)....

It's late, and we have no place to stay! The girls live in an all girl's dormitory, which is apparently strict. We look for a room at 12:30 p.m. at about 5 different hotels, and no luck. Then some local character tries to help, but those hotels are too expensive. He lets us crash at his place, which is about a 1 hour walk past the Latin Quarter, past the Bastille, a beat little room at the top of a tall thin spiral staircase. We crash about 2:45 a.m. , then he wakes us up at 5:15 a.m., because he has to work at 7 a.m. He made coffee at least, very civilized! Still dark outside, Dan sleeps for an hour @ Metro, where we hang out!

We start our day @ Sacre Couer (Sacred Heart), utterly beautiful church on hill, then the artist square... Mont Marte, is extremely cool place. We go to Pigalle "Red Light District," where I fall in love (infatuation) with a beautiful blonde woman of the night (but in broad daylight), "Ou est la metro" I blurt out to create a conversation. It's in exercise in futility, unless I plan on spending a lot of money that I don't have.

We visit the girl's residence on Blvd. Respail # 11! Before we lunch, Lynn takes us to Luxembourg Gardens and then to lunch which is great, and see Beth I., also 2 of the 3 girls I met in Amsterdam. We go to the top of the Arc de Triumphe, beautiful views, then the Aquarium, and old palace, then Eiffel Tower and sit on bridge over the Seine. We get us some 3 Franc red wine ($.75) and get a room for 20 F or $5.00 for 3 of us. We pick up Lynn and Gabby and walk to Ille St. Louis on Pt. by Latin Quarter, Cluny, Pantheon, and Sorbonne.

We head back to Pigalle which looks very cool all lit up, bigger than Amsterdam, different, more like a Carnival. A bit overloaded with so much, as it had been a long couple days, and go back about 12:30, and crash shortly after.

Free @ Louvre on Sunday… I am amazed…Venus de Milo, Mona Lisa, Winged Victory, etc. The Mona Lisa, was really covered up, encased in an extra case (Good thing with my cat burglar instincts/notions, ha ha). Then we went through the Tuilleries Gardens to the Jeu de Paume (Expressionists Museum) for 2.50 F (65 cents-student) Van Gogh, Renoir, Gaugin, Monet, Manet, Pizzaro, Lautrec, etc. I've had more art in two weeks, than my first 22 years combined.

We see Sue S. from our Bruges program, on our way to Notre Dame Cathedral. It is raining a bit, but a beautiful walk. It's huge inside, and I take a few pictures, as in Museums. Take about 30 pictures of Paris… decide against the zoo in Viscennes, because of rain and darkness. I take the train back with Andy @ 3:20 p.m., and arrive in Brussels @ 6:20, in Bruges at 8 p.m. Anjis and her friend give us a ride to Ridderstaat. Dan, is not in yet from hitching, left Louvre about 11:15 a.m. I crash after bullshitting for a while!

TODAY is exactly a month since I left Syracuse, Feb. 23rd on a Monday. Some great trips so far, in particular Amsterdam and Paris, but life in Bruges, the people and events, have been great… always something!

I hope, I am giving as much as I am getting, as we all have our different strengths and weakness, personalities, adventurous or not. The cerebral and artsy… it takes all kinds. The basketball has brought 5-6 of us together, with our own distinct bond, but also, a way to bond with some of the grads as well…

Classes have been ok, as the teachers are very understanding. We talk of Carnival in Köln this week, during Poly Sci. class (Mancke's class). We decide to go there Friday morning. We also have an 8 day trip to Britain coming up…

We have a waltz lesson at the grad residence tonight, I dance with Patty M. And Judy for an hour, it was a lot of fun… structured, but loose at the same time. The basic waltz steps can help you, or guide you in almost every form of dance I learned (and put into practice whenever I had the chance).

Stop in to see Malcolm with Lisa and Mary Rose (Dublin), Malcolm had hurt his leg Saturday playing soccer. Stay there for a while 'til 11 p.m. and back at Ridderstraat, stop in to see Sue S. for a while and listen to the Jacque Brell cassette, that I picked up while hitching to Paris. I really have this romanticist side of me, constantly with French café music in my head.

I am doing my paper for Kormos's class, I tell Kormos.

I take it easy today, and it is Cheryl B.'s birthday so the girls are going out later. Some days are like a blur, can't all be a party.

Friday Feb. 26th- We have a new young teacher, who the girls seem to like. He seems like a good guy, had him twice today.

I go out with Tom, Lilly, Sue (who studied here 2 years ago) and her friend, a teacher from Alberta, Canada, and we go to the Cactus.

The Cactus, I would say is my go to bar/café, .I think from the very first, the co-ed restrooms, variety of Trappist beers, etc....

Later, we walk Lilly to the train station, as she heads towards Paris.

Thurs. Feb. 26th- Made it to Tsoukalis's class....We play some basketball today, with me, Bob and Richie against Dan, Mike and Andy, split 2-2, rode bikes there and back... it was great... a wonderful mix of local transportation, and our basketball routine...

Nancy and Sue are in from Amsterdam, on their way to London... but, we are getting ready to go to Koln (Cologne), tomorrow. We have Mary Rose, Malcolm, and Davey O'Brien over for supper, and then we go to bars and pub next to Terrehalle, and then King's Disco to meet the girls. I dance with Nancy as if there is no tomorrow, then off to De Goezeput and meet 2 Belgium girls, who are planning to go to America (Perige-little bird, and Kate), then, I crash, as I have a big trip tomorrow for Fasching (Mardi Gras..) in Koln(Cologne) !

ROAD TRIP-COLOGNE (KOLN)

"Carnival in Cologne" (Fasching in Köln) here I come, hitching by 11:30 a.m.-via Ghent, Brussels, a ride by a fellow that worked for CBS, Köln (3 rides), final ride with a girl going to meet her boyfriend! I am there by 4:30 p.m. (5 hours) and it's 8:30p.m. before Danny shows up at the Cathedral (Dom), and 9:30 p.m. when Mike arrives by train.

We finally get started, head out to the University area, end up at bar with a lot of people partying. Meet about 10 Germans and 1 American, who buys us drinks all night! Sue an American from San Francisco, and Elmer, her friend from Heidelberg we also run into. The streets are bustling with activity, all the bars, cafes are packed, and music is everywhere. We finally, move on to another bar, which is noisier, and meet more people 'til about 3 a.m. Take a Mercedes taxi (a rich person's car back home) to the Dom (main cathedral)!

We end up sleeping outside and in front of the Dom, for about 2 hours (freezing) as we climbed over this work area wall, outside of sight of anybody. It is freezing though and we wake up and go in subway for a while to get warm, while Dan and Mike sleep, I keep lookout. They head back to Bruges by train @ 9:42 a.m. Are we crazy, one night partying in another country!!

I am supposed to meet Elmer and Sue, but they don't show at Neumarket, at or near the Hertie Store. I hang around and watch the parade, very nice, beautiful sunny day! As I am leaving town, I see this very nice park full of these amazing, athletic Afghan Hounds, they looked to be training for something….,WOW, what a sight!

I take a tram to outskirts of the city and I start hitching by 12:45, and I get a quick ride to Aachen, then Brussels (2 students) Japanese and German, visiting an American there! I take a train the rest of the way to Bruges, after all, there's a Carnival like Party at the Belfry tonight!

I got back about 7:15 p.m., exhausted, eat, change my clothes as I go as a PIRATE, with my handy plaid Sabena blanket as a sash. I have no money though and I am exhausted, so I leave early about 12:30 and crash, it's 2/28/1976.

It's a nice day, Sunday, Lilly, Sue, and I go out to Loppem to see Brigitte at her beautiful little cottage. She has a couple goats, chickens, roosters, and her dog Mora, who doesn't seem to like me. Brigitte makes Borsht (a vegetable soup concoction) for supper, and wine. We sit around and talk, very relaxing... Head back about 9 p.m. My local friends from Bruges are becoming pretty close to me now and I to them, I am so lucky...

Upon return to town, I go to De Kogge (Painters Place) where David O'Sullivan happens to be singing, and Malcolm is there too! A little later Richie and Lisa pop in, but I am broke and tired, leave at 11:30 p.m.

It's another beautiful day, and most of us are going to England tomorrow by ferry from Oostende. Sue and Lilly leave for Paris, Nancy and Boodie go back to Amsterdam, leave tonight, so we have to see them off at Cactus for drinks, meet Johan (Ghent U.), and Yule (girl).

I am actually leaving at 1:15 a.m. in the morning Wednesday, but it might as well be Tuesday. I still have Kormos's class, but Mancke's was cancelled (not really I skipped), as I had to pack still. Hell, it's for a week, and I bring a lot, and of course, we have to see ourselves off at the De Goezeput later tonight.

ROAD TRIP-GLASGOW, EDINBURGH & LONDON

I leave Bruges at 11:20 p.m., 15 minutes to Oostende, then 1 ½ hr. wait for ferry, all together 23 of us going over, 22 to London, and I am going to Glasgow. Well, I have gotten very close to Tommy P., and he's back home, he thought it would be great for me to meet his family...

I meet Ely from Peru, on her way to live in London for a couple years. We stay up almost the whole night talking, sleep a bit. The ferry is probably easier to take in the dark, especially after the pub, and duty free, and the Channel can be rough. Ely gives me her number in London to look her up upon my return from Glasgow.

I head out hitching from Folkstone after the ferry lands! I immediately hook up with Michael (student in St. Albans). Michael was born in Austria, has boarded away for many years. We landed at 5 a.m., but don't get a ride 'til 7:30, and in London by 10 a.m. We stay a couple hours in London, walk around a bit, then train with Michael to St. Albans (Hadrian's Wall) very nice, and it's his destination. It is back on the road for me hitching the M1 to Glasgow (4 rides and 9 hours). I am in Glasgow at 11:30 p.m. to Central Station, where Tom Patterson meets me, we have a meal at his home, get caught up, then I crash! It was a long day(s), train, ferry, and since I started hitching 18 ½ hours from Folkstone.

It's pretty cool, not seeing London really, to go to Glasgow to see Tom and his family. I am so comfortable traveling, hitch, train, hike, ferry, Belgium, France, Germany, Holland, England and on to Scotland. This is all winter travel mostly, 3rd week of January to 1st week of March, still much milder than back home. It is damp at times, slushy but overall no real snow!

I like Glasgow, but I don't know if I would I have picked it as a tourist destination if Tom didn't live here, not sure! Real Glaswegian's are they with very thick accents, and really a pleasure to be so welcomed by them! Meet Ann-Marie, Tom's sister and Tom's mom, we have a nice breakfast and chat, very welcoming. We walk through town for quite a while, then the proverbial pub stop "Macular Arms" (not bad) but I am really beat, from just getting here! Talk for quite a while though.

You Take the HIGH ROAD and I'll Take the LOW ROAD, AND I'LL BE IN SCOTLAND BEFORE YOU, and we are off to Loch Lomond. I am a creature of history, books, stories, movies and any adventure .Tommy and I were hitching there, and got there in 2 quick rides. The last ride, was like I was going to a foreign land in lore, and language, the truck driver spoke a different dialect than in Glasgow, or so it seemed. He was from Fort William, if I understood right…Tom was laughing, knowing I was completely baffled by the conversation.

We were visiting old friends of Tom's, who ran the Youth Hostel at Loch Lomond. My kind of place, the Hostel was beautiful and at an amazing setting. Jim and Margaret ran it, and they made us feel like royalty, they were so friendly. Tom and I took a hike up in the Heather, among sheep, cows and with Sheba, their dog. It was utterly breathtaking, the air, the views, the moment, and I had goose bumps being in such a place.

Well, just a day trip and we get back in one ride around dark to Glasgow. I meet Danny, Ann Marie's boyfriend "fiancée", as they are getting married June 12th! It's another fine day, and great talking with the family...

Off to Edinburgh in the morning, what's this, a stop at the pub with Danny and Tommy! So, I end up a little bit later start, after mixing my lager and whiskey, and meet a wonderful old hosteller, named Jimmy Stevey, telling stories of his youth and travels, it was so well worth it!

1 ride to Edinburgh from 3-4:30 p.m. , a bit hung over and cold!! I think I won't hitch to London, (we'll see)!!

I am staying at Eglinton Hostel for £1 ($2.00) meet an American girl Wendy, and go to sleep early though. Hostel is on Eglinton Crescent, near Darmeashaus and Haymarket. Walk through town, park, Princess St. I stow my gear at bus terminal, see Parthenon Observatory at Calton Hill, Old Calton Cemetery (David Hume, and Lincoln statue/mausoleum like), and go to "The CASTLE" that overlooks the city. There is no guard, but basic today, the big event is later this year, which is called the "Tattoo".

There was a great veggie place nearby, with Krish Rotatonies... probably the best food I've eaten over here....

Get bus to outskirts of town, Roundabout at Wallygord A1. Get going about 2:30 p.m., my 1st ride was from 2 Australians, about 150 miles (South of Dearhams) then 250 mile ride by Paul Davis, who lets me stay at his flat in London (Meet Phil and Win) at 89 Charlotte St. I am always open to meeting new people, which is very much a part of the experience. We stay up 'til 3 a.m. (made it in 8 hours; 2:30 p.m.-10:30 p.m.).

It's amazing, the luck of the rides and the wonderful people… Wake up early, but enjoy relaxing in a nice flat, get out about 11 a.m. I try to hook up with Ely (from the ferry), call her and we're to meet at 3 p.m. at S. Kensington Station.

I walk all over, 5 Museums and elsewhere, Trafalgar, St. James, Marble Arch, Hyde Park, Piccadilly, Oxford St. I meet Solomon, a Jew born in Babylon, coming from Israel, stopping in London on his way to Los Angeles (UCLA).

Ely, and I never hook up, and I head back to flat, but have trouble getting in. I finally get my things, but then I have to race to catch bus at Victoria Station, too late, take train for £2.91. Miss the right train car at 9:10 p.m., they untie the car I'm in, while I'm sleeping in E. Maidenhead, then Ashford and to Dover, and I almost miss the ferry.

Meet Edgar, a Dutchman while waiting for ferry, which leaves at 12:20 p.m. and in Oostende at 5 a.m. It actually gets there at 5:50 a.m. and back to Bruges at 6:04 (station). It is always a good walk to the Residence, tea and letters waiting… sometimes it's great to get away, and great to return. It's Tuesday March 9th (left Tues. March 2nd) a full week worth of travel…someday, I'll just visit "a single place" and branch out from there, with day trips, ½ days, etc.

I am a good student and make it to both classes, EXHAUSTED, HUNGRY and BEAT!! It really was a Marathon of sorts… not complaining, it always seems like there is so much to see… and I have the budget of "Oliver Twist"! Today overall is a good day, setting back in, and relax with fellow friends, and students, speaking of our adventures!!

Really a blur for a day or so, catch up on writing, square dance practice, for upcoming American Party, and basketball with the Grads. It's really the best conduit we have to exchange together, no overall common language but English and Basketball, which is becoming "Universal"!

There are visitors from Copenhagen today, Todd, Kay, Kate, and Sue from Wisconsin. Todd hangs in my room, as Richie went to Paris this afternoon, until Saturday. I take Todd to the Pick, and we have a volleyball game with the grads later… Have a great rapport with the grads lately, between basketball, volleyball, different parties, pub life, etc.

Miss class to do my first wash, after all these weeks, is that possible? I am so European now, ha ha! I did bring a lot of clothes... Actually, people don't shower and wash as much in Europe, hot water is not that common. Dinner at Jacobstratt tonight, these dinners at the grad residence are really nice, a little more formal than ours(Good thing I brought my "Thrift Store " sport coat), which are more casual and family style, with a couple different students helping Madame every night!

Girls from Paris are in today, so I go to meet them at station, Gabby, Lynne, and 6 others. We settle them in at Residence Hotel then we all go to the Pick. Later, I go to De Goezeput and King Disco with Gabby, Lynne and Judy H., partied and danced pretty hard, and of course had fun...

Today is the day that we are hosting an American Party for the College's International Grad students... We all help pick up the house, then pick up beer, with the Party starting at 8:45 p.m.

We had macaroni salad, coleslaw, hamburgers, ice cream, chocolate chips and brownies. BASH & BEER! Dance all night, I mean we square danced at the party, and I used some of my moves from the North Carolina "HOEDOWN", that I learned at the end of Outward Bound last year. It was a bit corny, for some of the Grad Students, but it was fun. Heck we don't normally square dance either... We were ultimately up all night, wolfing down salad at 4:30 a.m. in the kitchen with Mike K., Sue M.'s uncle from London who was visiting, Judy F., and Andy P. Andy and I stayed up to 6;30 a.m., just too wired to sleep....

Still somewhat hungover at noon, I then help pick up downstairs a bit, and drink some leftover beers and listen to music for a while back in my room. Todd and the girls leave for Copenhagen at 6 p.m. for 16 hour train trip. I am so beat, that I crash about 8 p.m.! Sleep for 13 hours, still tired, you pay to party. We watch "Take the Money and Run" and "Cool Hand Luke," crash early tonight too! Big trip coming up...SPRING BREAK!!!!!

INTERRAIL

Well with Spring Break coming up in the near future, I decide to hang it out there and pull off my biggest and longest trip yet. Noticing at the train station that there are train passes called InterRail Passes, with unlimited travel in up to about 30 countries within a month's time. You have to be 23 years or younger and from a European country, or in our case (Mike K.) and myself, being City of Bruges residents, as we had our Visas as local college students. The age was just raised from 21 to 23 this year, or I might not have qualified, having turned 22 back in February. The alternative was a Eurail Pass which was more costly and I didn't need 1st class....

I get my InterRail Pass, for 4,999 BFs ($125.00), which is good to travel by train from country to country, train to train, without a particular destination, allowing for spontaneity and freedom to get off and get on as you wish. The pass starts Saturday March 27th (for 1 month) and ends April 26th.

Mike K. is my travel partner for the break, and he gets a letter from Brigitte from Moissac, France today, about her time available for us to visit, He met her when she studied in the States the year earlier at SUNY Oswego. We leave earlier to visit her from March 30-April 3, because of her break from her school in Switzerland. We are leaving 2 weeks earlier for Spring Break, than our scheduled school vacation, but Hell, the travel is paid for the whole month!!

There is a Debate at the Bank of Brussels, ex-Rector Broughman vs. Aanis (Fr.) "VERY GOOD", Sue S. translated the French to English!

ST. PATRICK'S DAY, March 17th

We have an 11 hour Field Trip through Flanders today. We start at Oostende, Niewport (Locks), Verrine (Cathedral), Dixmuide (German Cemetery and Death Trench), where French officers sent Flemish soldiers to their death at Trench that German machine guns overlooked, as we were told, Ieper (War Museum and Cathedral) Kortrijk (Best Carpet Factory in Belgium).

Now we're back for the Big Festivities (not really), but go to De Goezeput, where Irish grad students David O'Sullivan and David Imman were singing and playing some great songs, both rebel and traditional. It's really a great touch of Ireland, but here in a beautiful Flemish Pub. Drink and talk to Pus, a girl from Kortrijk who was very nice!

One day's events leads to another with Scott Gillespie, a professional golfer over here to tour, staying with us now. He graduated from N. Texas St. at Denton (lot of nice girls there he says). Lisbon, Portugal is the 1st stop on the tour (he comes over 10 days earlier to travel...). He says if I make it there, I can caddy and hang together, we'll see? I am heading that way during break. We go out to Stokus Bar, meet Rudy and Chris and end up closing the PICK, surprise, surprise!!

(Photos) Bruges's Love Lake, Edge of town, canals, and views

Have to go to Ghent today to research my Term Paper for Kormos (Geography). I am going to compare the City of Ghent with my home town of Syracuse, New York. Hitch there in 45 minutes and I only stay 4 hours, and meet Johan who goes to University. Most of information is in Flemish and French, not easy to understand but interesting. Hitch back in time for supper, catch Godfather II for 80 BF, and relax after.

It is a beautiful day today, go to see a Michelangelo and Museum (a local treasure), windmills on the edge of town too. I forgot how beautiful our own town is. When we weren't traveling, we are fortunate to live in a large multi-storey house in a beautiful medieval town with meandering cobblestone streets and flowing canals. Every day was a marvel of exploring parks, churches, ancient alleyways, museums, shops, restaurants and bars where we all became connoisseurs of Belgian beer, chocolate, waffles and frites. And, in the background, there were the bells, chiming throughout the day to herald time's passing, filling the air with their soft music.

Later I play bumper pool in bar with Scot G. There's another dinner party at the Grad Residence, they have schnapps, beer, and wine at dinner, with Irish coffee, Guinness and after, dancing, What a day and night, and off to Lotus for party, meet a girl, and out 'til 3 am.

Spring today, Sunday March 21st, and I call America! I am really tired all day, "I wonder why"?

Scott splits for Calais, and perhaps I'll see him Friday in Paris. We have a group meeting after dinner at Residence, about SPRING BREAK, etc. I do some reading for my Ghent-Syracuse project.

Get my 1st haircut, 365 F ($9.12), by Frankie, a good job too. I picked up money for vacation 5,650 BFs ($141.00).

Play basketball tonight against Bob's Team from the Bruges's League, we won 52-37, came back and drank beers. Bob in particular loves these games and the connection with the grads and in this case the town team. These games are a battle, and they love the challenge, we have more experience growing up with it, even though we put our team together just since we got here.

Madame gives Mike K., and I some extra money for the 2 extra weeks we won't be here. Pack some gear for the trip, shine shoes and boots, chat with Judy H. (she's alright). Pack more the next day and call Ireland, about summer, and maybe a job in Galway!

CHAPTER 4

Spring Break

VACATION- THE BIGGEST trip within a trip! I can't script this too much, or at all, it has to take a life of its own. After all, it really has been a vacation already, but I do know more about Europe in the past 2 months, than my full 22 years of life before, living is learning!

LEAVE FOR PARIS! Enough said, as I say good bye to 3 girls from Nottingham (UK), Par, Gill, and Rita! Maryille is up from Paris, and here to visit Richie (from LA originally)!

From Paris to Frankfurt, train pass doesn't start officially yet, so a half day bonus ha ha. I left early, but a German girl I meet on the train puts me up at her place in Paris that she shares with a girl-friend, and a Frenchman (Goodwyn, Alleno, and Allen). So, now I catch the 7 a.m. to Frankfurt (6 1/2 hours), train to Hoffheim and bus to Wallau, to visit the Scott family.

The Scott's are from Syracuse originally, Pat Gavin Scott is the daughter of one of my mother's best friends, and her husband Alan is in the US Air Force stationed in Wiesbaden, W. Germany. Scotty, Pat and their eleven year daughter Linda are very happy to see me and have me visit in the small German village of Wallau where they lived.

Scotty and I have a drink or two at their home, he then makes a restaurant quality pizza for dinner (in high school he worked at Luigi's which is a very popular place back in Syracuse). We go out about 7 p.m. and meet a few of his friends at the local gasthof, and down some pretty good beers. Later we LISTEN TO INDIANA-UCLA semi-final NCAA Basketball Tournament (March 27, 1976, Indiana Undefeated and Win the NCAA's Men's Basketball Championship, and the last undefeated team still through 2019). All together it was a pretty full day and night, and I felt totally at home…

It's very nice being with the Scotts', Americans and from Syracuse, but equally as nice that they live in a village away from the base in Wiesbaden! It's a beautiful morning, nice like yesterday. We drive along the Rhine River to Loralei, Rudesheim, also a spot where Hitler controlled the Rhine River during WW 2. We started the day with a big breakfast, I felt so at home. I played Frisbee with Linda, meet some of their American friends! It's "Daylight Savings Time in France"… and I weigh myself at 160 lbs. with clothes on! Oh, to have conveniences and updated knowledge once in a while.…

All things change, and good things come to an end. I will miss Scotty, Pat and Linda, and their nice little village of Wallau. I am off to Toulouse in France to meet up with Mike K. Before I go, I hang around talking with Pat, and Linda comes home from school. I am leaving my film here, as Allen is a photographer with the Air Force and will develop it for me, which is very nice.

Catch bus to Wiesbaden, train to Heidelberg, which is beautiful, but can only stay 2 hours (quick tour) meet 3 American girls from Bath, England (via New Jersey and Connecticut), just barely catch my 7:06 p.m. to Toulouse!

Been on the train 14 hours, with a ways to go yet, beautiful again (4th day in a row), sleep a bit! Beautiful country side… Lyon-Avignon… dark, before that! Jura Mts., I change soon at Avignon… and meet Mike tonight at 8:22 p.m. in Toulouse.

I arrive earlier at 2 p.m. and catch 2:10 to Moissac, and I call Biÿou when I get there. Her mother and her are so nice to me and her father too, whom I meet later. We drive to Toulouse in the evening to pick up Mike, who was so surprised, and thrilled.

We are being treated like Kings!!! It is a beautiful here, with a view from on top of a mountain overlooking the town of Moissac, the Tarn & Garonne Rivers.

I get a sun burn while lying out as temperatures and sun are much hotter than what we've been used to!

We eat like horses, with wine at most meals, Vin Ordinaire (Table wine). The parents are so nice, but don't speak English "Quel Domage" (what a pity). One of Biÿou's cousins is visiting, her name is Mido. Mike and I are learning to drive a standard, the parents let us borrow , it's a Renault Deux Cheavaux (Biÿou doesn't drive) on small French Roads and Mountains, and her father is so nervous (I don't blame him). Biÿou's other friend and fiancé have dinner with us also, and it's an absolutely beautiful day and night!

(Day #6 of SPRING BREAK) April 1st "Fool's Day," that's us laying in the sun again, so hot and nice, the air, the smell, in the country side, like nothing I had ever felt, "fresh, clean, warm…". Listen to music and dance for a while, I take a long walk with Biÿou, voila, we like each other, "it's the air." I've never been so swept away, is it the place, the whole family, Biÿou, etc… We drive again, almost in to a ditch and it was hilarious, Biÿou and Mike pushing it (car), her cousin and I in the car laughing, It's like Heaven here. We walked through town, to the Cathedral, old fort from the 10th century, and Cloister.

Take a shower in the morning then Biÿou and I have breakfast to-gether, tartines. I go to town with Mike to pick up food with the car for our picnic today, flowers for Mama too! We visit Mido's village about 25 km from Biyou's, and picnic, a little cloudy but nice. Drink wine all day at picnic, then over to Mido's one set of grandparents, then another. We actually drive pretty well today, especially after getting looped on Spanish (Port) and French Wine. We bring back Josiane, another of Biÿou's cousins, and everyone is so nice!

Tomorrow Night is a Big Ball! Sunny every day so far!

Saturday, April 3rd, and up early and shower. We pick up Mido and then to their grandparent's house for lunch. We eat so much as usual, and drink a lot too! Josianne, Mido, Biÿou, Mike and I are all going to the Ball tonight. We have to dress up, but my pants aren't good enough, and I try a boy from the town's pants on, too tight, try papa's pants too big, everyone laughs. It is so funny, I am laughing too, even papa has a big laugh…it was worth just for that!

We make it to the Ball (big pants with a tight belt), and dance up a storm, Cha Cha, Bimbo, Waltz, Twist, Polka, etc. We drink champagne all night and have a great time. So many people, a lot of beautiful people, and papa went too!! Papa was very proud, but a little embarrassed as we were pretty wild…and in his pants, ha ha!

Go to 11th century church (it's Sunday) eat a huge lunch at Mido's house, champagne and wine of course… get a little drunk and take a walk in field with Biÿou and Mike. More of Biÿou's cousins are there, girls of course, Colette, Marie, Josianne.

Finally, we go home and relax, watch T.V. with Biÿou. Mido went back to school in Toulouse this night. But, there are more relatives, Biÿou's grand uncle and aunt, and great grandmother. We ride on a tractor, and visit Mido's mother, who is sick. I am actually driving the standard pretty good, and so is Mike, winding through the narrow and winding roads. Drink champagne when we get home and fool around downstairs. Didn't I say it was like Heaven here!

Mama and Papa's day off, we buy flowers and champagne for them, as they have been the ultimate hosts "French Parents to us." Mama Bissiere was like a mother to us, another adoptive caring mother the whole time this week. I don't think language is a requirement for caring for somebody. I wish I had taken the extra French class in Bruges, just to be able to communicate better with her. Papa, was papa, working mostly, but also genuinely happy to have friends of their daughter visiting. I will not soon forget the trying on of the different pants for the ball!

Well we are off shortly, eat, pack, shower, and buy batteries for my camera. Biÿou even packs a lunch for Mike and I. We are leaving by train to Narbonne at 12:30, and saying goodbye to Biÿou was difficult, as we became very close this week.

11th day, thus its April 6th!

Narbonne-Port Bon-Barcelona-Valencia (21 hours), Barcelona looked nice. A new stage, Spain, and going to Ibiza!!

Warmer, warmer, warmer, the further south we headed, also a different country, culture and terrain. Great people on the trains, a lot of families, always trying to communicate, but ultimately bog down, and a lot of smiles by all of us, especially the children. The ticket takers and customs are always so serious, suspicious of us backpackers a bit, but nothing too heavy! I can be suspicious acting, mischievous, but not in a heavy way either, ha ha!

We're leaving from Valencia by boat to Ibiza tonight at midnight. In the meanwhile we crash on the beach most of the day, meet a couple girls from California, Cindy and Suzanne. It's magical travelling, like a glow of happiness, and an acceptance of what adventures exist and lies ahead. Very hot, but breezy, later on when we walk thru town, stop at a couple cafes, as to kill time (we've been here since 9:30 a.m.). Valencia, is fairly dirty so don't mind moving on, boarding the boat at 11 p.m.

Mike and I run in to Miro, young fellow from Switzerland, and Poofs from Argentina, we met getting tickets and we get a cabin together. Easy, so easy to meet other travelers as we all stand out like an army of backpackers!

Never at a loss for new acquaintances, Esther from Quebec City, hangs with us for a while on the trip to IBIZA. But, my weakness, I meet an absolutely beautiful Spanish girl, but she doesn't speak English, we communicate un poro… que lastima. Esther helps, as she speaks 3 languages, but it's not the same, as the translator and girl become more acquainted, ha, ha! Absolutely fun filled time, music and singing as we depart, and "festival like" on the boat.

Everybody goes there separate way, girls anyways, as I still have Mike, Miro, Roberto, and a crippled fellow, also from my cabin. We get a coffee and find a place to stay at HOTEL EUROPA at 240 pesetas for a double. It was a very nice room, with a shower and bath. We made it, we're in a very famous resort Island! Majorca, larger and more famous, but for older folks, is nearby (4 Islands-the Balearics).

We're in pretty early, eat Tortilla Francesa (omelet sandwich), and walk around a lot. Later after resting and cleaning up a bit, take a walk to beach (deserted) we buy some wine and Esther comes over for drinks,and we then go on to a very nice bar, Myself Mike, Esther, and Miro. We were all feeling good and we're all best friends by now, bonds are easily formed, it goes with the travel, I know we are never short on fun…

The following mornings are sometimes slow though. Esther and Mike go to rent scooters, and I haven't gotten my act together as quickly. Adios, I go for a walkabout finally to see the town. Fantastic old fort with great views is my destination, and I run in to Miro, Roberto and Nicholas. Miro and I hike out to rocky coast, over the hill (4000 graves of old Carthaginians, dug in rock). Esther and Mike hook up with us, but Esther gets insulted by a Spaniard, and goes home. We all go to a small bar with excellent music, Mota Club/ Diaco a very cool place, with music and of course dancing. Meet Tommy, a German fellow a bit later.

Today is Saturday, and we decide to leave Tuesday not Thursday, so we get a ticket in advance. Cloudy today, go to San Antonio to rent horses (they're beat) walk around afterwards (we were faster than the horses).Sit in sun, walk through town, nice sandal shops… but very commercial, crash early tonight.

It's Sunday, and almost every place is closed, can't even eat almost. Decide to hitch to Las Salinas, very nice beach, sunny for 1 ½ hours then clouds move in with rain. Heading back by bus to Ibiza, it clears up, beautifully. We watch sunset in Harbor… absolutely beautiful, will be nice tomorrow we think. Have a couple beers, and talk at our Hotel and crash after reading.

It is great when I my get money back for ticket we exchanged, so I can get some food. Go to Las Salinas again, a lot of people today. It is sunny to start, then overcast and windy. We got a real nice spot for our wine, bread, and radio. Good rays, good times, we take a walk up the beach, and apparently it's the Nude Beach, and so it was NICE…. When in IBIZA, ha ha!

Do some wash when we get back, leave tomorrow at noon! A LOT OF GERMANS HERE, Tui Int'L Tours (German, biggest in the world I heard)!

Going out and it's our last night, meet a Swedish guy, and couple German girls and a guy from Andorra, and Miro. It is very expensive, very nice new bar, many girls, near Chino's (3 different bars near each other). I really don't have a resort budget…..

The boat to Alicante is supposedly @ noon today but it leaves at 5:45 p.m. instead, get drinking on again. Meet Doug (Buffalo), Mike (Vancouver), Harry and Judy (York, Eng.) on the boat. We land @ 2:30 a.m. hang around beach 'til a train for Granada @ 5:30 a.m. which is late. There is a theme in Spain so far…

Meet Scott (Dayton, Ohio), who goes to school in Valencia and on his way to Gibraltar. It's a 13 hour ride to Granada, and we'll stay the night without much time for touring, get a pensione for 75 ptas (pesetas).

MOROCCO, AFRICA

We leave for the port of Algeciras at the southern part of Spain, across from Gibraltar, in early a.m. and then boat to Ceuta 126 ptas ($2.00) 1 ½ hours. Ceuta is part of Spain, but in Morocco, AFRICA. We arrive @ 7:30 p.m., we know we left Europe, no question, the buildings, roads, people, clothing, mixture of languages.

We are looking to go a bit inward, travel to Tetuan, by bus @ 9 p.m. The bus we had paid for and were on, had to stop at the customs, and we all get off to get checked through. As we were checking through, the bus I just takes off and leaves us there at the BORDER (Customs). Many people had left their bags on the bus and now we were stranded and it was paid for!!! Very mad, in utter disbelief, but weary and cautious!

We meet up with Harry and Judy from the boat and also stranded by the bus., After spending 2 ½ hours at the Border, lost the 1000 pesetas for the bus, we start walking toward the nearest village.

Hell it's night, we just arrived in Africa, hearing crazy sounds, we bond with these 5 guys from Dartmouth (they study @ Granada), Harry, Judy, Mike and I. We are all walking along the very dark, hilly road outside of Ceuta and toward Tetuan, and we were very suspicious of the area for very good reasons.

In the next village we get a taxi with Mohammed to Tetuan, where we spend the night. Next morning, I buy a Jalaba (long full length hooded robe) to blend into our environment, a leather jacket (traded my jean jacket), leather passport pouch, traded other stuff, sunglasses, 3 shirts, scarf. I feel ripped off as I am trying to "Haggle," but they're the pros! Shortly later we take a bus to Tangiers. It is crazy at the bus terminal, begging, stalling, harassing, and staring all over town.

Tangiers is also Crazy, and Much Bigger. There are a lot of people, and everybody selling, anything and everything. You hear a lot of "hashish" "hashish," you want to buy? Come to find out, the police set people up that buy from the "narcs"on the street. I am wild and crazy @ times, but you get the feeling if it seems too easy, then it could go big time wrong. My instincts are safe and secure, right, as we are on their turf, and it's like no place I've ever been, it's not NYC, LA, Amsterdam, London! It's their country, continent, culture, and their customs, but you know it's not legal, and don't want to go down!

We (Mike and I), meet a young Swedish guy and German girl that we get along with and we all decide to get a hotel or pensione together. The Swede talks to everybody on the streets about Hash, I get pissed off because he's so obvious (naïve), no way or he's on his own I tell him! So here I am acting as the mother hen, but I don't want to be busted. The girl Anna is spacey too, keeps her purse slung behind her, and 3 different shoves against her, and I end up grabbing a thief's arm right out of her bag. No Problems, and get in her face a little too, naïve… 18-19 year olds probably… nice kids, I feel old, but street smart!

We meet a couple more Mohammed(s), anybody who speaks English wants to be your guide, take you to a Hotel, get a kick back (commission). I buy a fancy colorful shirt from one guy ($5.75), very touristy of me, but it was different, exotic….

We are bugged again and again, for hash, clothes, another jalaba, a room, bus, etc.. When in Morocco, be in a Jalaba to blend in….well I tried anyway, ha ha!

That night Ronnie the Swede wants to get in my good graces, so he invites me to enjoy the hash that he had earlier purchased. He is a friendly kid and I partake, it is very good, very strong, it was like tripping, and hits me hard and quickly. We are all friends again though, and the stress between Ronnie and I is over.

We are not in Kansas anymore, and all the sounds and smells are magnified after smoking. All night long, there is music playing with exotic sounds, songs, and voices throughout the night… I sleep with one eye open, and I dream that men were climbing up the walls with daggers in their mouths, I awoke, exhausted but alive!

Saturday morning, Mike and I leave for Ceuta, and back to Spain at Algeciras! Morocco, in particular Tetuan and Tangiers, are too much for now, even though I feel we can hold our own, too many people playing off you, too many Mohammed's. The Jalaba, doesn't cover the shoes or lower jeans, and as an obvious outsider, it is too hectic to relax… It is a 3 hour bus trip to Ceuta, via Tetuan, but there is no boat out of Ceuta 'til manana @ 11:30 a.m. We can't find a room, but meet some nice Missionary types, Dan and Cheryl. They are "Christians", and let us stay in their church. We get to take a shower even, after almost 5 days, and it's our first hot meal since France.

Come morning (Sunday) and down to the boat back to Spain, and Europe. Well, we need to move on anyways,

BACK TO EUROPE

Spain, France, Italy. Meet George, from Dallas, who studies in Madrid, 2 Portuguese (man and wife) from Lisbon, who wants us to stop there, and 3 girls from Bowling Green(Ohio), Jamie for instance was in my brother Dan's class at Bowling Green, who knows who you will meet!!

We get the train in Algeciras @ 3:15 p.m. and in Cordoba by 10:15 p.m., then the train to Madrid @ 1:30 a.m. (7 hours). We have to stand in the aisle of 1st class, and I catch a cold or bug. It's Easter, everything is packed, and we walk around for a while 'til our train to San Sebastian @ 12:15 (but late again 1:30 p.m.), arrive @ 9:30 p.m. (8 hours). We get a Pensione for 150 pesetas, with the help of 3 Spanish girls. It is a very nice city on the Atlantic coast, with a beautiful bay area.

It is Semana Santa in Seville, Cordoba, Granada and the rest of Santa Lucia, which contributed to the huge crowds on the train. "When in Spain, watch out for the holy days ", ha, ha!

Boy am I sick now, my throat is killing me! San Sebastian looks really nice though, but I need a big night's sleep! Take a cold shower, buy some food, and go to beach (beautiful) even though a bit overcast. We walk around town, great architecture, and a very comfortable city, not hectic, not too big, and very clean...

We are always on the go, since we left Ibiza, now off to Hendaye (Border), nice along coast up to Bayonne in France. We switch at Hendaye for Nice on the Riviera in 14 hours (6:15 p.m.-8:30 a.m.) miss the countryside, but great to arrive in a.m., and save on hotel!! There's always a tradeoff, short term satisfaction, and or long term expedition. Overall I would like quality and quantity, but I am in it for the long haul, not just Spring Break, or my last semester...

Very nice morning, love the countryside in Spain, and South France. In Nice, it is gorgeous, very classy beach, all stones. It is a beautiful day, with beautiful people everywhere. I crash on the beach for a bit, stretch out, air out my clothes, not quite what they want, though! Somehow I lose a pair of socks, as I was reorganizing, "my loss is the French Riviera's gain" ha ha!

On to Monaco at 6 p.m., ½ hour away... It's a beautiful little country, "like a jewel box". We hike up to the Casino "Monte Carlo," have to go inside and at least play the slot machines. We try to check in to the Absolutely Stunningly Classy "Hotel de Paris", just across the street. We walk in with our backpacks, and I ask with a straight face for a room? Startled at first, but not mad, they tell us the price...The prices are a little high for our budget, but thank you!

The Palace is across the harbor, but when in MONACO, you must visit the palace, and the guard. I asked if Princess Grace was home, they were polite and said she wasn't. I am an old movie fan, and Grace Kelly was an American Beauty first, before she was Princess Grace! Monaco is very famous for the Grand Prix car race, right through these same streets. It was a very cool and magnificent place, the buildings, setting, and the people, "small and precious more than quaint"! It was way too expensive to even think about staying!

Italy is only 5 miles away, this area is so special, beautiful, and quite expensive. We leave for PISA at 9:47 p.m., meet Ann from Wisconsin on train, arrive at 3 a.m., walk around town and sleep in station for 1 ½ hours. We're only here half a day anyways... But what do you see, the LEANING TOWER, of course. Tower is great, and the Cathedral and chapel, next to it. Try to find Maureen M. and Mary Jean (Mark L.'s girl), but can't locate them. Happen upon potential new friends constantly, and their friends become your friends, or at least traveling partners...

We are on a train to Florence by 2:30 p.m., and in 1 ½ hours we'll be there...

Florence is a Beautiful city, the Ponte Vecchio (oldest Bridge over the Arno River, with shops built along it), Mt. Belvedeere, camping grounds, as I hike around within a short time frame because my train pass is starting to wind down, and the end of Spring Break is approaching.

I meet up with Bobby, Billy, Reed, Mark, and Jennie at a little restaurant just off a beautiful and busy plaza where I am eating pizza, spaghetti, and drinking vino. We are old friends after a while, and we are all taking the train to Genevé @ 1:10 a.m. meet an Aussie (Rick), and Yank (Larry), in train station, and we're all still drinking wine!

The train is so crowded, that we have to stand and a couple guys make a fuss, trying to see 2 of their friends in 1st class. One of the guys rip maps off the wall, and yells at the conductors. We hop off train while moving in Bologna to run ahead to another section of the train, and the local police stop us, check our tickets, passports, and arms for needle marks. They hold up the train while detaining us, they are extremely serious and it is absolutely crazy!! They finally let us board after a twenty minute delay….

We meet a lot of nice people on board… really nice German group from Duisberg. Finally, I get a compartment to relax, sleep, get up in Milano, it's pouring, thought my stop, get off, but hop back on in time!!

There is snow all over Switzerland, stop in Friburg with the 3 Americans, drink more wine, and beer, leave for Genevé, at about 5 p.m., but sleep through, and have to catch 8 p.m. and arrive at 9:30. I am so tired it's ridiculous. I fall asleep almost again, but make it to Geneve, and I take bus #4 to Bijou's Residence @ Rue Hugo de Sanger. Bijou is sleeping but she gets up and makes me soup as I seemed pretty sick and exhausted. It's raining and cold out, 1st bed since Monday (4 days)!

Lousy weather around, and feeling crappy, as I walk around in the morning , and go back to Bijous's. She is working on a term paper, so is Mike. Everything is super expensive here in Genevé, and my funds are running low. The U.N., Lake Genevé , etc., I will see when I re-turn. Crash early but Bijou and I can't sleep…

Thank you again Bijou for your hospitality and friendship…"Au revoir a mon ami" !!!

Off to Wallau in morning (8 hours) this is my 30th day… Train pass is about to run out, as Spring Break is ending. I take a non-stop train to Mainz, change to Wiesbaden and bus to Wallau, #902 for 1 ½ DM. Scotty developed my pictures, not all came out (most are good). These are my 1st rolls in Europe, after getting camera for Christmas. It is so good to see the Scott family, Linda, Pat and Scotty, eat a Syracuse style "Luigi's" pizza, watch T.V., read and crash, it's like my comfort zone.

End of vacation, 31st Day, sleep great, but not long. Wake up to see Linda before school, eat, sit around talk with Pat, leaving on the 3:54 p.m. bus to Wiesbaden, train to Köln, 6 p.m.-6:20 , then to Bruges, 10 p.m. and home..

Meet Rosamunde from England (Brighton). She stops in Bruges for a couple drinks and rushes back to catch train to Oostende. I stop in to Cactus and a lot of the guys are there, and it was very nice to see them.

(Photos) Pisa, Rock of Gibraltar, Tangiers (Me in Jalaba, pouch and shirt-in-set) Florence-Pont de Vecchio, Palace in Monaco, Monte Carlo, Heidelberg, me on Neckar River in Heidelberg, City of Nice on the French Riviera "airing clothes"

I still have this cold since last Monday in Spain, 8 days now! Hang close today, 31 days away, no place like home, relax and catch up with everybody. Meet Patty from Heidelberg, a friend of Sue S., and 2 guys with her, and Marie, from Auburn, New York, visiting Diane. I hear that Tom P. is sick back home in Scotland, and I will try to contact him, call or write, etc. I get caught up on reading all my letters that came while I was away!

MEMORIES OF OTHERS

It was a lot of fun sharing stories with others, like Sue M., telling me about them sleeping on tables in a train station in Munich because the nuns wouldn't let them back into their convent-hostel late at night. Her experiencing a divided Berlin, travelling by subway trough eerie, empty East Berlin stations guarded by dogs and soldiers. In Paris, having a frustrated waiter give up taking their dinner order by slamming down the order pad and pen on her table and telling them to write it themselves . Singing throughout the "Sound of Music" tour in Austria.

It's refreshing to hear other's experiences, and to share your own as a way to generate ideas for future trips, and staying connected.

CHAPTER 5

Semester End: The Final Weeks

I WRITE LETTERS home and send a resumé to Bob W. in Galway about a job. Bob and his family are from my hometown Syracuse and he is my step-grandmother's nephew with a great job at the Wilson Sporting Goods Plant there.

Professor Lory's class is OK, but will I ever feel better? I stay in most of day, after talking to Professor Kormos about my paper, he gives me an extension and I don't have to type it...YES!!!! I start my paper the next day after classes (April 29), and tomorrow is actually the last day of classes.

Beth I. and three of her friends (girls) are visiting from Paris, what great timing, even though my paper is due tomorrow! Friends and or fun usually came first. Beth and I take a nice walk thru town, and get caught up on our respective study abroad experiences, again from a different program and city,and another voice heard from....It is such a beautiful day, too!

I get caught up with class work, studying and my paper. My paper is due for Professor Kormos on May 6th, the first extension, but he extended again!

We have a big field trip to the Delta Works near Rotterdam, Delft, and the Kuekenhove Gardens (every color and size of tulips). We drink Heineken all day... when in Holland!! When the weather is also great it's a bonus!

I played tennis with Art, Richie and Christian today at a private club, and basketball as well. Where was this club before? It is always nice to tie in local activities with my fellow students. Art in particular, I hadn't had a lot of interaction, but a very good guy, sharp, smart, etc.

With time winding down on our Bruges study abroad experiences, and probably life here in town, I seem to be finding activities and places that were earlier unknown to me.

Sat. May 8th- A couple of people arrive from Copenhagen, actually a brother and sister that Danny met, they're from Santa Cruz. We went up to Knokke to go to the beach because it is such a beautiful day!

Sunday May 9th I play tennis at the club again, hang around with Art, who I have finally gotten to know better.

Also, I have to remember to call home, it's MOTHER'S DAY! My mother is excited to her from me, and to tell me about her plans for Ireland this summer. She is flying over in August, because she wrote and found some long lost cousins on both her mother's and father's side of the family.

I handed my paper in to Professor Kormos, on Syracuse, New York (USA), compared to Ghent, Belgium! It was a nice little project, similar sized cities with prominent universities

Final exams start tomorrow... study all day!!! Exams last until next Tuesday (1 week- 5 exams). I miss ½ day trip to visit multinational company which Prof. Manche set up because I was studying for Prof.Lory's History test tomorrow. I study all day and night, but take a break to see Kris and Paul visiting from Santa Cruz, and off to Paris.

Prof. Kormos's test is coming up, and I study all day and night for it. I remember to call Ireland finally, about job in Galway hopefully (nothing yet)!

Come to find out, I did very well on Kormos's Geography final, as I am one with that subject, and he made it interesting.

We have a couple nice girls visiting from Copenhagen Program, there's Kim from (Eau Claire and Milwaukee) Wisconsin and Diane from California (Pasadena) they stay in my room.

We go out to Carnival Musical with rides, games, food, and music which is really a lot of fun and a fantastic distraction from tests and papers. Later we go to De Goezeput with Carl, after getting stoned beforehand. Carl has always been an enigma, or difficult to comprehend/figure out, but that wasn't mine or anybody else's job, ha ha!

Kim and I definitely hit it off, perhaps the other distraction I needed during exam week. Kim is so peppy, wholesome, and a free spirited party girl.

SUNY Oswego graduates today, and they have a little ceremony for the 8 of us seniors (diploma and a rose) VERY NICE!!I still have a couple exams left, but I will enjoy this moment…still somewhat anxious, about whether I really graduated!

The girls, Diane and Kim are heading on to Amsterdam…I guess you can't have everything…there always seems to be a "Richochet Effect", from the up you have a down, but bounce back and or move on, and I felt like this was part of who I was …100% all in with that person, that place or thing, 'til the next!!!!

Study for exams with Professors Luka and Tsoukalis- US and EEC @ 3:30 p.m. tomorrow!

THE KING

5/16-King Baldouin is in Bruges, "a big deal", and I went to see him. The main square below the Belfry is a good spot for viewing, as it is very busy in the market square with great energy! Sue M. told me how she collapsed in laughter as much- taller- than- her Katie put her hand over Sue's eyes just as the King of Belgium was passing by....it cracked me up big time to think of it!

It reminded me of other pranks, like us guys taking all the furniture from Christian's room and replacing it with mini, paper versions of the pieces. He was a good guy and clever as hell in his own distinct manner. Sitting down on his paper chair and laying down on the paper bed as if it was the real thing...hilarious...Our residence/ home was a vast labyrinth of potential intrigue, mishaps, and additional pranks. We always had visitors, co-ed friends, strangers, some more mature as an uncle or so, but it was all fair game. Madame would let us know if we crossed the line in her own controlled motherly manner, sometimes with a glint in the corner of her eye...

The exam for Professors Luka and Tsoukalis is very tough (Pass/ Fail). Economics is tomorrow, but Kim (Milwaukee) comes back (skip a lot of studying) hang with her a lot, as we get along like long lost friends and lovers. Judy and Mike K. hang with me later studying 'til 5 a.m. in my room, Kim, cool too! Last final, really hard time, I feel terrible (blew it a bit), go out to De Goezeput bar and King Disco to drink it off, dance and have a ball with Kim and others. We are never at a loss for letting off steam and or enjoying life to the max.

Big Study Trip tomorrow (but no studying), we leave @ 7:30 a.m., after being up late the night before with Kim! Kim leaves for Paris in the morning. Kim and I have had a great time together, and I think we will miss each other, but on to the next adventure....for both of us!

(Photos) Bruges-View from windmill, Cathedral, Flemish Flag, Market Square, Day trip to Dixmuide-Tower of Flemish Nationalism, King Baldouin visiting Bruges, Cafes just off Market Square, View toward North Sea, Belfry from a far

Good or bad timing as the big soccer match between Liverpool and Bruges for a European Club final is tomorrow when we head out! The town won't be same with us gone, and with Liverpool arriving it could be even more chaotic....We started seeing the visitors in the last day or so, prepping so to speak!!!!

STUDY TRIP-European Economic Community, ET AL (May 19th)

Our group goes to Bastogne (Battle of the Bulge-in World War 2, "Nuts"- by General McAuliffe), to Luxembourg City, pretty and the weather finally clears up.

At Metz, we stay at Hotel du Globe, very nice (73 F/ room, $16 double w/ Mike K.). We go out for a pizza at a really beautiful restaurant with Mike, Carl, Richie and Larry. Later, I was accused of stealing lamp @ the Hotel!!! What would I do with a lamp???? Apparently they did a room check and our room was missing a lamp. There are souvenirs (blanket from Sabena Air lines-made a great kilt and a sash in 2 different costume parties), but a lamp is furniture.... I have done a lot of crazy stuff, but that would be silly/ridiculous!

We visit the Ecology Institute, then a guided tour of Metz by 2 pretty girls to the Cathedral and Robert Schummer's House, then lunch at big restaurant , where of all things I get hooked on sauerkraut, remembering I don't eat meat and have to wing it off the menu sometimes... It usually creates some interesting and often far fetched scenarios or discussions, not just because of the language, but culture too, with the whole restaurant involved at times, ha ha!

Strasbourg then for 3 days, stay at Hotel Hanong (116 F per dbl.-$26) very nice, take a walk around with Mike K. , we were such good travel mates on Spring Break, but have done a lot of our own things since. Also, get caught up on my Journal, which is difficult to keep up with as I am living it....and it's been hectic lately, trips, exams, visitors etc.

We go to the Council of Europe in the morning, as we can tour the facilities and sit in on a presentation. They take us to beautiful restaurant for lunch (herb omelet, quiche, Riesling wine) then a Tour of Strasbourg. Later we go out near the Cathedral to a bar restaurant with Beanie, Suzie, Katie, and 2 others, partied upstairs too!!

Today is a free day, and it rains, C'est la Vie... ! I take pictures of the Cathedral (it's gigantic and beautiful). A bunch of us go out later to the same bar, outdoor café as the night before (Richie haggling with Senegalese) then to another bar. We get comfortable pretty quickly in the different cities, venues, etc. Doesn't mean we don't ad lib, and have some fun....everywhere it seems!

Off to the Black Forest in South Germany. Beautiful, we stop at All Saints Valley and we take a picnic at Baden Baden, and between Heidelberg.

We have so much wine, a recurring theme you might say… nobody's driving, well except for the official bus driver(Thank you, Danke, Merci beaucoup…), but not one of us. We arrive in Heidelberg and see Patti, Sue S.'s friend who had visited Bruges. She studies here, and maybe we'll see each other later, I was getting the vibe.

Dash…what a great nickname (Carl), Debbie and I get pissed (bit drunken) on the Neckar River looking towards the castle. Others in our group rented small paddle boats for short trip on the river, but I felt wiser not to after a couple drinks…

I take off on one of my solo walk about trips later that night and run in to Richie and a British fellow. British bloke takes me to a student bar, while we are there, these 2 frauleins want nothing to do with us (must be "mein slecht deustch sprecken"). I head out into the night, very lost until I meet Patti, who is like my guardian angel, and we talk and have fun on the streets 'til 3 a.m.

I must say I have been blessed with some of the potential mishaps turning to positives at any hour or place, and in different cities, countries, continents….May the Gods continue to watch over me….

We head out fairly early to see the castle, partying early too… meet all these lovely German school children at the castle. They are enamored with me, about thirty of them surrounding me at the bench I am sitting at. They think I am funny, a crazy American, but nice (I had a great double exposure photo with them). Have a fantastic day, have lunch with Patti, her friend Mary (Michigan) Sue S., Mike, Dash (beer for me).

Leave Heidelberg for St. Goar, on the Rhine R. (the Loralei) ,and we hang on the Riverbank most of the day. Leave St. Goar, for Rhine Distillery, then Bonn (W. Germany's capital) for lunch and conference with W. German Foreign Minister and then on to Aachen that night!

We visit Aachen Cathedral for a while, which is amazing (there are many Charlemagne relics and valuables), and then off to Waterloo Battlefield where Wellington defeated Napolean! I feel one with the history not just the place, as I love history and geography, and at times feel like such a part of it.

We get back to Bruges about 6 p.m., after 8 full days. We have a few visitors, and I have a couple letters (Kim from Wisconsin/ Copenhagen)

PROCESION OF THE HOLY BLOOD (Bruges)
5/27-The annual Procession of the HOLY BLOOD is today! This is an amazing event with great characters, costumes, floats, etc.. They have commemorated the arrival of the RELIC of the Holy Blood from the Crusades in Bruges for centuries on Ascension Day. It is of course religious, historical and a significant display of Pride and Devotion.

A few of us hiked up to the rooftop of the Europa College's main building for a phenomenal view of the procession. What a privilege to be in this town and this is another reason as this was spectacular.... It was ALIVE, the history and the pride, and the way it was presented and appreciated!

Later, I call the Walsh family in Galway, Ireland about visiting and a possible job. I get a lot of things together to leave Bruges soon, and off to another new stage of my life...post college, post academia, at least for now!

APPRECIATION DINNER, 5/28
There is a Party and Big Dinner tonight, with Presents and Appreciation for Jeremy, Madame, and Bob.

Jeremy has been great, a cool, sophisticated, British professor and academic representative for us. He has always been very approachable if we needed someone to talk to, always with a cleverness, sincerity and friendliness.

Madame has been like a mother to us, with a strictness, yet guiding type of persona. She always held us responsible for our chores, like our group dinners for instance. She had an amazing work ethic, always preparing this and cleaning that, while a mother to her own teenage son, Bart. When you saw her smile, you felt happy for her, and proud if you had something to do with it.

Bob has been like a big brother, with a Midwestern dryness, salt of the earth and a regular guy. He looked like a lumber jack from Scandinavia…and how about our basketball games, always the competitor!!!!

So for our Big Dinner, we have shrimp cocktail, fritters, Dover sole, salads, strawberry shortcake and wine for dinner. After, more wine (a lot!), then more beer, (also, a lot!). I party with Judy F. and Reenie until 3 a.m. talking about some memories, recounting adventures and misadventures, and what's next.…

A FRIEND'S REMINISCENCE

This semester and this time in our lives would stand out forever, and bond us all together because of it.

A dear friend shared some of her personal thoughts on our time together. "My semester in Europe was magical. I barely passed my courses at the College, but I got an incredible education. Traveling and living with 29 fellow travelers opened my eyes to new experiences, places, people, and I have 29 people in my heart who I will always regard as special friends, even if we don't see one another. I gained confidence, learned that I could maneuver my way through countries, transportation and customs. I experienced a connection that has helped me understand the world so much better, and in a personal way".

I GRADUATE!!!

I get a C in Economics from Jeremy, so I officially graduate, and call my mother to tell her!!!!! WOW, PARTS OF 18 YEARS OF MY LIFE IN SCHOOL, NOW I'M SCHOOLLESS!!!!!!!!!!!!!!!!!!!!!!!

HEADING IN NEW DIRECTIONS

Only 3 more days left in Bruges, as I hang around tonight and it's settling in, that the others are already heading out of town! Beanie, her brother (Dooper) and friend (Joe), leave for Amsterdam. My roommate Richie, leaves tomorrow, he heads out with Dash, as they fly from Paris the following day back to the U.S.A.! I really feel bad that everyone is leaving, Pattie M. and Jim fly home today, and Judy F. is also leaving for Amsterdam.

It's almost like your family is breaking up, Bob, Reenie, Larry, Patty Ma., Marcia, Sue M., Walter and friend Peter (Edinburgh) leave for England tonight. We all go to Pick and De Goezeput, before they leave. Rob, left earlier for Paris!

Monday, May 31st It is the last night for me in Bruges, for a while anyways. Mike K., Debbie, Walter, Katie and Christian have left. Cheryl and Helen leave today for Poland and Berlin. I go out with everyone to the Italian Restaurant that is near the Cactus for pizza. Later, I go to Bob and Chris Werner's for a little party (all graduates) and Bob's sister in law. Bob gives me his address, so does Catherine, from Zurich (Christoph's wife).

Our grad friends and acquaintances were so welcoming and cool to be with, and great ambassadors for the many countries they represented.

Our RESIDENCE and MADAME, Really has been our glue, our base, the most common and cohesive element(s) that we shared. There was always something going on here with visitors, parties, dinners, returning from nights on the town at all hours, etc. Leave for a weekend, a week, or a month, and come back with stories that we shared, and people we brought back with us, or who would come at another time. Word got out to visit Bruges and Ridderstraat 12 (Like the Embassy).... There was intrigue, internally and externally, relationships with townspeople, grads, amongst ourselves, from our travels/adventures, or just strangers in the night...

THIS IS AN EVERYMAN'S STORY, NOT A GOSSIP COLUMN.... HA HA! Catch me sometime after a couple Trappist Beers......☺

I do some shopping and take some photos of pubs (of course). I take the air in, the memories, all fantastic. I could not think of a bad or sad moment until now, but for all the right reasons, the deep rooted connections to so many wonderful people, our residence, the college, and an absolutely amazing town, and a special time in life (21-22 years old in 1976 EUROPE)...WOW!

CHAPTER 6

Summer (Part 1)

6/1/76-I LEAVE BRUGES by train with Christian @ 9 a.m. arriving at Köln @ 1 p.m. From the edge of the city we start hitching until 9:30 p.m. in cold and rain (hard) try 3 different spots to hitch and finally a truck driver takes us to Mannheim (we were going to Frankfurt), but anything for a ride... We crash along rest area at 1:30 a.m., as it finally stopped raining...

Wednesday June 2- We wake up about 8:30 a.m., nice, but then it rains again. We start out hitching to Stuttgart, then Munchen, no luck, head to Frankfurt, then Nurnberg and Munchen. Get a quick ride by a truck to just before Nurnberg, figures it starts raining and it's getting dark. Give up outside and ask people inside, and we get a ride right to the Munich (Munchen) Youth Hostel (6.50 DM) with breakfast included, we got there right before closing.

Thursday, June 3rd-Christian is on his way to Greece in a.m. and I stay fairly local.

Dachau (CONCENTRATION CAMP) is my destination, by train and bus. I grew up learning of these concentration camps, The Holocaust and "Man's inhumanity to men, women, and children". The imagery was very surreal, sad but respectful in a modern style gallery with photos, the barracks and ovens though, were "SO REAL"! This is the most important place I have visited and I will always remember because of the significance. You leave a part of yourself there, at least I thought so....

I go out to the Olympic Village and Stadium from 1972 Olympics... Stadium very interesting modern design, futuristic, compared to things I was familiar with. After I got lost looking for the youth Hostel, I meet Karen and Robin from Texas, and Mike from New Jersey. Guess what? Judy F, Beanie, Dooper, and Joe come in later!! It is great to see them, hadn't been long, but still a nice surprise.

We go to the Lowenbrau Brewery for a 9:30 a.m. (never too early) tour, meet Robin, Karen and Mike there. It was a very decent tour, girls couldn't drink their 2 beers each, so I helped them (they weren't used to drinking in a.m.). After tour, we go to the Treasury (Crown Jewels) Residence of Bavarian Kings. We follow that up by going to Schwabing, which is a cool area, university like, and on to Englisher Park for a picnic. A lot of walking is not unusual, later on to Hofbräuhaus (3 Dbl-litre) to sing and drink, which sounds like a good combination. Meet up again with Judy, Beanie, Joe, and Danny. See Bob (guy I almost got arrested with in Italy),and meet Rhonda, a girl from Oswego who had studied in Italy. Forget what time Hostel closes, and almost missed curfew, we had to race back.

Sat. June 5th- I walk to Town Hall for the Glockenspiel @ 11 a.m. I am still a tourist, and when in Munich (MUNCHEN), see and do their things.

Of all things, I run in to an old high school acquaintance Jim C., based in the area with the American Army. I don't know who was more surprised him or I, but it was a short lived mini reunion as we were going in different directions.

Then I see Robin and Karen, and the three of us go to Deutsches Museum (fantastic),then they go to Dachau, I go to Nymphemburg

Castle and Garden (beautiful, but Castle closed though). Meet Dan from Los Angeles at the Hostel, we sit around talking, while Beanie and gang left for Salzburg in the afternoon.

I Leave Munchen (Munich)after 4 days, and start to hitch to Salzburg, but end up walking from Bad Reichenhall to Salzburg, about, 20 KM! My first ride was after 2 hours, and then her car broke down. I take a campsite near airport, about 1 hour walk from town, and it cost about 5 schillings (80 cents), with showers! See Beanie, Judy, Danny and Joe at Hostel in town, along with Karen and Robin, and Jill and Anna (N. Zealand), who I met hitching. I meet Marriane from San Francisco, and another girl from Texas. We all go to Augustine Keller Beer Hall (GREAT), outdoor area, beautiful evening!

I walk them back to their Hostel , called Nonntal, then I have to head the opposite way to my campground, "NO CURFEW FOR ME", but a ways out of town!!!

I wake up @ 8 a.m., but it takes me a couple hours to get out of camp. I run in to Judy @ RR Station and I end up going to Helbrunn Castle with Judy, Beanie, Joe and Danny! (Beautiful gardens and water displays @ Helbrunn) Then I go up the big hill to the fortress in the heart of Town, as Beanie and gang went on to Innsbruck!

I went to Augustine Keller again with Robin, Karen and Myra (Australian). We meet 4 Turkish guys, who buy us beer and radishes (trying to hit on the girls). So, I walk the girls back to their hostel, partly as bodyguard and friend. I get lost, going back to camp, and I have 30 min. to run 6-7 km, as they were watching my backpack at the campgrounds office. I make it at last second by running the whole way and sweating like Hell!

Early up 7:30 a.m. and out of camp by 9:30 after a shower and start hitching to Berchtesgaden. I end up walking from the Austrian border to there, then 4 KMS up to Obersalzburg. I catch a bus up to Kelstein/Eagles Nest (Hitler's Hideout), 9 DM roundtrip. It was beautiful on top of the snow covered mountain, but eerie, as well. After all, to me it tied in with Dachau as a complete contrast to that brutality and inhumanity to a beautiful scenic getaway for DER FUHRER.

I end up walking back to Berchtesgaden from the 1,880 meter (6,017 feet) high Eagles Nest, and then to Königsee, a beautiful sea in the mountains with a nice town, about 5 km out. I walk another 3 KM, until a Canadian girl and I get a ride to town and then I sneak in her YH for free (save $5.00). I walked about 30 km again today and I am exhausted, so it was nice to have a roof over my head and some company.

I am off to Bad Reichenhall by train, walking then to the Autobahn, about 6 km, ride to Nurnberg which is near the E. German border at Coburg. I get invited to Norbert's house, with Carola , who goes to the the U.S. in 2 weeks. Then on to near Kassel, about 120 KM from Frankfurt, I get a ride to Wallau, and arrive around 10 p.m. at Scotty's, we BS a while as usual, getting caught up on their village news, family, and my adventures!

Scotty gets me up early to help Jim from across the street to unload his truck. We work 4 hard hours and I make 50 DM ($20), Scotty helped, Kaiser and Linda, too. I finally take a shower and then we go to Scotty's softball game in Wiesbaden at the U.S. Air Base. You needed dollars and could get some of the staples of the States, like hot dogs, hamburgers and sodas. Later, back in Wallau he makes a Luigi's Pizza, again!

I am very sore the next morning, as we look for Scotty's friend Gerhardt and find him in Gasthof (Pub)! Gerhardt's a big German and we drink from about 7 p.m.-1 a.m., playing match sticks and I lose twice. I also meet Siegfried (butcher) and Dietrich (construction worker)! I met Klaus, Ruth, and Christine earlier at Gerhardt's.

"STRAWBERRY FESTIVAL" today on the Rhine River!! Scotty and I go to opening of new Firehouse first and then go to Festival in Erbach on the Rhine, also with Mike and Gail, Bill and Sharon Moore with baby Alana (from Denver), Gerhardt, Ruth and Christina.

We drink champagne, Rhine wine, sugar and whole strawberries, and have a big salad and fruit. Leave early, but buzzed after drinks, and bumping cars with Christina and Linda. We go back and play tag and Frisbee, at least Linda, Christine and I.

Today is Wallau's 50th anniversary of their Volunteer Fire Dept. and there's a nice parade. There's a big Beer Tent, Scotty, Pat, Gerhardt and I have a few drinks, while Linda and Christina go on the rides. Later, we go to Gerhardt's, with Bill and Sharon Moore for a drink, then over to Scotty's for pizza. "Vie Gehts" (V Gates), How are you? I learned today!

Leaving Scott's today, say my many thanks and goodbyes. I am leaving with Jim to Liege in Belgium, and he buys me lunch, and a couple bucks for train to Bruges ($7.50). Jim is very nice, like they all have been to me. I arrive in Bruges about 7 p.m. at our residence, and there's a sign to go to a restaurant where Larry, Reenie, Patty Ma, Sue S., Helen, Cheryl and Diane are. Well, I am there in minutes because I would not miss a reunion.

Diane, Reenie and Patty, fly home tomorrow and leave for Paris tonight (So glad I caught them). Larry is off to Brussels and Greece, Helen and Cheryl to London, Spain and Riviera, Sue S. is going to Paris and London.

I had 6 letters, 2 from England, 1 from Ireland, 3 from Mom. I get a lot of things packed in the morning, go on a picnic with Helen, Cheryl and Sue at park with pond and gazebo (near prison) Later go to De Goezeput and Pick for a while, do my wash 2nd time by machine, and then go see Jeremy at the College!

Judy H. comes in at night, Judy F. during the day, and we all go out to Chinese Restaurant for dinner (a treat)! I have Chinese omelet with shrimp, rice, some pineapple and fried rice. Sue S. leaves for Paris later.

I am leaving for London (Eng.) tonight. I meet Mike from London, Sally (Wisconsin), Marie and friend from Sweden, all on the ferry. I have over 50 Kilo's (110 pounds) that I am carrying in my backpack and shoulder bags, some of which I am shipping home when I get settled.

ENGLAND

I stay up all night on the ferry bullshitting with Mike, who is very laid back and travelled a lot in his day. He helps me with my bags, and as the girls leave for YH, I go to Mike's place in Camden Town. I eat and take a bath, and it's cool to leave most of my gear here at Mike's.

I take the tube to Prislip Manor to visit Don and Ann Galleries (Beanie's friends). Don is in the U.S. Air Force, and stationed over here and married to Ann who is English. Meet Ann's mother, brother and sister in law, stay up talking for a while, then I sleep outside which is nice!

I sleep late until noon, exhausted from the travel must be?

Ann's brother and sister in law fly to the States today. Don and I go to club at his base today, drink Budweiser, then we drink Pernod (like licorice), then scotch. We started at 5 p.m. and get quite the buzz, but meet a lot of people. We go out to a private flat for a party with a lot of local English girls and many USAF guys, and it seemed like an American type party with the music, the talk, the vibe. Later, Ann stopped down with Joe, a friend of hers and Don's, who just arrived.

We get a flat tire on the way home, and I end up directing traffic, but from the wrong side of road....surprise, surprise!!! We finally leave for their place about 1:30 a.m., and I end up sleeping outside, with hardly any clothes on, as it's such a hot summer's night(IT RAINED, of course). I wake about noon, while it's still raining, and I am soaked!

Don and Ann take her mother to the hospital (appendix or gall bladder). We go to a party (all GI's and English girls), really crowded. We then go to a beautiful English Pub 'til closing at 11 p.m., and then back to the Air Force Pub. We meet a few people from yesterday, and Denise, Darlene, and their husbands. When we head back, we stay up and BS 'til about 3:30 a.m., and I am in the house tonight...

Wake up about noon again, go to open market next to Wembley Stadium, when we come back and I take a bath, also hang around talking to Denise's husband (Joe). Beanie and Dooper show up, and

Denise, her mother and father stop in. I am offered a ride to Brighton with the mother and father, the Taylors. So off to Brighton, as I say my goodbyes, we leave at noon, and get there by 1:45 p.m. They are so nice, they feed me and put me up in Denise's old room. I feel a part of so many families, like I am a recycled visitor, relative, or drinking buddy, ha ha…

Wimbledon starts today and I am not there, but the buzz is everywhere. It's gorgeous here at first, but clouds up. She starts me off with a huge breakfast, then a visit to their local grocery, and I am off to the bus station (via Mrs. Taylor), to go to Shoreham to visit Rosamund W., but she's not home (a Teacher). I hang around town, stop back a while later, as I go to the beach (stony), meet old Welsh man (drunk) named Robert (I give him 50 p). Rosamund turns up later, and we talk and have coffee, meet her flat mate, Michelle. The three of us go to a pub, and I try a Bitter, a Tankard, and a Guinness. I didn't really care for any (I have been spoiled with the Belgian and German beers). I haven't yet acquired the affection for THE GUINNESS yet, perhaps when I will be in Ireland, itself ? We have a great time though, the affect is still there, walk to beach, and go back to their flat finally!

The next morning I go to Brighton, and will meet up there with Rosamund at RR Station about 5 p.m.(after her work). I had gone to Prince Albert Pavilion (beautiful, like a small Taj Mahal), and what a gorgeous day. Do a lot of walking, get fish and chips, and hang on the beach (crash a bit). When Ros gets here, we go for ice cream, then to a restaurant for dinner (strawberry milkshake for dessert). We walk thru the Lanes, a famous small old street with shops, and back to the beach for a sit, stony but nice. Later we catch the cinema, "Dutchess and the Dirtwater Fox"…Ok. We top it off with a beer, and back home to Shoreham by 10:45 p.m.

London, today, as I leave for Ireland, tonight! We eat breakfast, then we go to Brighton to lay on the beach, very hot and sunny .We pick up food for a picnic that we will have in Hyde Park. First, we hitch to London, rush over to Mickey's place(Mike) in Camden Town, where my gear is. The picnic in Hyde Park is beautiful but rush around a bit to say goodbye to Ros, as I had to get my ticket to Holyhead (£6.80), from London. I'm off to Easton Station carrying 50 kilos, and just make the 9:15 p.m. train.

I meet 40 little Irish boys on the train, who are from Dundalk near Northern Ireland. It's a 5 hour train ride to catch the boat, and these lads will be fun.

The boat doesn't leave until 4:10 a.m., instead of the 3 a.m. scheduled departure. These Irish kids, are wise guys, the bunch of them, "Hey Mister, you got a fag", looking for a cigarette? They seemed about 11 years old or so, and reminded me of my own rambunctious youth ☺

IRELAND (SUMMER PART 2)

We arrive in Ireland at 8:35 a.m., my first day in Ireland is after 5 five full months in Europe (Jan. 24-June 24th). I run into Beanie and Dooper at the RR Station in Dublin, so we walk around a bit, as they are on their way to Donegal (Sligo).

I am going to visit an old acquaintance from Syracuse, Patti Bland. Patti and I were in elementary school together at St. Patrick's, and I had not seen her in eight years. Patti has been studying and now working in Dublin, and lives in the Ballsbridge area. What a great reunion, a lot to catch up on. It's been 8 years, all of just before high school, and the college years, exactly! We of course are in a unique setting, Dublin, Ireland, and us coming from Tipperary Hill in Syracuse, New York.

My memory took me back to our early teens and pre-teen years from 3rd grade thru 8th grade. Part of that time Patti was at the brunt of much verbal and or suggestive bullying, both from fellow students and even some of the teachers/nuns. I was not an innocent bystander, as I could be a wise guy and at times emboldened, but now had a blaze of embarrassment and being totally apologetic to her, when I first met her. This was probably my most humbled time in my life to this point, and I was prepared for any rebuttal or vindictiveness that she might bestow on me.

Alas, in what might have been the most open arms welcome, one could ever receive, she embraced me for who we were and both had become. We were like long lost friends, and could move forward without hesitation and with a new found appreciation.

Patti, I would come to find, was so comfortable in her own skin, and her surroundings. Her current friends here and former roommates in Dublin all seemed like they have known her for a life time, as she had a way to endear you to her.

Getting on with our time together and my visit. Patti gives me a great tour, starting with a walk around Dublin to Trinity College, Christ Church, St. Stephen's Green, Dublin Castle, and we stop at the student association to get half price stickers on my International Student I.D. We of course end up at a pub, and just miss happy hour at O'Donaghue's, which is very near St. Stephen's Green and in the heart of Dublin. We stay for a couple pints anyways, as it has great atmosphere and I feel at home with its feel of the pulse of the Irish Capital.

We leave for Ballsbridge Inn, where Patti used to work (very hot inside), as it was a beautiful, but hot day. I meet Katy and Una, who are Patti's former flat mates, and they seem like a whole lot of fun. After a while we all go back to Una's and Katy's place to hang out, BS, and party, and then ultimately back to Patti's about 3:30 a.m.

Today is another day and I meet Ann and Breda, great girls who currently live with Patti. It's always nice to meet new people, especially when they are friends or roommates with someone I know, and cute as hell....

We do normal stuff, such as the Market on Henry Street, and see "One Flew over the Cuckoo's Nest" for 85 pence, what a great movie. I had seen the play in Boston, a few years earlier in 1973, while visiting Patty C., when I was with my old friend Deacon. I remembered my earlier prediction of Jack Nicholson playing McMurphy in a movie if it was made....!

I am never stationery for very long, as we go to RR Station to pick up my gear, because I am taking the bus tomorrow to Galway. Back at Patti's, Breda has a salad ready, and I repack for the next trip, then we go out to Ballsbridge Inn, and Horseshoe Inn after. But I am in for a thrill, as we end up out to Leopardstown for late night snacks, drinking, and dancing. I tried Lancers (beer) and loved it, the taste very strong too. Again dancing, the music, I felt right at home…"those that can't play, dance" is my motto! I swear dancing is universal as is the music that stimulates the dance, as is the alcohol that fuels the motivation.

It's pretty far out, about 6 miles or so. We hitch back without Breda, and get back about 3:30 a.m.

THOUGHTS OF HOME

My brother Kevin and Kathy are getting married today back home in Syracuse today! I didn't know about it before my trip to Europe, and I always figured this was a trip of a lifetime. If I went home, I wouldn't have come back, but I was torn and felt guilty, with my brother getting married, and Kathy is so great, so cool and very dear to me! They know I am there in spirit(s)! I really love them both so much….!

I am off for Galway today, to visit the Walsh's, and maybe find a job? It's a 6 hour bus ride, half price for a student at £2.70 ($1.60 per L).

I say more goodbyes to Patti, roommates, friends, because I have so many hellos, how many I could not count!

It's a beautiful day as I arrive in Galway at 6:15 p.m., left Dublin at 12:25 p.m. It was a nice ride, 2 ½ hour actual drive time. I finally meet the Walsh's (my step grandmother's nephew, also from Syracuse), and we eat, talk, and meet the kids later. Very nice family, we play tennis that same evening with Bob, Karen, and their neighbors, Ray and Joan from Cleveland. Galway has a Wilson Sporting Goods Plant, so there are a decent amount of Americans, mostly management level.

It's another beautiful day, what a great stretch of weather, but very windy. We all go for a ride to Silver Strand Beach and the water is warm, beach is nice with a lot of people on this summer Sunday. It's fun playing with the three kids, soccer with the oldest boy, and swim with all three. It's a lot of fun being with a family, as I have had my share on this trip. When we get back, we play tennis after I call the States (Kevin and Kathy's wedding was great, says my mother)! We eat a big supper, and then I go for a walk with the kids in to town. I get along with the kids as well as with the adults, and they like having a visitor from their home town .

I start job hunting today, calling an employment agency, but no hope without a work visa. I took a long walk around Salthill, see a mixed rugby match near Leisureland. There's a tennis tournament, so Bob, Ray, Joan, and I can't play, and because it's hot as hell again. It's apparently the hottest June in six years, so we hang in yard relaxing.

It's been great having a home base here in Galway with the Walsh family. I am so at home here and speaking the language even makes it even easier. Like taking a walk along the promenade at Salthill, and then a walk to downtown Galway barefoot, as I am getting my sandals repaired that I haggled for in Morocco. Sit a while in Eyre Square, no Herald Tribune in town again. It's hot again at 84 degrees, as Sheila and I walk to Leisureland for an open air pop concert, which was ok.

Later we take a ride to Spiddel along the Bay, after Bob gets home from work. He had my racket restrung at the Plant, very nice and convenient. On the following day, we actually go shopping in Spiddel, and I buy an Aran Sweater and wool socks, at Standens, "Best and Cheapest Sweaters in Ireland". We watched a bit of Wimbledon, women's semifinals, and men's doubles. Later we go out to watch a mixed soccer game in Leisureland.

We watch on TV at Bob's club, the men's semi's at Wimbledon, as Nastasi beat Ramirez, and Borg beat Tanner. Later, I walk along the bay in Salthill, and write a lot, about five postcards tonight.

It must be time to go, when I walk in to Galway, and there's no Herald Tribune again. Walk to beach in Salthill, and Evert beat Cawley 6-3, 4-6, 8-6 in Wimbledon Women's Final. I play tennis with young Bobby, and a couple of the men. I end up being offered a ride by Gary N., who works at the Wilson Plant, to Clifden, as he's heading that way. I meet Dave and Suzie from Lincolnshire, UK, as well that day.

July 3rd, my brother Dan's birthday today!

I am leaving to the north with Gary. I thought I would go to Achill Island, but end up at Rossnowlagh, in Donegal. Sometimes you go with where the ride takes you. After Gary's lift, I hitched a ride with Connor Britton, who runs his father's hotel on the beach, which is a surfing beach per sé, and I meet all the family and friends at the Hotel Disco at night. Robin and Sue, Willie (Connor's brother) Jerry, Rosie, Mick, Beńat (French) and a few others, getting buzzed on Guinness! A great bunch here and I finally crash in my tent, much later…

The day was great, earlier walked a few miles along beach, which is beautiful and big. Connor and I won a couple games in pool and I feel like I found a new friend…..

It had taken 4 rides to get to Rossnowlagh, but absolutely wonderful, good to mix it up!!

BICENTENNIAL BACK IN THE STATES, SUNDAY JULY 4th

I am still in Rossnowlagh and it's beautiful out, relax at beach all day with Robin, Sue, and a few others. Beach is packed… hot Sunday, not the Holidays here. Actually they have music and dance tonight at the Franciscan Friary! It might as well be their Holiday, here… Beautiful Summer Sunday at Beach Area!!! What a fantastic area, and place in time, great people and country!

SLIEVE LEAGUE

It only gets better if that's possible! I am off to SLIEVE LEAGUE, 1,972 FT. High SEA CLIFFS on the Atlantic Ocean, which are the highest in Western Europe. Hitch through Donegal, Killybegs then on to Carrick, and stay at Youth Hostel there.

It rained most of day, and when I get up to the Cliffs, it is "SO FOGGY and RAINY", I can only see the Cliffs for a few seconds it seems. Seriously, you could not tell where the edge was, then all of a sudden it cleared up... and it was straight down to the waves crashing against the rocks at the base of the Cliffs. It was actually scary, because I was hiking around on my own, as I hiked up from the Hostel.

I could have disappeared with one wrong step between the fog, rain, and wind sweeping up. As amazing as it is, it was equally treacherous and precarious to view. This was no tourist spot it was more mountaineering and exploring, ha, ha. It really starts pouring and when I was maneuvering around earlier I took off my raincoat and forgot it there, shite!!

Meet a few folks back at the hostel when I get back, and I was soaked at the time. I had walked about 16 miles today, between hitching (3 rides to Carrick) and hiking up and back from the Cliffs. The other travelers are 2 French girls on bikes, 2 Dutch girls, and a couple Irish guys.

Still rainy in the morning, walk about 4 miles, stop in Ardana and buy an Aran Sweater (£9.50), walk a bit more. It's an absolutely beautiful valley between Carrick and Ardana. I look to take a boat out to Aranmore Island (20 min. ride for 20 p), leave from Burtonport, after 3 rides in all. I have a bad blister from my boots, with all the rain and hiking, and still raining. I stay at the YH right off the pier, after landing, then walk for 3 ½ hours (9 miles or so) around the coast. Really cool lighthouse and beautiful cliffs. Ran into the two Dutch girls and Irish guys I met at Carrick. Also, meet a fellow from S. Africa and his girl from New Zealand. Another adventurous day, with a good 16 miles walking I reckon.

As usual, I am on the go next morning, getting a feel for a place but not digging in, limited here anyways!

I take the boat back to the mainland, and get my 1st ride about an hour later, after walking a few miles. After a ride to Bumbeg, I walk the coast road here in N. Donegal which is gorgeous, beaches, mountains, and lakes (Mt. Muckish) a few more miles then another ride near YH @ Bunnatton, near Port Salon. My last ride was right to the Hostel door from Ramelton, then I settle in, and go for 5 mile hike to Port Salon, beautiful beach on Bay, and walk 5 miles back. Putting more miles in today, another 18+, after the blister, I decided to wear sneakers today, boots were soaked! It took 4 rides today, and I hang around the hostel, after it rains most of the day again…

It was like a marathon today it seemed… 9 rides to Achill Island YH, almost 12 hours on the road. I am rather beat as it was raining the last 4 hours! Still a great distance with great rides, no complaining here!! Most of the day it was nice and didn't have to walk that far, probably 9 miles, or less. At the hostel, there's an American, 4 Germans, and a Frenchman. It's a little out of the way, and not so wonderful! I left my map of Ireland at Bunnaton YH, and forgot another rain jacket, which could be disastrous. I call them up, and they'll mail it to me at the Walsh's house in Galway, that's grand.

Beautiful scenery through most of Donegal, driving thru Knock (Our Lady appeared there), it seemed really commercial though. This is not my kind of place(a bit tacky, no blasphemy) I don't mind the hike, that's not it!

Friday July 9th Looks to be a bad weather day, but sick of rushing around. I decide to walk to Achill Island, and from the Hostel it's about 6 miles, which is relaxing for me. I get a ride after 4 miles, by a German girl and 2 Irish fellows, drive me all over the Island, stopping to let me take pictures while I am standing on some small mountains and cliffs. It rains like hell again, and I am glad I am in their car. After touring around with them, they take me right to YH door, and I almost leave with them to Westport (then on to Ben Lettery YH). But, I meet Clare Murphy from Australia @ YH and we talk, and I stay. A bunch of us go to Pub down the road a couple miles, there's a couple Germans, an Australian, a Frenchman, Canadian, 2 more Germans, and an Irishman, we have a great time, it's a nice night!

When we go back, I have some tea, because I am starting to feel sick (stomach and fever) or was it a "bad" pint? I stay up 'til 5:30 a.m., beat and sore. It rained all night and very windy, It was like a nightmare that wouldn't end.

I must have finally fallen asleep, out of pure exhaustion. It's always worse when there is no one to help you, or the comforts to console you, just suck it up and get on with it,but it felt like a monster inside me trying to get out!

Well, raining again, not much sleep, time to move on... makes sense. The hostels are not meant to be your home, as you are supposed to be out all day. Leave with Johan (German), and he gets first ride and I get a ride soon after, all the way to Galway (wanted to go to Ben Lettery, weather still too bad).

It was a quick trip to Galway, about 2 ½ hours which is fast, and it felt great to be able to relax and recuperate.

There was a BOMBING at Salthill Hotel (July 9th, Friday). Everyone is scared and worried, it was probably the IRA, they're saying. Overall, in all the time I have been in Europe this was the most political life changing moment that I experienced. It created an edge that one could not forget.

I babysit tonight, as Karen and Bob go out, but even I am on my guard.

My mother is coming in 3 weeks, flying in to Shannon Airport, her 1st time flying, and it will be a nice Reunion!

7th day in a row of rain today (Sunday 7/11) and I am leaving tomorrow to the South, towards my cousins in Rathdowney. We sneak some tennis in with Bob, Bobby and Ray (Bob's boss). Great to be with a family, the rain and trekking catches up to you. They have a huge supper tonight, popcorn, ice cream and Pepsi too, (JUST LIKE HOME)!!!

Tomorrow, I start starving again, it's pouring so hard, I stay an extra day, catch early bus tomorrow 9 a.m. to Roscrea, only 16 miles from Rathdowney. I call my cousin, Eva Keegan, and she's expecting me. Still play more tennis with the WILSON people, the evening is lovely, but I play poorly again. Called Patti B, in Dublin, who is on her way to Galway, leaves on the 28th too...

IRISH COUSINS

The bus is a bargain £1.70, ½ fare... but all places aren't served by the buses. Just 16 miles to Rathdowney, and I call my cousin at # 179 Daly Terrace (a friend who has a phone), Eva my cousin, her brother, and her daughter Catherine, pick me up and bring me back to their home!

Their home, but my roots, my heritage takes a new turn. It's a special occasion for them as well, their American cousin, and we are all excited, nervous slightly too!

I am very grateful to them for coming to get me, everybody doesn't have cars, or phones even. So this is extra special, as they come from very humble means, but proud.

Meet Eva's son John, who is 22 as well, Jim her husband, and Catherine who is 5. Eva is my cousin on my mother's side of the family, the Kilcare side of the family from Donaghmore in County Laois. Eva's mother would be my grandmother's sister Bridget Kilcare Daly. My mother's father's side, the Moriartys are from nearby as well, Upper Church area in County Tipperary!

We settle in and get to know each other a bit. Eva wanted to hear about my mother, and where we come from. I wanted to know about them, who they were, their family, and how many other cousins, uncles, aunts, there were etc.

Later I go out with cousin Johnny to a local pub, O'MALLEY'S it is, and we no sooner arrive when a young beautiful woman calls out to my new found cousin "Hey Johnny ,play us a song" upon passing a guitar over to him. I then felt immediately at home and the drinks started flowing....

We then head out to a hurling match in Port Laoise. And I also meet Kay, John's girlfriend, and Ann, a neighbor (a nurse in Dublin). Rathdowney lost in Hurling in the County final 7-5 for under14 years old. It was a very tough game, hadn't seen it since I was younger up at Burnet Park (Syracuse). I remember men playing it on the upper field at Burnet Park, just above the zoo...

My mother's father Michael Moriarty was a great hurler I would come to find out. I remember an older cousin telling me he (Michael) played on an All American Irish hurling team, and went back to play in Ireland around 1913 or so! In 1913 he married Mary Kilcare while on this prolonged trip. Michael had come over to the US in 1906 when he was 21 years of age, and having the opportunity to go back must have been, "a dream come true".

A good chance of a ride to Dublin either tomorrow or Friday with Jim, he's a Lorry driver (Truck driver). I hope it's on Friday, because I want to go to Thurles on Thursday with Eva's neighbor. I also take the opportunity to send some things back to the States £ 1 for 1st 2 lbs., and 20 p each lb. after, $10.00 with a 22 lb. limit!

It's my first full day here, Wed. July 14th, and I play with little Catherine, walk around town with her and Eva. I get my luggage sorted out and meet some of the neighbors, and a couple more cousins. Kay, John and myself went to a couple pubs, and then to a Hooley, which the whole town looked to be at. Ann Bergen was inside, the nurse from Dublin, and we dance a bit. I even tried a bit of the IRISH DANCE also, as we were a wee bit buzzed you might say! John and Kay had snuck in, and saved the 80 pence!

I am here three weeks now in Ireland, July 15th as I wrote a letter to mom, updating her and especially that I found our family (Cousins). I also wrote postcards to Tom in Glasgow, Marty, Vince and Mo back home. Get my gear ready to leave for Dublin tomorrow with Jim. It is actually the 1st day in 11 days that it didn't rain, but it is cold and windy.

Leave with Jim to Dublin, who is such a great guy, down to earth, he's proud to give me a lift. We're in Dublin in 2 hr. 45 minutes, and it was a great opportunity to just be with Jim.

Call Patti when I arrive, and we go to a movie "Sherlock Holmes Smarter Brother" with the actor Marty Feldman for 95 p, very funny. Afterward we head to The Lincoln (Pub) where I meet Isabelle from Bordeaux, but just a passing fancy as I am with my friend Patti. Patti and I finish up at the Ballsbridge Inn before going to her friend's place.

We end up at Una's, Kate's, and Mag's flat, where I meet Mary too. Breda was at a wedding in Killarney. I feel like one of their friends, because I am Patti's friend. Individually I think I had a thing for all of her friends, as they were all so vivacious, and fun loving, but being accepted and within the extended group had more meaning and depth.

Coming back to a place one's visited already, it's nice to feel comfortable, like you know where you are, and feel like you have friends. Patti has been so welcoming, like we've always been great friends, and I respect that, and appreciated it immensely.

A little touring around town, go to Phoenix Park, Dublin Zoo, we just walk around it, giraffes, rhino, kangaroos, tiger, lion, elephant, wildebeest, etc. We see the President's Mansion, and have a picnic across from it. It is a nice day with a lot of great things within walking distance, and we also see the GARDA, the National Headquarters of Irish Police. I take a wonderful photo of Patti with an older gent and his Irish Wolf Hound, who are walking past.

Go to see "Return of Pink Panther," 95 p, it was OK! When we get back to Patti's, Breda is back, Patti goes to a party, Breda and I just hang out. I start reading the book "CENTENNIAL"! How ironic, during the BICENTENNIAL! Sunday, a nice day to hang around, get stoned with some of the girls, Ann Byrne, Breda and Patti, read a lot earlier, newspaper, Time Magazine and my book!

Some more sightseeing at St. Michan's on Church St. and seeing the Mummies in vaults. I shook hands of 700 year old body of a Crusader... We just missed getting in to the Guinness Brewery, as we didn't know what the hours were or have a schedule. Meet Patti's new flat mate, Angelina, and Mags is over as well... Patti and I have our "TEA" (supper) at Dolores's, Marianne's, and Margaret's. We B.S. and watch some of the Olympics (Montreal).

Today, we make it to the Guinness Brewery on time, after meeting up with Patti. We watch a movie and get a ½ pint (Patti gave me hers also! Thanks!!) Visit St. Patrick's, Lovely, but not well kept, not Catholic, Jonathan Swift belonged!

Patti and I, Breda and her boyfriend Gerry from back home, and with Dimna, we all go out to the Horseshoe House Pub!

See another movie "Barry Lyndon", beautiful Irish scenery but a bit long. We see Mags at Ballsbridge Inn a bit later, and it just seems so natural and routine to close out at a pub. Overall a quiet day, earlier read a lot... Patty baked cookies, brownies and a tart, which was wonderful!

Thurs. 7/22 Patti makes Breda and I a fine meal of scallops au gratin, salad, chocolate chip and peanut butter cookies. I am on a reading frenzy too, with my book... funny it ties me to home via history. We go out to JURY'S, a big hotel, for a meal and a drink... Expensive, but a nice change with Patti, Breda, Dimna (Breda's friend), and on to Horseshoe House for a drink, and then Mags (Kate and Una) but she is sleeping, too bad we wanted to watch the Olympics... PUBS close @ 11:30 p.m. approx.!

Off to the South, figure it's cloudy as I head out towards Waterford, while Patti and Mags go to Tipperary! I take a bus to get me out of town (Bray), 7 rides and 9 hours later I'm in Waterford, in Tramore, about 10 p.m., with a fellow from Mississippi who works at Waterford. We meet up with his Irish friends in the pub. I crash on beach about midnight, the stars are out!

I'm not in the area to see the Crystal Factory, more to see the land, ocean, towns, pubs and people!

I get a good sleep, 'til 10 a.m., pack up and get on the Cork Road at 11:30 a.m., 2 hours no ride, then walk up a ways, and get a ride right to Kinsale (past Cork), almost 100 miles… I go to the hostel and get a cold shower. The very nice Irish girl (Anne C.) and Dutch guy, Bart from Amsterdam, who gave me the great ride, might see them later at the PUB called the SPANIARD, that we had heard about.

Very, very, nice here in Kinsale, one of my favorite places so far, just the feel, the looks, the terrain and the bay provide wonderful views in a picturesque setting… not big, but friendly and colorful. There's an old fort, overlooking the Bay. Spanish were here years ago, darker hair, perhaps!!

Well I do meet Ann and Bart again, at the old fort, and we go to the SPANIARD together. They are very hospitable, buy me a few Guinness', and it's a very nice place with tremendous atmosphere, and the people all seemed to be in the happiest of moods.

I was almost too late to get in to the hostel, ran back 1 ½ miles… It really cleared up the last couple days, sunny in day, stars at night!

Off again, cold shower and change clothes (limited wardrobe) 4 rides, 7 hours later, and about 11 miles walking, and I am in Baltimore on the south coast. I have to wait 2 hours for the next boat to Cape Clear Island which is only 60 p, and I meet John from Long Island, and his German girlfriend. Ride is about an hour, and I meet Eva B. from Munich, we end up together at a small barn up a ways from the hostel (She didn't have a youth hostel card). So, we make ourselves comfortable in the loft of the vacant barn, and later head up to the PUB, "Paddy Burke's". We had our own as well, Paddy's Whiskey, drink before the PUB, then a couple Guinness's. We crash about 1 a.m. at the barn, as we didn't have a curfew which was nice!

The Island is nice, and it is a Gaelic speaking, but not that many people living here. There's a lake, cliffs, the Bay we arrived in, and of course THE PUB!

We had visitors, John and 3 Germans came over for a while too! John comes back over in morning, with hot tea from the hostel, what a nice neighbor. We've established roots it seems with some of the other travlelers. We also visit the hostel which is pretty big, have fish (Mackerel), then John and 3 Germans, Eva, and I go to the lake (pond), where there are little wild donkeys roaming around. We go hang at the hostel again, talk with a few people, Dutch girl, English guy, 2 Italian girls, Irish guy, 2 French girls and a Swiss guy. Have to clean up, go to house and get Eva, Uvay, Thora, and Birate. We've now, adopted the house (vacant) across from the barn!

This is our best day, we go to Paddy Burke's drinking and singing Irish songs, later back to the house and get stoned with Eva, Harry (German) and John. Harry plays flute, nice! Then we all go down to fire at campsite below!! Very cool setting...at 6:30 a.m., 2 people, Harry and Fille (German) try to get in our window, and are completely stoned as we're like "the place" to crash now, no rules!

Nice day at lake with Eva, then her, John and, I go to the restaurant/pub. We hike out towards the old castle which was on its own little island.

We go to the Pub as usual, later... we have new guests at our house, like the German Embassy now, 4 more come in during middle of night, drunk and loud.

Wed. 7/28-5 more days until my mother arrives... I am heading that way to meet her at Shannon Airport, but slowly!

Take a bath in the lake, sunny and clear, nicest day in 3 ½ weeks, some days have been partly clear. John, Eva, and I take off by boat @ 9 a.m. to Baltimore. We all plan on meeting in Glengariff, 3 rides (2 cars of French people brought me here), 1 ½ hours or less, then Eva. It's a tourist town, Bantry Bay is pretty, but again Glengariff, not so good, TOURISTY. We meet up with John finally, and the 3 of us get a ride to Sneen in one lift. Sneen is nice, view behind town towards sea... PUB "The Ole Ceiling", stay at B&B with Eva and John also got a room for £2.50 which included breakfast and run by a nice woman.

Today Eva is heading to Dublin, we had a great breakfast, scrambled eggs, toast, bread, cereal and tea. Eva, and I discussed staying together, but we knew we would split up sooner or later... She was as refreshing a person as I've ever met, fun, bold, earthy still!

John and I get rides along an especially magnificent stretch to a beautiful beach at Caher Daniel. I stay 4 ½ hours, sunny and hot, with nice Irish Folks, the Brady's. Then 3 more rides to Barranfore and on towards Dingle. Go through outskirts of Killarney, Ring of Kerry is beautiful, the most up to Waterville, from Kenmare. I went to Staigne Fort, a 2,500 year old Celtic Fort. Get a ride to Inch on Dingle Peninsula, then right to Dingle Town about 10:15 p.m., it's raining. I walk outside the town, town seemed busy, almost hectic, my pace was slow and exhaustion! I find a field just off the road about a mile outside of town, no lights or noise.

DISGUSTING

I crash in the field, after an all day hitch, with a couple nice stops (6 rides in all).I couldn't sleep very well, rained all night... no tent, just on a tarp with bag and backpack!

I wake up just before dawn it seemed, more dark than light. I am completely soaked, my bag and me, and slimey things from head to toe...but not quite light enough to see what they were. Struggling to stand up, grab my things and start walking towards the road from the slushy swamp, as it is getting brighter.

Now, I see what it is....there are SLUGS all over me and my sleeping bag, backpack! "DISGUSTING" dark, squishy, and sticky as I attempt to clean myself and my things, or free it of the slugs as best I can (it seemed like hundreds of them)!!!!!!!!!!!!!!!!!!!!!!!!!!!!!!!!!!!!!

I am on the road before 6 a.m., and can't think straight, wet and cold, freaked out... and I just wanted to get as far away from where I just woke up.

Luck would have it, a car was coming and I basically jumped in front of it. It was barely even light yet, but these guys were going hunting, saw me in the middle of the road, wet, sleepy... I don't know what they thought. Great guys, and seemed as if they were lifesavers of a sort...they were on their way towards Killarney and they can take me all the way.

Raining still most of morning, as I walk thru town, (touristy), and I don't stay long, 4 more rides and I arrive into Limerick around noon. This is a road trip day... feeling still disgusted, damp... I wanted to keep moving, on next to Bunrratty Castle, Durty Nelly's, on to Mt. Shannon thru Ennis, then near to Scariff, and on finally to Mt. Shannon YH, after 9 rides and 12 hours approx. (and hundreds of SLUGS)!!

Beautiful, huge hostel (worth the long day's journey), and cold shower, NICE EVENING, it seems! I go to the local pub with 2 Dubliners, but there is more action at the hostel, everyone sitting around singing, a priest and all. We fit right in with our mood from the pub and continue with them singing and laughing all night....

Go to harbor the next day's afternoon... read and relax, when it cleared up, cloudy and windy earlier. It's a beautiful like last night and I stay in tonight and have tea with 2 Germans, Rhinehart and Korin whom I met in Kinsale camping, we sit and talk quite a while. I am leaving tomorrow for Limerick, and Shannon Airport, and I plan on spending the night at the airport, to be there on the morning my mother arrives! They fly in at 10:30 a.m. Monday.

Sunday Aug. 1st leave Mt. Shannon for Shannon Airport, no hurry, I have all day... My mother and Bette, fly out of Niagara Falls at 11 p.m. tonight direct to Ireland!

I get a ride from the 2 Dubliners who were staying at the Hostel, to Killaloe, 15 miles more to Limerick, then another 15 or so to Shannon Airport. I am there in three rides, at about 3:30 p.m. I reach the airport but way too early... I know how to relax, take a load off. I catch up on some major reading, Irish Independent, Herald Tribunes, "Centennial", finish the "Massacre" Chapter 7, up to page 523.

At midnight I go to the Lounge to sleep, and then get up walk outside and I try sleeping in the grassy area near the edge of the runway, but get startled by a plane landing, or was it taking off, ha ha! I return inside, wake up about 6:30 a.m., and talk to some Irish folks waiting for their relations from New York. I woke up in the Lounge earlier, and it was like these folks around me were watching out for me and were so friendly.

MOTHER ARRIVES (AUGUST 2nd)

Mom and Bette come in @ 10:25 a.m., so great to see them both. My mother has never flown before, and I wanted to make sure she saw me immediately after leaving the plane! It's been over 6 months…… It was so cute when she saw me and how she reacted, and I was so broken up and in tears when I saw her! She's a trooper, a great traveler, a lot of cross country bus trips back home, but flying is different! She just seemed a little lost, tired of course, raring to go, none the less… We hugged and cried together with happiness, joy, and love to be together, also to her relief that she landed ok, and seeing her long lost son.

They had arranged a rental car from Avis, a 1976 Capri (white), it is £ 17 for a full tank of gas, and Government Tax. It was £ 10 week for insurance, which we did not get. Bette is all set to drive, it's a standard (I don't do much, just in the South of France), plus it's on the left side of road here. Funny, it reminds me of the first time I hitched in England, from the ferry towards Glasgow… started out on the right side of road, or the flat tire while visiting Prislip Manor after the partying…wrong! Ha Ha!

We go to Bunratty Castle and to Durty Nelly's for drinks… thru Limerick, Tipperary, and stop at the "Rock of Cashel", and had a nice guided tour, and on to Thurles, and have supper at Mona Lisa's! We get to Rathdowney about 8 p.m., and after visiting a short while with Eva and her family, we check in to the Hotel n town! Mom and Bette are very tired as we have a couple drinks at hotel then settle in for the night.

I stop at pub, and John and Kay there, we chat a while over a couple drinks, I hadn't just flown the ocean, but I know their jet lag...

Tuesday, August 3rd today, we have got relatives to meet, and some history to catch up on!!! I miss breakfast, because I overslept, bathe, write some letters, and cards, then off to Eva's. We have different relatives expecting us, Eva got the word out, and from my previous visit, set the stage so to speak!

We visit my grandmother's birthplace in Donaghmore , meet Eva's brother, a Daley and one of her sisters (12 of them total), later a step uncle (Kilcare), step aunt too!

We also meet an old friend (about 95 years old) of my grandfather, who calls him "A Great Hurler". My mother was really tickled to talk about her dad! It was like her dad's spirit came through her, and was so genuinely special, and real. They spoke like it was yesterday, like going back in time to the late 1800's, early 1900's, when they would have been boys and young men, as my grandfather was born in 1885.

We are driving, 8 of us in the Capri into the countryside. It is quite the tour and great fun, but more importantly a "family experience"!

We stop at the pub in Rathdowney for a couple, then a late snack at Eva's. John and Jim are both there too, so we all get caught up!

Mom and Bette are here to see Ireland, not just the relatives! At noon, the next day, we head out to Dublin! We stop at Eva's to say goodbye, but we'll be back in a 1 ½ weeks. This is a good time to step back from the emotions, seeing my mother, my mother meeting her long lost family etc. Now to see some of the country we're from, for my mother's benefit.

After reaching Dublin, we go to the zoo, see the President's House, the GARDA in Phoenix Park, then shopping for some Waterford Crystal for mom's friend back home ($130.00 for 16 glasses) Kildare Goblets and wine glasses. I buy an O'Leary Coat of Arms wall plaque for £ 5.95. We take a walk to St. Stephen's Green Park, Dublin Castle, Christ Church, Ha' Penny Bridge, O'Connell St., and Henry St. (where Mom bought Crystal at Arnott's). I was veteran of the tour now, from my previous walk about with Patti, and it went pretty smoothly.

We drive to Howth to spend the night, a beautiful harbor town just north of the City. It's a very nice evening, and we go to the Abbey Tavern, where they have Ballad singing, it's quite a special place, with a variety of different shows from time to time. What a wonderful day, Rathdowney to Dublin, to Howth!

Tomorrow, we head south to Powerscourt and Glendalough. We leave our B&B at 11:30 a.m. and stop in to Ballsbridge to visit Breda at Patti's old flat, but Breda was not home! I wanted to say hi and introduce her to my mother and Bette.

There was a very large horseshow going on and it was very crowded.

We head down to Powerscourt Gardens and Waterfall, a very beautiful estate and mansion, not too crowded but a bit cloudy. From there we go to Glendalough, a a very small, beautiful village with 2 lakes, hills, St. Kevin's Church, Monastery, St. Kevin's Cell, a round tower old church, and a grave yard. St. Kevin was a 6-7th century monk, and this place was once a center of learning for thousands of students… all in a beautiful valley setting. Obviously, sentimental for my mom, as my brother name is Kevin, and her religious background (being an ex-Catholic nun)!

We continue out to Wicklow and finally get a B&B, but we have to split up, not enough rooms here, but we find another B & B for me as well. After we settle in and go out for fish and chips for dinner and then crash by 10 p.m.

Friday Aug. 6th we're going to Waterford, Dummore East, and Tramore today by the coast from Wicklow, a very scenic route. Also, go thru Enniscorthy and Wexford. Bette and Mom stop over about 10:30 a.m., kind of nice for them to do their own thing at their pace at the other B&B… We have a big day on the road, end up in Ardmore, Co. Waterford, and split up at B&B's again. We then go to a real nice, big, crowded pub, and end with some nice singing and drinking, or was that drinking and singing, ha ha!

We had driven through Wexford, Enniscorthy, and stopped at Arthurstown (my father's name is Arthur, by the way), on the way to Waterford, and Waterford Glass, we stopped in Dunmore East, which is nice, and so is the weather. In Tramore, we ate Fish and Chips, didn't particularly like the place, though. I don't know, maybe I am getting spoiled with the wealth of beauty, history, and continued adventures, and it just takes more to get me interested. That being said, sometimes the simplest thing, person, or fork in the road can be precious.

We go through Dungarvan, then Ring, and on to Ardmore, all along the beautiful coast road. It was a very nice evening, cloudy inland, but clear around sea, and it was a great day. On to Kinsale, Cork, and Blarney Castle tomorrow!

We're leaving Ardmore about 10:30 a.m., and take coast road most of the way to Kinsale thru Cork. We got a B&B about 3:30 p.m., and cloudy now. Go up to Blarney Castle, and kiss the Blarney Stone, Bette and I. You bend over backwards, lying down reaching across a gap or space between the wall and the walkway! A poor lady got sick, literally and figuratively puked, kissing the rock!!! One of the guys working there was laughing earlier, and was saying how the workers piss on the rock at night, and all the tourists kiss it one after another!

The area is nice and so is the weather. We head back through Cork to Kinsale, and eat dinner at Jim Edwards, where I had Grilled Salmon, chips, salad and an extra side salad (£ 2.35). We go out later to the Spaniard (where I had been earlier on my trip) about 10 p.m., crowded out to the Street, and about 99% young people (good) but I don't want us to stand with Mom and Bette. Mom has a ½ and ½, and her face turns red, I have never seen her have a drink, she says "Don't tell your father".

Funny my mother is 59 years old, and I had never seen her have a drink before this, and it was only a half and half…..We go to another pub at 11 p.m. (99% older people) we can sit, and everybody is singing.

What a great atmosphere... both places! We come back, and talk to Mr. and Mrs. Breilly, who own the B&B... what a beautiful evening!

Day 7-Sunday, Aug. 8ᵗʰ We are off towards Killarney today and the peninsula below it. Looks like a beautiful day, we end up in Bantry, and there is a beautiful sunset and rainbow near the bay....It's not always planned or is it typical to have an exact destination...I love it and the ladies are all in☺

We had driven the roads south of Roscarberry, (nice), and thru Glandore, Leap and Union Hall, very pretty. Continue thru Baltimore, Schull (gorgeous) and the peninsula, it's fabulous along coast road to Goleen, Brow Hd. And Mizen Head, up coast road on Rock Island, the other side is gorgeous, rugged scenery along Dunmanus Bay. You can see Cape Clear Island (where I stayed with Eva B.) clearly from past Schull to Goleen.

We stop early tonight, no pub or restaurant, just the B&B with very nice folks! There were such Beaches all over...

Today is the nicest day since Mom and Bette came, what great timing because this is such a beautiful area to appreciate. We leave Bantry about 11 a.m. (late) stop at the Bay.

Glengariff (couple hours), along Ring of Beara, down to Castletownbere, then along to north side (Beautiful), Healy's Pass and Glanmore Lake (excellent) and thru Kenmare to get B&B at Muckross, up the street from Muckross Hotel. We stop in Killarney, to eat, shop, walk around, and drink (I am such a good influence). There's a lot of people in town, all the pubs are jammed, Danny Mana and Laurel's for Ballads, all too crowded though... we go to Hotel with music and seats (nice). Again, all considering the nicest day yet, the weather and tour!! That's really the 2 best days in a row!

Tues. Aug. 10-The rain doesn't let up today, the Ring of Kerry, Drumloe Gap, Lakes of Killarney, and Muckross today? Muckross Abbey, House and Gardens, tour Waterfalls... "Ladies View"and "Meeting of the Waters" @ Weir Bridge, bicycle race passes by!!!! We end up in Tralee, and get B&B and eat! Time to drive out thru Dingle Peninsula, Connor Pass (Beautiful), thru Dingle town... looks different at daytime, than the rainy slug infested night, when I was hitching and sleeping outside ...ha ha! Go to Ballyferriter, Dunquin (Ryan's Daughter, the movie,) Slea Head Beach! We don't get back to Tralee 'til 11 p.m. exhausted, but happily... what a long, wonderful day!

Well we didn't make it to Ring of Kerry yesterday, but we saw a lot of great places... today for sure, and up to Clare by the Tarbert Car Ferry. Tralee, was a rip off at the B&B, £12.00, charge me a double or £3.00 per person. We go to Lough Caregh, thru Ballaghasbeen Pass to Ballinskelligs, Waterville, Dereynave, Sneem , Ballaghbeama Pass on to Dunloe Gap. I go horseback riding up to the Gap for £ 2.00, but I had a beat horse, losing a shoe...I felt bad for the horse, this was a rip off, he was so slow, I could have walked faster.

To Killarney, Listowel and Tarbert for a car ferry across the Shannon River for £1.80, after waiting ½ hour for 9 p.m. ferry. Kilrush is this day's destination or place to stay, the whole day as a product is our destination. We stay at a beautiful big house with a nice old lady running it, with a nice garden, and an orchard as well! Meet John C., from Milwaukee, I share room with him for just tonight. Meet him at the pub, and do him a favor, as rooms are in short supply.

Day 11, Thurs. Aug. 12th, looks like another Beautiful day... I slept well, the ladies are doing great, and we go up coast of Clare to-day into Galway. We needed reservations for Bunratty Castle and the Medievil Banquet, but fine just visiting the area and we have to get settled in and we get a B&B nearby. Call the Walsh's in Salthill, and Eva to tell her we'll be back in Rathdowney tomorrow night.

Delia runs B&B, her brother Keane is at St. Brendan's College in Bristol, England.

We take it pretty easy today, nice day again, and we drive along coast road of Clare, thru Kilkee (nice beach). Spanish Point with a nice beach, and Lahinch with a nice beach. The climax is the Cliffs of Moher, which are fabulous, and O'Brien's Tower overlooking the Aran Islands, Galway, the Bay and the Twelve Bens of Connemara. We get a B&B in Salthill on Devon St., which is the Walsh family's Street. Standans is closed, we can go tomorrow to exchange sweater, as I had gotten the 2nd sweater in Ardmore, and Mom and Bette can shop! The town is packed, and it's a very nice evening. We spend a lot of time talking as our time together is winding down. At the B&B, Bette sleeps on floor, as there is only one bed…

Visit Ashford Castle in Cong today, very regal, especially for the West of Ireland, it seems. Then we pop down, or up to Upperchurch, where my mother's father is from near Thurles, and then to Rathdowney.

Before we go, we visit Walsh's for a while in Salthill, and they were so happy to meet my mother, after the time they've known me. My mother knew a bit about them, from her step mother, Mae.

On to Spiddel where I exchange my sweater, get a pair of Aran wool socks, instead. Mom and Bette shop, sweaters of course!!!

We go to Clifden, Kylemore Abbey, Cong, Twelve Bens, Connemara Lake, Kilary Harbor-then on to Upperchurch!

(Photos) Shannon Airport, Kylemore Abbey, Ancient Celtic Fort on Ring of Kerry, Harbor at Cape Clear Island, small lake on Cape Clear "Ice Cold Bath", Cliffs of Moher, Cows near Port Salon,-Donegal, Dingle Peninsula, 12 Bens in the distance-Turf in the foreground

We meet a cousin, Ned Griffin's wife, Peggy (Ryan) and daughter, Mary. Ned is in the hospital with a bleeding ulcer. It's very funny trying to locate Upper Church, and Milestone (Griffin's live on top of Mt.) down and up small winding roads, with scarce signage, etc. John Griffin, Ned's brother is down visiting from Dublin, but we don't get to meet him. Ned has 5 kids, and they are very pleased with meeting some American cousins.

By the time we got to Rathdowney, it was 10:30 p.m., good thing I called earlier to reserve rooms. Go to Forger's Pub, John and Kay, there and there's a Dart Tournament going on!

Sat. Aug. 14th Looks like a nice day. We go to Eva's then visit relatives, Jack Kilcare (my mother's uncle), his sister Liz (Paddy Purcell), Nanny and Paddy Bray, Eva's sister Mrs. Bowes. Go to Erril, with Paddy Bray for a couple drinks. Later on to O'Malley's in Rathdowney, John and Kay are there singing... when pub closes we go to their friend's house and drink a lot of whiskey....well themselves, their friends and myself!

Sunday, Aug. 15-Mom flies home tomorrow!!!

I wake up early, with an Irish head, sick during the night. It must have been something in the whiskey... ha, ha. The man at our hotel was not very happy with me for some reason. We go over to Eva's (Reminder: Eva's mother was my mother's mother's sister, or Bridget Kilcare Daly) then out to Jack Kilcare's, and to Eva's other "deceased" uncle's place which is a vacant old cottage. I walk inside and turn to the right into a room, where there on the wall, is a full size framed black and white portrait photograph of a woman.

Oh My God, "IT'S MY GRANDMOTHER", Mary Kilcare Moriarty!

My mother had a passport size photo of her, in a cute frame that we grew up seeing around our house. It was another even more so "Special Moment" as much as anything I've ever been a part of!!!!

This is my mother's mother, her "ESSENCE", more than just a photograph. My mom was so surprised and happy like a school girl, it was like seeing her mother, who died when Mom was very young, about three to be exact! She was beautiful, and is beautiful, and they gave us the picture, in its frame. It was more valuable than any souvenir possible, a part of our "ROOTS".

(Photo) Mary Kilcare Moriarty circa 1914., My mother's mother, and the FIND of ALL FINDS, then & now ☺

Afterward, we drive to Nenagh to see Ned Griffin. He's in the hospital there, and it's a very nice moment for him when we arrive! Word had gotten around, about us being here then leaving to tour, but that we would return, etc...

We're winding down with Mom and Bette's time here! We go on to New Market on Fergus to a prearranged B&B. Take it easy tonight. We stop in Ennis for a while, eat at Chinese Restaurant, I have curried shrimp, eggroll and chips, which for me, a last good meal for a while....

Last day of Mom and Bette's Holiday in Ireland!

They fly out at 2:30 p.m., check in @ 12:30 p.m., we leave Fergus an hour before. I will miss Mom and Bette, we've had a great time and formed a good team. I would say, things went pretty smoothly on the whole. Summary: 4 nights in Rathdowney (1st 2 and 2 of last 3) 1 night in Howth (Dublin day), Wicklow, Ardmore, Kinsale, Bantry, Muckross, Tralee, Kilrush, Salthill, Fergus. Over 1,700 miles travel by car... mostly B&B's, and the 4 nights @ Hotel in Rathdowney. All total fourteen days and nights, a fabulous and amazing adventure with my mother, and what a "BOND" ☺

It's a rare opportunity to share a trip like that! I know of friends, or couples, families with young children, but to tour around with my mother for a couple weeks, was amazing, a special bond we have now!

Mom and Bette leave and will arrive in Niagara Falls @ 4:30 p.m. today, with the time difference. Mom gave me the rest of her Irish £'s, and treated me great, "Like we are Somebody's..." She knows how to travel, it meant so much to her... Ireland, her roots, flying, seeing me after ½ year, seeing how I can handle myself, and me her, very special!

She knows I am grown up now, not perfect, but that's her boy (only 1 bad night @ the Hotel). We don't know when we'll see each other again, that's still open!

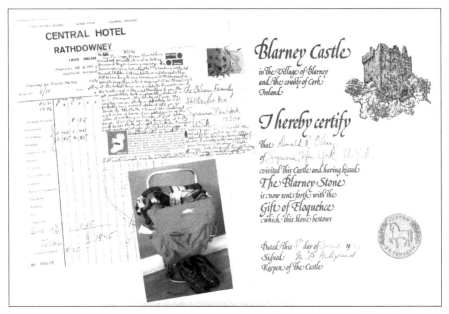

(Photo) Misc. memories in Ireland, Rathdowney Hotel, Blarney Stone, post-card to home Backpack –hiking boots plaid blanket/kilt w excerpts from my journal☺

NO SCHOOL

For the 1st time in parts of 18 years (1959-1976), from Kindergarten-College, I am normally getting ready for the end of Summer, and going back to school. This is a European Tour Marathon, school is done, Summer is over, and onwards now…!

Back to the moment, I meet a girl from Bowling Green University (from Cleveland, Ohio), where my brother Dan went to college, and who I saw at Kylemore Abbey, but now on the bus from Shannon to Limerick. I start hitching from there, wait 3 ½ hours, then one ride to Ballsbridge. Stay with Patti's old flat mates, got in around 10 p.m. Wow, what a hot and humid day….

I realized Patti didn't get to take my extra clothes home with her.

Blarney/O'Leary, Patti B in Dublin, mom & I at Trinity, mom at airport and at O'Malley's with cousin Eva K.

Tues. Aug. 17 Hot, but nice today, and I ship a couple boxes of books and clothes home, 22 lbs. for £5.40, $10.00! It worked out great, as I could send packages right from Ballsbridge, and I pick up a Guinness T-shirt, my ticket to Holyhead which cost £7.00 for the 8:45 p.m. ferry. I walk thru Dublin for the last time, and just make it to Dun Laoghire for the ferry.

I had said good bye to girls in the flat, what a great bunch of people, maybe I'll meet Angelina at the "Big Concert" in Stevenage/ Knebworth (North of London) Rolling Stones, 10 CC, Lynyrd Skynyrd, Todd Rundgren, etc. maybe at the front gate. It's a big 12 hour out-door concert from 11 a.m.-11 p.m. on Saturday, August 21st and KNEBWORTH is the site of the concert!

As I pause and gather my thoughts and prepare to continue for who knows how much longer… It seems up to this point I am getting along with all kinds of people, kids, adults, older and younger, many with different languages and cultures. It didn't matter from Belgium, France, Spain, Morocco, Italy, Netherlands, Germany, England,

Scotland, Wales, and now Ireland. Whether it is locals, travelers, families, groups or individuals, my experiences have all been friendly, fun, at ease, on a Monday, Wednesday, or a Saturday, during Winter, Spring, Summer, and now heading slowly towards Fall.

It's another day, and some are more routine, and less exotic, or fascinating, but this is not a vacation, it's more like a "Life's Journey"! To be in a new situation almost every day, or a week at a time for about seven months is challenging. Making it interesting is never a struggle…Onward!

BACK TO ENGLAND -SUMMER PART 3

Now I am off to England on the boat from Dun Laoghaire to Holyhead. I meet Ole Bjarne, from Oslo, Norway and we talk all night. He is going on to London, and then he is flying to Oslo tomorrow. Perhaps I will look him up he suggests if I make it to Oslo. I meet Kevin and Dee from Ireland on train, but split up on train in Birmingham, maybe see them at concert at Knebworth (Stevenage) as well. Nice girl from Arkansas on train in Bristol, as I head to Newquay, Cornwall (Nice Town-and beach on ocean) she says.

Well it's even nicer than I expected, but talk about crowded. Also, it is sweltering today, and I didn't get here 'til 3 p.m., left Dublin last night @ 8:45 p.m., that's 18 ½ hours on ferries and trains. I lie in sun and walk around a bit. It's a beautiful evening here as the sunset is radiant overlooking the beach.

I leave here tonight for Cardiff in Wales, or Salisbury, depends on the trains…

I will call Roz in London tomorrow, my brother's friend from Syracuse, lives in London now!

Off to Par, then Reading, to Salisbury, as I wanted to visit STONEHENGE, with an excursion at 11 a.m.-1:15 p.m. One of the most unusual monuments I've ever seen, besides all the wonderful sculpted architecture in Europe… These are massive individual upright stones brought from further away, which you can walk around and admire. Stonehenge, is quite different, it's out there, too!

Salisbury is a lovely town on Avon. I crash for a while in the Cathedral Park, and then catch a train to Oxford, after changing @ Reading. This week long train pass Brit Rail, is addicting, like the Inter Rail... you always want to use it. I walk around Oxford, which is a beautiful old town, with many colleges-Christchurch is the biggest, Magdellan, Trinity, etc.

I try calling Roz again, but roommate answers at least...

I crash along canal for the night, near the station in Oxford, exhausted, my 1st sleep since Monday Night in Dublin (10 p.m.). Where I end up sleeping is random but somewhat hidden, too tired to care.... Wake up at 9:15 a.m., feeling rested, but dirty (4 days with no showers/bath, and it's really been hot).

Try calling Roz for the 3rd time at work, not in yet.

Take 10:30 a.m. train to London at Paddington Station 11:30 a.m. and finally reach Roz, and we'll get together for lunch at 1 p.m., on Old Compton St., where she works at Charisma Records. Tube to Piccadilly Station, down Shaftesbury Ave, left on Wardrous St., Rt. on Old Compton St. # 70.

The concert is tomorrow at Stevenage.

I finally meet Roz, very nice, and we go to lunch (Guinness), across the street from her office, and at the pub 'til 3 p.m. We go back to her work and hang around 'til 6 p.m., finally Roz and I go to her home/apartment.

I adapt, very easily, the people I've met, have for the most part been so nice, in almost the full 7 months I've been travelling, school, breaks, Summer etc.

Meet Andy (Nottingham), Grant (Australian)-married, Bob, who is Roz's boyfriend. We sit around talking and drinking all night, even Roz's old pen pal visits with his wife. I finally take a bath after 5 days, they all probably appreciated it!

KNEBWORTH FAIR (Stevenage)

Sat. Aug. 21st looks like a scorcher for the concert! I'm up at 9 a.m., Roz about 10 a.m., it rained a bit which makes it somewhat humid. Very nice of Roz to go to the concert with me, easier and great company for the Rolling Stones, 10 CC, Todd Rundgren, Hot Tuna, Lynyrd Skynyrd, and the Don Harrison Band.

Roz and I get to KNEBWORTH FAIR, about 1 p.m., there are so many people and we miss the Don Harrison Band, and about ½ of Hot Tuna (who I like quite a lot). There are long breaks, Todd Rundgren is good, and there is a buzz building up for the upcoming acts..

It's a beautiful day, Airplane Acrobatics, Giant Helium Balloons, Jugglers, and Dancers. Thousands upon thousands of people are sprawling all over the grounds, a virtual sea of scantily clad women and men from all over Europe, and world travelers passing through.

Lynyrd Skynyrd is GREAT, with added fervor from some Rowdy Southerners from a local American Base. They are very close to us and waving a Confederate Flag the whole time it seemed. I did kind of feel right at home, at least the rowdiness and loving the music….:)

Starts to get dark, way before 10 CC starts at about 8:30 p.m. and they were excellent and play about 1 ½ hours. There is a 1 ½ hour wait for the Stones, not 'til 11:30 p.m. ,which is 4 hours later than the original schedule.

The STONES ARE AMAZING, and play just about everything! We had some wine, get stoned during 10 CC. What an EPIC DAY!!!!! Altogether we are there over 13 hours for the LARGEST CROWD in England's history 170,000 people from what I heard. Castle in back of 200 acre field, with a huge mouth shaped stage and set up!!

After leaving the concert grounds we get to Stevenage at 3 a.m., and then to King's Cross in London by 4 a.m. The TRAIN AND TRAIN STATION is WALL TO WALL, with very tired and burned out people.

Roz calls Bob to pick us up, and we're home by 5 a.m., what a long, but amazing end to yesterday!!!!!!

Just hanging around today, it's hot and nice. Bob and Roz go to the Park, Andy and Grant stay home, and I repack, leave some things here, leave tomorrow for Windsor (Eton), and Bath Spa.

Go to Windsor, visit Castle... it's enormous, see State Apts. the Queen is at home in the spring mostly! Just another gorgeous day, hot as hell though! Visit Eton College, meet German girl (from near Frankfurt) and walk around with her thru college and town, take pictures i.e. Warrant for Charles I (Stuart) to be decapitated. I go on to Bath @ 4:30 p.m. arrive @ 7:15, it's a very nice city, old, with river, bridges, and the 1st King of England was crowned here in 972 AD, there's Bath Abbey Church, Roman Baths, nice parks, nice shops, side walk, St., etc...

Leave Bath about 10 p.m. by train, and would like to come back some day as it is beautiful and historic. On to Bristol, on way to Cardiff,

WALES

I get there at 11:30 p.m., and I was lucky to catch it @ Bristol, it was an hour late. I walk to Cardiff Castle, to the park behind it, and crash under tree with my sleeping bag and pack, just out of view on a hot starry night!

I wake up when I hear people talking and walking, just on their way to work (Tues.) at about 7 a.m. I am pretty much in the heart of town. I walk thru the park, into castle and then to RR to catch train to Swansea and then up to Llandurlod Wells. I hope to be well on my way to Scotland, towards days end!

Arrive in Swansea, a big city, not bad, industrial all along south coast up to Swansea! I take a bus out to Langley Bay, on Gower Peninsula, past Mumbles, nice little town. It's a hot, beautiful day, beautiful beach, with lots of people. The tourist office told me Gower Peninsula was voted the Most Beautiful Stretch of Land in England!

Meet a little motorcycle stud who lived in States for a while in

Massachusetts. Then I meet a lovely lady on the train, who was flying to Hong Kong tomorrow and then on to Nepal to teach at the RAF (Royal Air Force) school for 3 years. Meet a Merchant Navy man, flying to New Orleans tomorrow, then to Caribbean and a Christian Scientist as well. The Christian Scientist talked from Crew, England to Aberdeen, Scotland, and gave me all these books. I accepted them to be polite, but he was a decent chap.

SCOTLAND

I arrived in Edinburgh @ 5:25 a.m., then Aberdeen 7:40 a.m. but leave thru Aberdeen (big, not bad)!Really hot again, nice coast from Edinburgh to near Aberdeen.

My train pass runs out today 12 p.m. Inverness is nice, but touristy, fairly big. I almost camp out 1 mile from center, but £1.25 too much, go on further down Loch Ness, and sleep on the Loch. I take a bath in the loch which was quite cold, but clear. Midges attack me the minute I got here, but sun is setting and I'm not about to find a new place to sleep. Go to sleep about 9 p.m., just to get away from midges. I cut my legs up bad also trying to find this place to sleep, so maybe the midges like the blood, I don't know (like no see-ums). Invermoriston is the name of the town and or crossroads that I am just outside of (nice old bridge and house).

Wake up 8:30 a.m., midges aren't too bad, it was like a nightmare last night! It's a bit hazy out and take a couple pictures in town, then hitch to Kyle of Lochalsh, to take ferry to the Isle of Skye, 53 miles, then 42 miles up to Uig on Sky, a small town where you take ferries to Hebrides (Islands N.W. Scotland).

Tomorrow, I think I'll go to the Harris and Lewis Islands for the day, with Susan, from Newfoundland, the ferry costs £2.90 return. I camp out today, very windy and this nice English family helps us, and we talk for a while, and have soup and coffee with them. Later, after set up, we go to the pub for a pint and meet a couple of American guys... It's been a beautiful day, very windy, BUT NO MIDGES!

Start the next morning, get cleaned up, and have coffee and sandwich with our adopted English family, who are also taking the ferry to Tarbert. We leave our packs in their Van, which has many comforts, and the ferry heads out at 9:30 a.m. and arrives at Tarbert 11:30 a.m., returns 5:30 p.m. and UIG at 7:30 p.m. tonight. It's a bit hazy on boat, can't see much going across, weather always an issue around these islands, and the coast.

"STANDING STONES" are, like Stonehenge, but on Lewis Island, and are much less accessible than Stonehenge.

Well, hitching is no good!! We walk 3 ½ miles out of Tarbert (North in Lewis), relax then head back to Tarbert. I walk in the other direction, down Harris (supposed to be beautiful beaches), but don't get far again. Relax and sit down on side of hill, by a little Loch. I buy a pair of rough wool socks in Tarbert, and run into girl from München that we met at Uig hostel.

The sea is really choppy heading back from Tarbert, the tent is still standing though! Even though our adventure was cut short with no rides which is actually part of the adventure!! We go right to the Pub 'til 10 p.m, when they close!! The wind has calmed down a bit, when we get back to my tent, should be a good night's sleep (less howling without the wind).

Sat. Aug. 28th- It's a nice day to start, clean up, take tent down and start hitching together, her and I. We soon arrive in Portree, and split up with her going to Broadford, and me, who knows? I get a ride by a couple, all the way to Glencoe, with them going on to Glasgow (him on to London then) I wasn't planning on going so far, but Fort William was too big and commercial. It was a beautiful drive between Portree and Glen Coe, I see Six Cuillan (Mts. on Sky beautiful, rugged and good climbing), beautiful lochs and Mts. on way to Fort William.

I decide to stay at Glen Coe Hostel (no shower), and meet up with Howie and Chris from Ann Arbor, who I met @ Uig. I call Tommy's house in Glasgow, and he's living and working @ hostel there now.

Howie, Chris and I hike down to the pub in town, about 2 miles down the mountain, just a short jaunt. Really dark on our way back to the hostel and a bit buzzed. We think we are hearing things "Bagpipes" in the field just beyond the hostel, and we are drawn to it and lay down to listen as this big fellow is wailing away. It was pretty amazing, like out of Brigadoon, in a mysterious mythological setting that comes to life, but right in our own back yard.

They were a couple from Winnipeg, Canada staying at the hostel as well! They were travelling around to different festivals and competitions, and had a big competition coming up.

August is almost over, it's the 29th, cloudy and chilly, and by 8:45 a.m., I am on the road. I get a couple quick rides then I walk 7 miles or so, finally a lift right to Oban! The sky is overcast when I arrive, looks nice, good sized town, and wait for hostel to open, and shower! I'm pretty tired, 4 ½ hours to get here, only 39 miles, not a lot of traffic...

Take a nice hot shower (5p), and change, walk around town, up to the Folly (an unfinished Colloseum). Meet a couple girls from the hostel Helga (Australian born German) speaks French, German, English and Italian, and her friend Gurnund, Australian Italian who speaks 5 languages. We end up walking around town together, with a Beautiful Sunset over the Harbor. Helga gives me addresses of friends all over Sweden, and in Munich, etc...

Going to Mull? Wake up 8 a.m. then I go to bank and store, decide to take 10 a.m. boat to Mull, it's a 45 min. cruise for 80p, I just made it!! Hitch at Craigmure, wait a bit, get a ride right towards Iona Island, Ancient Center of Christianity in Europe with St. Columba, there's a 6th century old Abbey and Nunnery. Also, beautiful white sand beaches, with great views of other Islands, Staffa, etc.

Get a ride with an older South African couple, who are very nice, I leave with them after a couple hours, to Salen, then up to Dervaig, beautiful scenery, the whole time. I hitch to Tobermorey, a gorgeous town, harbor and mountains. I meet a couple Scots, 2 Italian girls and a couple older Scotsmen. Leave for Oban tomorrow? I had 3 rides, all day! A Beautiful Day-An Interesting Day!

Just missed 11 a.m. ferry to Oban, and it takes a while before getting a ride. They were just taking the gangplank down as I approached, wait for 1 p.m. ferry, I suppose….

I walk first six miles out of Oban, past Connel, towards Crian Larich. Meet a nice fellow from Stockholm, then a ride by a Scot, but French born woman, who is married to a Chinese doctor. She now lives and works in Hong Kong, but is on a 5 months World Trip. She has a son who's a doctor in New Zealand. She is "Quite a Woman", takes me to pub, and have a whiskey and water, to a Chinese Restaurant in CRIEFF, where I have chop suey soup (shrimp, bean sprouts, mushrooms, etc.), King Prawn foo yung, lychee ice cream and lemon tea. Woman speaks chinese to girl, eats with chopsticks like they are extensions of her hands and fingers.

We take a side trip to Glen Eagles golf course and hotel (£18, a room the cheapest), beautiful, affluent looking area. Jack Nicklaus and Johnny Miller etc. are there for Double Diamond matched tournament. Funny, when I left Oban, I was heading to Loch Lomond, what a difference a ride makes! Now I plan on St. Andrews tomorrow, where will I end up?

After our wonderful tour today, she lets me off at hostel in the middle of the night, it was hard to find, and then looks for a Hotel for herself! Maybe, I'll see her again, and her mini (2 rides total today)!

My first September that I am not in school in 17 years! Hopefully I'll stay 3 more full months on this continued adventure!!!

Wake up cold and tired, look at my map, and chat with old fisherman at hostel, then on to Rt. 91 and St. Andrews. It was raining early, and cold and windy now, it takes 4 rides to get to St. Andrews. It turned into a beautiful day now, a beautiful town, beach, castle, harbor, and of course the "Historic" Old Golf Course. I tour around, have to see golf course in particular, nothing like any course I had seen, narrow, sandy, short, a lot of tall grass, "A Shrine to Golf"!

I'm back packing, camping, hostelling, hiking, and hitching, not on a golf holiday, so excuse the golf simplicity….

After a while, I head to Glasgow, and in 5 rides, and 3 hours, there by 7pm. I see Tommy at the hostel, and what a great surprise, as he didn't expect me! It seemed his family didn't say I called, worth the surprise!

Meet May, from Montreal, and we all go out to drink, and with David from Aberdeen too. Later, Tommy and I stay up talking for quite a while, as we had of catching up to do since I was here in early March.

I learn a new word today Sheisse, or "shit" in German, as I was planning on my shower that I learned one stall was too hot, and one, the one I chose was just right! Anyways, as I was showering, another guy comes in, and yells "SHEISSE", as he walks into his "hot as hell shower"! I just know what he meant, language aside, ha, ha, ha! We laughed about it later with our hostel mates and Tom of course. People you meet at the hostels are potentially best friends and co-adventurers no matter their language or nationality.

Anyways, my 4 day intervals for taking showers continues, and I do a walk about with May after. I then meet up with Tommy and Christy (from München) at Museum and Art Gallery at half twelve. We see The Group of Seven from Canada landscapes, which are very nice, also there are Van Gogh, Rembrandt, Gaugin, Picasso, Rodin Statues, etc.

Relax at hostel, reading the Herald Tribune, meet Kay from Australia, Frank from Milwaukee, Keith (Australia), and Mary from Nova Scotia. We go to Gresham Hotel pub, with very good music, and a lot of fun, after a great meal at the hostel. We continue drinking back at hostel with May, Mary, and Tommy 'til 4 am, what a Great Day! It helps to know the proprietor…..

Off to Edinburgh today for a day trip, get a ride by a Glaswegian (prearranged by Tommy), also May, Kay and Kristy. We walk thru town all day, the castle and other hill. Could not get tickets for TATTOO at Castle, with Pipers, Bands and Exercises, Very Famous! The city is packed for the festival! I go to a very good vegetarian restaurant

"Hendersons", on Hanover St., had curried cauliflower, potato salad, cheese and dates (apples) RATOUTOUI, and fresh whole wheat bread, great for 88 pence. Great little shops near castle, Holyrood Palace, (the Queen's Residence) great bakeries, and beautiful weather. Hitch back to Glasgow at a little past 6 p.m. and there by 8 (43 miles and cold now!) Say goodbye to Kay (Aussie) at hostel, maybe see her at BRAEMAR Highland Games tomorrow 10:30 am-5 pm, a long hitch for a day. May, Frank Camer, Aussie and I go to Gresham's and talk about Australia. I am also interested in Kibbutz in Israel, from May (she had one) I plan on checking in London about Australia…

I wake up at 4:45 a.m. to get an early start for Braemar. Take bus to outskirt of the city to hitch, very cold this morning, a couple rides, then a busload of drunks going to a football game in Aberdeen (from Denny) pick us up before Perth. We are part of the crew now, drinking and singing, way out of our way, but too much fun! We have to get to outskirts of Aberdeen now, pretty buzzed on 6-16 oz. cans, by 11 a.m., 2 more rides and in Braemar by 2:30 p.m. I meet Kay (Aussie) there and we hang together for a while, she had taken a bus up from Edinburgh for the big day.

See the Queen of England (Liz), drive by with Philip on the street about 10 feet away from where I'm standing, everybody waving and cheering. We see her again later at her Royal Box across the grounds.

The Gathering is Fabulous, and Braemar itself seems quite nice within the hills, a valley like setting. The Queens Royal Box is right there near the events. There is quite a lot of energy in the air, with music, tossing the caber, sprint races, etc.,

I had some experience with Scottish Games back home, actually working at them for three Summers in Liverpool, New York on Onondaga Lake. Tossing the caber is not for the faint at heart….

We hitch back near the end of the day and get 2 quick rides to Stirling (1st Perth), then another to motorway, darkness now, and get one more ride to small town near Glasgow by a fellow from Nepal, but he takes us all the way straight to the hostel instead (10:30 p.m. and beat, but very appreciative)!

Sunday September 5, May is going to Stirling by bus for the day. I am taking it easy, for tomorrow I leave Glasgow after 4 days and 5 nights, I catch up on reading the Herald Tribune. Frank, the American comes back after 5 hours trying to hitch to Carlisle. Meet 2 fellows from Tennessee, 2 German frauleins from Hanover and Braunsweiger (N. Germany) at Gresham's, maybe visit them if I go to Northern Germany. Otherwise, not very eventful, Fish and Chips closed, and they are great too!

GOODBYE TOMMY

Hitch south today, say goodbye to May, Frank, and of course Tommy. Will I see Tommy again? He was one of the first people I met in Europe, in Bruges, back in January and visited him and his family here in early March.

(Photo) Scotland: Glasgow,Loch Lomond, Oban, Braemar- the Queen, St. Andrews, Tobermorey. England: Concert at Knebworth with Roz & The Stones, Stonehenge , Brighton

I get to Penrith by 12:45, Keswick in one ride. Keswick is nice, in the Lake District (touristy though), and I go past to Grasmere, Ambleside, and Windemere, etc. to Kendal, on outskirts of Lake District, which was gorgeous. There are hostels all along the way, in Kendal YH by 6:30p.m. (4 rides-154 miles)and on to York tomorrow?? This hostel is nice, only 80p (standard), then I can relax and read all night.

I would love to come back to the Lake District, just going through made me appreciate it and its beauty. With more time, you learn of the people, places and history.

I am on my way to York today, again hitching! I arrive there in 4 rides, 3 ½ hours in 88 miles, and I'm at the hostel. I check in at the hostel for £1.00, leave my pack to walk around. I meet a couple girls from Toronto, and we hang out, walk to York Minster, it's the biggest Medieval Church north of the Alps, and it's in great shape. I end up losing the girls, and walk thru the old streets, buildings, churches, castle, SHAMBLES (famous old street and buildings). The city is surrounded still by fortress wall, (Old York).

I meet a Flemish boy named Rudi from near Leuven, 2 girls from Innsbruck, Eva and her friend, very nice girls, we talk about me visiting! It's been a great day, good travel, great architecture and history, very nice people I meet, and the hostel is great value!

Hoping to visit Nottingham, Sherwood Forest, and see Gill Bennett, etc. Wake up 7:45 a.m. semi-hot shower, after 3 days of hiking. Guess what though, I made it all the way to Cambridge instead, decided to bypass Nottingham, Sherwood Forest and Gill Bennett, to my regret!

It took me 6 rides, the last 4 were short, and the hostel is filled up, the person in front of me was the last one in! I meet Paul Clarkson (Toronto) at RR Station, who was at York hostel, and we decide to stay at YMCA, £2.80, like a B&B or a hotel, so a treat, but more expensive. We meet a fellow from Trinidad, very strange, very hyper, a couple Germans, and 2 Englishmen at the EAGLE PUB, and another Pub, on River Cam. It's a beautiful old town, with Abbot Ale, a strong local drink.

After breakfast with 2 Germans and Paul, I do a guided tour of Cambridge for 80p, The Old Colleges of King's, Trinity and St. John's. I walk around a bit more , then back to YMCA to get packed, and off to London! I walk a ways, then 5 rides and tube to BARON's Court (Roz), always great to have a reunion. We sit up and watch TV after catching up on the last couple weeks…

Fri. Sept. 10, Rearrange my pack, clean boots, do wash, I go to bank, then to NUS Student Travel. I go out for a walk to Leicester Square and Piccadilly for a bit. Happening places, shows, shops, pubs, discos, and a lot of people! I get a 90p Balcony ticket to see Jesus Christ Superstar at Palace on Shaftesbury in Piccadilly.

I meet 5 Americans from Bucknell and Penn., who are studying Economics in London. John of this crew and I are meeting up tomorrow to hang out day tripping.

The play (musical) is excellent, it runs from 8:40 p.m.-10:50 p.m. or so! It was raining before the show and after, and the Tube is packed going back to Roz's, and I got drenched… In the morning I have to go to Victoria Station for info on Copenhagen and ticket to Belgium from London £6.90. Upstairs, in Grovesnor Hotel Victoria, I stop in to room of 3 fellows from Bucknell (Rm. 429), Hank, Gary and John. John, Hank and I go to Tower of London for 80 p (20p in winter time), there were 7 executions by loss of head, back in the day…, oh the good old days !!!!

I can't help but wonder what I would have been like back then, commoner, an adventurer? Just imagine for a second, a minute, but don't lose your head!!!!!

From there, walk to Piccadilly and stop at Drury Lane Theatre Royal, and get £1.00 Balcony seat for CHORUS LINE, (my cousin Thommie Walsh, from Auburn, NY is in it back in the States with the original NYC cast). Meet 3 guys and 3 girls from Syracuse U., in front of me, hook up with 2 of girls after show, and go out for coffee. Ran into Andy as well, raining again, but the show was EXCELLENT.

Have to catch up on some things today, sew my best Levi's for example. Laurie, from SU comes over with Andy, which is nice, and great that it's cool with Roz. Tomorrow try to see Equus, if not, then I head to Belgium.

Get my gear in order after breakfast, walk to Madame Tussaud's Wax Museum on Marylebone St. near Baker St., walk thru Hyde Park and Regent's Park (Queen Mary's Garden). It's raining all day and later, a character on the street tries to sell me ¼ oz. of Hash but he's way to hyper, and I have no £'s left.... I go to see Equus at the Abbey Theatre on St. Martin's Lane near Trafalgar Square for only £1.00, student rush-1 hour before show begins. I got 2nd row seats, normally £3.50, there were American students all around me. There's a fellow from Santa Cruz, CA next to me. An obnoxious girl from Long Island begins to walk out after first part, just leave, but not loudly!!

I walk all the way home after the play, 1 ½ hours to Roz's that is! Walking fits my budget and schedule it seems, and It also helps me know my way around the streets and landmarks along the way.

The next morning I say goodbye to Grant and Roz, thanks, you've really been great!

My 3 months in Ireland, Scotland, Wales, and England are coming to an end as I leave for Belgium today, via Canterbury. Late start, I miss 10 a.m., and get 1:10.p.m. train , which gives me only ½ hour at Canterbury. I realized that I left my rain poncho at theatre last night (they didn't find it, as I rang them up earlier). Now, no poncho, and I left raincoat in Ireland!

BACK TO THE CONTINENT

Arrive in Dover @ 3:20 p.m., I am taking the ferry boat which leaves at 4:45 p.m. for Oostende, Belgium, arriving at 8:05 pm. I sneak on the train from Oostende to Bruges and arrive at Hotel Ridderstraat about 9:30 p.m. after the long walk from the station.

There's a visitor, a College of Europe grad from Bruges, who happened to be over, and we chat a bit before I crash. He was a student here about 6 years earlier.

In the morning I sort through a lot of mail from a variety of people ,my mother, Eva in Germany, Sue McGrath, Karin in Copenhagen. Karin wrote and asked if I am visiting, and that I am very welcome to!

Wed. Sept. 15, I walk around Bruges, go to the bank to deposit $50.00 check (thanks mom), read a bit of some of the magazines and books left at the Hotel. I get everything together that I am ultimately taking home. I find myself a good pair of shoes to wear (from the things my former classmates left), because I am leaving my hiking boots! I get haircut near Van Eyck monument, 165 BF ($4.00+-) I stop in to the Cactus, Rita and the crowd from the Lotus are there. Meet Meika from Oostende who spent a year in the States, mostly Colorado. We had a good time on 11% TRAPPISTS Beers, and we seem to have a liking and an attraction for each other....

I saw Jeremy Cooper earlier today at the College on my walk, it seemed so long ago that we were all here as students, and it's all part of the PAST already.

I go to the bank in the morning and withdraw all my money, except the $50 that I just deposited! I have things like a train pass and flight home to purchase (When and from where are unknown so far)!

I see Bart for a minute and then later finally run in to Madame, and we talk for a while. She says, there might not be a program next year, because of a rise in the cost. That would be a huge shame, as I know the richness of her hospitality, and kindness, and of course the amazing setting that is Bruges. What a shame if is not available in the future, and more sincerely a loss for Madame.

CHAPTER 7

Fall 1976

I DO A lot of thinking about my next destination, how and when, perhaps Copenhagen (Kobenhavn, or K Ø). Also, about when I fly home, and from where, and I decide on Brussels to New York on Dec.10ᵗʰ!! That gives me almost a year, or at least parts of all 12 months (Jan. 24-Dec. 10, 1976).

After, I stop in to the Cactus to rendezvous with Meika, and meet Frances (Brigitte's fellow), he came after her. He is a nice guy, has a house here now, it's been 2 years since he was back, also his friend Carl! The girl bartending I had met at the Lotus Bar party a while back, which was a great time.

I hit it off with Meika, and we're out 'til past 2 a.m. Meika speaks 5 languages, and English like an American. Rita and Johan are at Cactus too!

Fri. Sept. 17ᵗʰ I buy my Interrail Pass for 4,990 BF ($125.00)! My train leaves for Copenhagen at 5:57 p.m., and Meika will see me off at the Station.

First I have to arrange everything, write some post cards, Diane C., Dan D., Tommy P. and Aunt Nell Moriarty Halpin (Thanks for the graduation money). Meet a fellow named Laurent, a land surveyor, who knew Sue S.

Meika is waiting on the Platform for me, and I see Ulla, from Finland, Tommy P.'s old girl, on her way to Finland. Ulla and I get a compartment together where we meet a couple Australians in our short lived 1ˢᵗ class seats. I get out of Belgium without paying the ½ tariff, 205 BF (over $5.00)! There are 2 Austrians, Swedish girl, Ulla and myself for 14 hours to Copenhagen (8 hrs. more to Stockholm).

DENMARK

Sat. 18ᵗʰ I am still on the train to Copenhagen, Ulla is going all the way to Finland, and she will be there Sunday night, and Swedish girl too. Take train on ferry from Puttgarten, with a beautiful sunrise crossing the sea, arriving in Copenhagen about 9 a.m.

I call Karin and Karoline who visited Bruges back in May when we hung out for an evening, and they invited me to visit them in Copenhagen. I call from the train station and finally reach Karin, and they are more than happy to have me. It is raining as I walk from the station to their place, so I stop at TIVOLI, to get out of the rain. Tivoli is an Amusement Park, and tomorrow is the last day for the season, lucky I stopped in!

I meet Karin once again, Henry (friend), and Karoline again (her roommate), who is very nice too! It is so great to be welcome in another city and country, instead of just hostels or B&B's/Hotels. It's a savings, but it's more of the comfort and knowledge the people I am visiting give me.

I shower, then they have a visit from Bengt and Greda from Jutland (Karin and Karoline's home), and we eat and drink wine. I walk around with K&K to Christiana, which is like a big dirty commune (especially for Copenhagen), stores, pubs etc., a couple beers at a café, then back home (their apt.) Karin has to work the night shift tonight (nurse) 11 p.m.-730 a.m. I sit around drinking with Greda, Henry, and Karoline here, and then out to see a jazz band at MUSKETEERS, where 4 drinks (beers) for 28 Kroner ($4.80), plus 8 Kroner cover charge. It's crowded, with a very nice atmosphere, and we stay from 9:30p.m. - 2 a.m ., Karoline and I walk back, but they meet up again later, I am beat, haven't slept but 1 hour on the train since Friday morning.

I slept 'til 2 p.m., finally wake up, everyone else has been up quite a while. We (Karin, Karoline, Greda, Henry, and myself) watch an old American movie on T.V. "Devil in Miss Jones" starring Jean Arthur and Charles Colburn, and enjoying it! I walk with Karoline and Greda to Palace of Queen Margaret, then to Fountain Statue, and to the Mermaid (Hans Christian Anderson's), and get a shot of "Old Danish." (Gammel Dansk) in the a.m., which was a typical local drink!

It starts raining again, but nice out though. I catch up on some writing cards and reading, because we go to the last night @ TIVOLI GARDEN, which costs 5 Kroners, 6=$1.00 approx. It's all lit up, crowded, music, rides, games, gambling, restaurants, fountains, gardens. At the end, a Big FIREWORKS display... Karin working nightshift at hospital, Karoline the early morning shift, so I went by myself.

It's my 3rd day in Copenhagen, and I really like it here. Greda and Bengt go back home to Arrhus, the 2nd largest city in Denmark, in Jutland population about 250,000.

Bengt and Greda wake me up to say goodbye, which is nice... Later, I go to tourist info, and to Christianborg Palace, and the National Museum, with Viking and early Danish History. I walk everywhere, then to the Carlsburg Brewery by 2:15 p.m., just in time for the English speaking tour. They give me 3 beers at the end, which is better than most brewery tours. Meet 4 Americans, 3 girls and a guy, and end up walking around with the girls, one from St. Lawrence University (northern New York State), Oswego State, and Univ. of Oregon (Kim, Terry, and I don't remember), plan on meeting tomorrow for lunch and to the Botanical Gardens.

I go back to apartment and no one is home, 'til Karin comes and we talk, she's working again tonight. A friend of Karoline calls and invites me to their party. It's a 40 minute walk and I left at 9:30 p.m. There are 2 couples, and Karoline and myself, drinking wine, sharing pictures from trips, and a lot of conversation. I walk home about

1:15 a.m. until 2 a.m. ,it's a good hike as Karoline stays at their apt. because it's near her Hospital for work in the morning.

Karin makes me a nice breakfast in the morning, an omelet and great coffee, and we talk etc.

I have to meet the American girls at 1:15 p.m. at the Student Cafeteria, near the ROUND TOWER. I see Kim and Janet, meet Mary Joan (Minnesota) and Joan (Syracuse University) and 2 guys, one from Rockland County, the other Danish. Dave, Mary Joan and I go to the Park at Rosenborg Castle to hang out, and the three of us get stoned, then we walk around after.

Kim and I almost get together tonight, but she can't make it. I hang around with an older couple at Karin and Karoline's, who are over for dinner, and are parents of a girlfriend of Karin's in the States. I am so tired after dinner and just want to read after!!

Tomorrow, I leave for Stockholm, and leaving backpack here. Tonight is Karin's last on nightshift, then Karoline's starts tomorrow night.

I meet Dallas from England, who spent time in States, and loves it (lived in Tempe, Arizona for a while). He works here as a dishwasher in a Chinese Restaurant. I don't get going until 1:30 p.m. and go to Swiss Photo Exhibit at Town Hall, to Ny Carlsberg Glypto Museum for Impressionist paintings, Egyptian Mummies, Rodin Statues, etc., and all were very good.

Kim from St. Lawrence doesn't meet me at Student Cafeteria, so I head back to visit with Karoline, Karin and Henry, and relax and read!

Today, sleep late 11 a.m., and out by 12:30 and arrive in Helsingor (Elsinore) by 2:30 p.m. I see Kronberg Castle, where Hamlet supposedly came from. It's a beautiful day for travel, and Sweden is just on the other side of the Sound!

I meet Raoul, a Brazilian from Rio, nice fellow, and we go to Hillerod, Fredericksborg Castle, former Residence of Frederick, now after fire, it is a Natural History Museum, begun by J.C. Carlsberg, who founded the Brewery, with 2/3 profit of Brewery going to Science, 1/3 profit of Brewery to Art.

I will meet Raoul at Central Station in Stockholm tomorrow at 4 p.m., as he's off to Copenhagen tonight for a date. I head up to Stockholm, leaving Helsingborg at 11:15 p.m. arriving to Stockholm at 7:47 a.m. The trip was very eventful for the duty free is like the reason some Swedes come over, and drink a lot during the trip.

Sept. 24, It is Daddeo's Birthday (my father), 73 today!

In Stockholm it's a beautiful day, hazy and cold at first. I walk around old town, the canals, palace etc. to the "highest building in Scandinavia" the T.V. Tower, with a nice park near it on a lake.

Meet Raoul as planned and walk around, he can't get in touch with the daughter of India's Ambassador, she's in U.S. We meet at a hamburger joint, with the daughter of the Russian Ambassador to Sweden. Her name is Median, blonde and pretty, exotic but friendly. These two want to see a movie, and I am invited (Mickey Spillane movie, with Chris George and Yvette Mimeux), but I decide not to, and grab train to OSLO @ 10:05 p.m.

I meet 4 Swedes that are in the Army in my compartment, and they were pretty rowdy, ha ha. There were many other people, with many conversations, and in different languages, and many drunks on top of it. Well it is the weekend….

NORWAY

The train arrives in Oslo about 8:30 a.m. Being spontaneous has its benefits when you have a train pass, as long as I see the scenery between Oslo and Stockholm on the return trip. I save the night's lodging cost, and get there at the ideal time, early and all day to walk around!

Try to visit with a friend of the girls from Texas, Karen & Robin that I was in Munich and Salzburg with. Marthe, was an exchange student with Robin in Texas for a year.

Arrive in Oslo @ 8:30 a.m., it looks beautiful out! I continue on to Heistad to visit Marthe, south of Oslo, 2 ½ hours by train near Porsgrunn. She's not there, but I meet her mother, and have coffee and a snack. Marthe is working at a nursing home in Oslo. It was a very nice side trip and sweet, meeting her mom.

I call Marthe and she meets me at the train station, with her friend, and we go to a get together of their friends, A"Christian Fellowship". She lives in an all girl residence she advises, and she's never met me before now, so I'll have to find a place to stay…

I call Ole Bjarne who I met leaving Ireland and on the ferry, and he will put me up! Marthe takes me out to his place, near the University at the Resident Dorms. Ole and I stay up late chatting and snacking after I get there.

It's funny, Martha was a so nice, and I never knew her. It works out better staying with Ole, though. After 2 nights on the train, I slept 'til 11:30 am. We stop out to where Marthe is working, the nursing home, but she has to go back to work at 4:30 p.m. and is going out with her friends tonight. We all took a bus to a wooden worker's town, and a nice hilly park looking over Oslo on an absolutely gorgeous day.

Ole and I then go to the Mountain overlooking Oslo. We take an Old Tram car to the top of the mountain for a fabulous affect, and there are many walkers with little rucksacks. Cross country skiing is so big here, as you see people skating on boards with poles, preparing for the snow it seems. We are at the "Highest Observation Tower in Scandanavia" at 1,929 feet above sea level, with a tremendous view and a beautiful sunset. And we go to the SKI JUMP from 1952 Olympics, "Fabulous", in a tremendous setting. Overall it's been a breathtaking and exhilarating day.

Later we play Monopoly (an international version, no Boardwalk and Park Place), after we return to Ole's place.

Marthe was tentatively going to meet me today, but I was ½ hour late, and I waited 1 ½ hours for her at the Palace. I walk to the Museums, 1) Open Air 2) Viking 3) Kon Tiki, but too late for the Fram or Maritime Museum. Open Air was the best at 5 Kroner ($1.00), other two were 2 1/2 and 2 Kroner. All three were a slice of their life, a view of their History. Marthe had to go in at 4 p.m., to fill in for her co- worker who was sick.

Open Air- old style Nordic Homes and Village, Lapland Exhibit, 12th Century Stave Church, and seeing what life was like 8 centuries earlier was very interesting!!!

I am on my way to Bergen tonight, at 11 p.m., arriving at 7:35 a.m. Many Americans, young and old, many drunks, one character has everyone cracking up. There were many different conversations, in different languages again... Quite a group of waiters for a train, a party train and it's only Monday!

WHAT SCENERY, Lakes, Mountains, Rivers, snow- capped peaks, and cliffs all the way to the city of Bergen. That's just from right before VOSS, as it started getting light about 5:30 a.m. I slept a bit until then, as it got uncomfortable (no compartment), and the characters woke me up, no worries...I've been a bit of a character myself on occasion!

I walk thru Bergen for 1 hour to Tourist Info, then catch Tram to MYRDAL at 9:40 a.m. and arrive at 12 a.m., from there a beautiful 12 ½ mile slow winding train to FLAM.

There is turquoise blue water streaming down waterfalls, as we descend down mountain to the beginning of the Fijord. It's raining as we get there, we play Frisbee in the parking lot, there's Laurie from Santa Cruz, an Aussie, and myself. The Ferry ride is 2 hour 15 min., thru the Fijord, meet a lot of people, the twins, Carol and Lisa from Detroit (met at Carlsberg Brewery) Ann and Marcos (he's an Argentine living in Stockholm), and some other nice Americans. I've never seen scenery like this, rain or not...

We take a 1 hour bus ride, winding up the mountain with fantastic scenery... waterfalls everywhere... we go from Gundarven to Voss. Going to stay at the hostel here in Voss, most of us are... It's like a ski resort hotel, outrageous, 30 Kroner ($5.65) with Breakfast included... "ALL YOU CAN EAT" of hardboiled eggs, breads, butter and jam, cheese, coffee and milk. Remember, I don't eat meat, so sometimes I leave things off menus that don't pertain to me, ha,ha!

I take a long hot sauna with Laurie and Lisa, as we relax after a great day, talking about our adventures… and then a cold shower… It's all very natural!! Lisa, and I go for a walk thru town, and pick apples on the way back.

Wake up @ 8 a.m., early for me, but hostel routine, eat breakfast for 1 hour, and Full! Talk with John O'Donnel (1974 college grad), who played basketball at University of North Carolina with Bob McAdoo, and against David Thompson at North Carolina State. Also, in high school, he was All State with John Shumate, Gary Brokaw and an Ulrich at Don Bosco High in New Jersey. I went to high school with Ulrich's sister Jane, small world.

I say goodbye to Laurie, Lisa and Carol, and play Frisbee with John and Aussie again. It's absolutely beautiful here, hostel is right on the lake, snow- capped mountains in the background. I walk around and up to FOLK MUSEUM on the mountain side, with a beautiful view.

I go back to Bergen at 12:52, with Jim from Edmonton, Babs from Miami, and Nitza who is from Israel. We go to Aunt Klara's Apt. (Bab's Aunt) and she feeds us 'til we're full. Take a funicular up to Floien, BEAUTIFUL SUNSET, and view…. This is the West Coast of Norway, but the way Bergen is situated, and Fløien as well, it's a spectacular view, and we walk back down the mountain and up to Aunt Klara's to eat again and we have a great time. There is a lot of laughing, eating, and joking! She is really a wonderful woman, as she took us all in for the day, and a couple meals.

We are all of us, on the go though, 10:30 p.m. train to Oslo, arrive 7:10 a.m., 8 a.m. to Copenhagen arrive 5:36 p.m. Don't sleep from Bergen because we are all so wound up, energetic and going different places soon. I leave Nitza and Jim in Oslo, but Babs, Tim (Aussie), and I go on together, at least to Helsingborg, where Babs departs (another relative) Tim and I plan on meeting in Munich for Oktoberfest, rendezvous at the Glockenspiel at the Marienplatz. Kurt, fellow from

San Diego gets off at Copenhagen with me, he'll also go to Munich, but takes the 6:10 p.m., and myself 11:10 p.m. I have to go to Karin and Karoline's flat to get my backpack, shower, eat and say goodbye! Great girls, Karin even packed me food for the trip. I will definitely write them from Greece and wherever else!

(Photos) Fijord-Flam & Gundarven-Norway, Me at Fredricksborg Castle in Hillerod-Denmark, Tivoli Gardens and Carsberg Brewery in Copenhagen

GERMANY- Oktoberfest

Friday, October 1- Oktoberfest Time!!!!!! It's the last 3 days of one of the Biggest Parties in the World, it started September 18th... I change trains in Hanover @ 8 a.m., meet a girl from San Francisco. Finally, get in about 3 p.m. to Munich, and I am so beat, slept a bit last night, as I had a compartment to myself. I call Eva in Starnberg (met in Cape Clear Island in Ireland), but no luck reaching her, and no vacancy at this hostel!!

Meet Karen from Calgary and Jeff, from New Brunswick, end up at hostel in Pullach, south of Munich, about 20 minutes. It's a beautiful place, a CASTLE, and it is packed, and full of the energy from all its worldwide visitors.

I have to meet Tim from Tasmania at the Marienplatz at 8 p.m. under the Glockenspiel, and start our evening's festivities.

We all go to the FEST of course!! Also, meet Margaret from Tasmania, we go to HOFBRAU Tent, the place was packed "Thousands of Drunks", we mostly get a feel for the place. It's 3.95 DM ($1.60) a litre, have 2 ½, as we arrived late, it only goes to 11 p.m., from noon it starts! Good start for the festivities, hop back on train to Pullach. Tim is staying at the other hostel that I stayed at before, which is the main Munich Hostel. The train is full of so many drunk hostellers, last train at 11:30 p.m., and hostel closes at midnight.

I wake up at 7 a.m., raining a bit, but I am psyched! I had a letter from Judy @ Poste Restante. Meet up with Tim again at Marienplatz, and a new member, Mary Beth from Ontario. We go to St. Peter's Church off Platz after a couple beers at Augustiner Beer Hall and then to Englishener Garden, as Karen and Mary Beth go to Deutsches Museum. Me, Margie, Tim and Jeff, get a little lost in Gardens, until we find Pagoda and get a beer.

We then go to meet the other 2 girls under the Dragon Heads at Oktoberfest! We try Paulaner Beer and meet a nice German Family, sitting at the outside tables, drinking fast, and then buzz over to HOFBRAU HAUS TENT!

The HOFBRAU HAUS is like American, Canadian and Australians

everywhere. I am a bit pissed by the time we get there, meet a jerk of an Australian, making advances to Margie, and he says that he's an American, with a bad accent, just an asshole! Margie had met him earlier in her travels, so she knew enough about him.

Back to the station, which is packed with locals and travelers, we just catch the last train back to the hostel. At the stop before ours, there's chaos, and pushing to get off. All of a sudden a girl traveler got pushed off between the train tracks and the platform. We never found out how she made out, but she got hurt pretty bad, from what we could tell. People were clueless at first, then a lot of screaming, it was very sobering. She was an Irish girl from Dublin, another girl mentioned

The police and ambulance arrived quickly! Everyone was upset, screaming as train started to pull away from the station. The train had left early, before the doors were closed. Another Dublin girl was in shock, and had a cut forehead, just chaos!

Sunday Oct. 3, This is the Last Day of Oktoberfest. Karen and Mary Beth go to Dachau and the Olympic Stadium, Margie to Nymphemburg Palace. We go to Mathausen Beer Hall, Tim, Jeff and I, and then to Fest Grounds, walk around, quite a place, Gigantic Fair with 8 Gigantic Beer Tents. By 4 p.m. we're in our 3rd Tent, and meet a nice girl from Toronto selling postcards with her German boyfriend. We're getting a great buzz, and I feel great, meet a fellow from Boston, a bit nerdy, but who are we! Tim and I stay there, Jeff and Bostonian get a table at HOFBRAU Tent, and we meet them later.

Supposedly it ends at 8 p.m. on the last night, but no it doesn't. The Hofbrau Tent is not packed, anticlimactic after last night, I guess. Meet a couple nice servicemen and some real jerky ones, and we get real pissed. I run in to Kurt from San Diego, but out of Copenhagen. I lose Tim and everyone somehow, and I am singing and dancing until I saw the Aussie asshole make a mocking gesture. Infuriated, I dove over the railing to his table below, which was the last thing I remember.....

3 German girls and 2 guys find me about 1 a.m., lying on a sidewalk, and help me up and to the train station, but the last train to hostel was gone. I had a big cut and bump under my left eye, and my head was killing me.

The Train Station is all locked up, but 2 different guys help me sneak in the station so I can hang out there 'til morning, as the next train is in 4 ½ hours. I end up in an idle train and fall asleep. After some time, the train I am sleeping in starts taking off, but not where I need to go. I realize I had to find my jacket, wallet, passport, as everything had fallen out of my pockets when I took my jacket off! Last night I was trying different sleeping cars on for size, and I finally find everything, Yes!!!!! I have to hop off this train, as it wasn't mine. I was a little bit freaked out....

Most of last night, was really Monday, the 4th. I take the 6:30 a.m. train to Pullach, and it's a really beautiful day, and I'm alive but exhausted, as I get in the hostel before breakfast, hungry and thirsty. I also, quite obviously look like I got hit by a freight train, or a waitress at a beer hall, what a shiner! There were more than a few comments from other hostellers, that I looked like shite....But it was just OKTOBERFEST!!!!!

I had a letter from my mother today, seven pages with an always important twenty dollar bill.

Everybody seems to be splitting today from München/Pullach. Tim, Karen, Craig and myself, are going to Füssen, "Disney's Castle" at Neuschwanstein, while Margie waits in München for her sister. Mary Beth goes on to Luxembourg, and is flying home next Saturday.

FUSSEN/ NEUSCHWANSTEIN-LUDWIG

It is beautiful here in Füssen, green pastures and hills, snow covered mountains, Lake, and the CASTLE(S)! This is where the idea for Walt Disney's Fairy Tale castle for Disneyland came from!

I am taking it easy tonight, tired and dirty, wonder why? Need time to gather my thoughts, and relax. Oktoberfest was CRAZY, 3 straight days of hard partying, especially the last 2 with life changing chaos and some catastrophe!

I never saw Eva in Munchen (Starnberg), and she was expecting me, I tried, but partying took over!!!

I plan on seeing the Castle at Neuschwanstein tomorrow, and picnic if it's nice out. Wake up at 6:45 a.m., breakfast at 7 a.m. Walk up to Castle at 9:30 with Karen, Tim, Ray (other Aussie), Craig (State of Washington), and Heidi from Steamboat Springs. It's quite a walk, overcast, rainy, but I like it. It is a nice change from the city and the hectic partying. This is Ludwig II's Castle, "Crazy Ludwig's" Fairytale Castle. Very ornate, picturesque, plus how it is set within the Mts.

The actual castle and interior were very nice, but I have seen so many palaces, castles, mansions, museums, etc. in the last eight months. But the setting here, is what really stood out for me, amazing in the countryside, between the mountains and lakes!

I meet Bob from LA on bridge behind the castle, and we go hiking up to the peak of the Mountain, a 1 ½ hour walk up trail from bridge. There's a cable car you take down for 4 DM, with amazing views, especially looking back to the Castle... Meet a nice American couple living in Frankfort, and walk back to Füssen with them. I stop in a bakery, and get bit by the dog of the owner, just a scratch though... The owner spent 11 years in Montreal, he tells me after apologizing I think, as my German is better than my Flemish, but not as good as my French or Spanish... ha ha! He also tells us to go to Disco in town later, and why not....

Margie is at hostel when I return, Roger too, from Melbourne. They seem to be hitting it off, and I liked her quite a bit, C'est la vie. We have a big dinner together and go to pub and disco later, curfews at 9:45 p.m. No drama, just hanging with fellow travelers, talking about who's going where, and when, and with whom, etc...

(Photos) Munich or Munchen-The Hofbrau House Beer Hall, Glockenspiel, Eagles Nest at Kelstein (Hitler's Hideout), Konig See near Berchtesgaten, and Dachau Concentration Camp

I'm a little set back and confused, no denying though. After much thinking in morning, I decided to go to Paris, to check on flight home!! I am thinking at latest Dec. 10 from Brussels, I only have $280.00 left for a little more than 2 months including transportation back from Greece!

Karen, Craig, and Bob, go on to Garmisch, Tim stays again and on towards Copenhagen, he's been a good mate, Margie not sure! I'll miss these folks it's rare I become attached so, but we shared some great and wild times in a short while, 5 days or so, between our time in Munich, Pullach, and Fussen!

Lives were changed at Munchen/Pullach, a real crossroads of travelers coming together for a particular spectacular event!

I get in to Wiesbaden at 5:36p.m.and have to wait 'til 10:35 p.m. for Paris train, and arrive in morning. I would like to visit Scott's, but maybe on my way home in December, or Friday morning after Paris, I am too exhausted to think!

Meet an American Air Force fellow on train (Charleston, SC) and we talk a while, but too tired, and sleep most of way to Paris, arrive at 7:30 a.m., BEAUTIFUL DAY (Oct. 7th, Thurs.). I store my pack in locker, get a map and ask for directions... not many francs, so I walk all day.

I book my flight to go back home for December 10th , out of Brussels at CIEE, 49 Rue Pierre Charron, off Champs Elysee. Then, off to Arc de Triumphe, and over to Gare Montparnase and take train to Versailles. Fabulous gardens, fountains and palace, and a nice day too! Funny while taking a nap at the gardens, a dog almost bit me, nipping and pulling on my pants. That's the third dog this year, in Loppem(Belgium) with Brigittes's dog, Fussen a couple days ago, and now Paris...

It cost 2.50 F, ½ price to see everything, great still to have student card, getting my money's worth ha, ha!

Meet 3 girls from San Francisco, having a little trouble with some French lads, which I interrupt, but no problem, as I act like I am there friend and looking for them. It's like I haven't been a tourist, since forever...

I walk again, now to Gare de l'Est, 1 hour 20 min, and meet a Canadian from Winnipeg, named Horst, who's on his way to München to play hockey. Meet a guy from S. Carolina, who spent 11 years in Israel, because his parents were Baptist Missionaries. I finally catch the 23:00(11:00 p.m.) train to Wiesbaden, then go to Wallau to see the Scott's arrive 8:30 to a.m. Scottie, home unexpectedly, just got rid of a cast on his ankle (sprain), his back hurts again too! He got a promotion recently though, which is awesome.

Their landlord died back in June, two weeks after I left. What a terrible shame that he fell from the roof of his barn. He was not a young man, but very able, and always working on something.

Linda just turned eleven on Wednesday, and had a friend over. We eat breakfast, and I clean up, repack things, and do some reading.

Most important, I leave my ticket to USA with them. Gerhardt, his wife, and Christina come over, Jim his friend too! We had a big supper, and I played a few games with Linda and Joanne, her friend. I almost feel like part of the family, sharing the moments, with friends and neighbors.

I am actually leaving tonight for Innsbruck, supposedly 23:20, actually 0:25 to Mainz and 0:55 to Innsbruck, always adapting. I am beat, as it's my 3rd straight night on trains.

AUSTRIA

I am going to visit Eva in Innsbruck, who I met in the York Youth Hostel back in early September. It's Saturday, October 9, one week to make Greece! Eva, not home at 7:30 a.m., she was mountain climbing come to find out. I run into Cindy, from Pullach hostel, then Dan from Ft. Worth and his camping companion, a girl from New Zealand! We walk around Old Town, Golden Roof, up to Tower and then to the recent 1976 Olympic Ski Jump. I was remembering Oslo's (1952) and I thought both are magnificent especially in their mountainous settings!

I finally get a hold of Eva, and we meet under "Golden Roof", the symbol of Innsbruck!

Eva, her friend Kirsten (also York YH), and I go to nice old Gasthof (16th century) I am tired, as usual, after 3 nights on trains. Plus, the girls stay in a girl's dorm, I have to camp outside of town. I go back and get sleeping bag at train station as hostel closed by now as well. I settle at campsite about 1:15 a.m., and crash.

5 days in a row, the weather is NICE!! Wake up at 8 a.m., meeting Eva at 9:30 a.m. in Center of Town, near Monument. Kirsten has to study, 3 can be a crowd anyway. Eva and I go for a long hike into the mountains, 2 little lakes up there, walk almost 2 hours to 1st lake. The lake is very nice, surrounded by Mts., as is Innsbruck! The downhill, slaloms, and bobsled are right across on the other side of

the mountain from our picnic. We have a very nice picnic, beautiful setting, day, and girl. Eva is good at taking care of me. She even packed food for later for me. We eat and relax and get cozy, just the right day for it.

We walk farther up, what a view and what a girl. I don't believe how nice it is out, and we stay up to the mountain 'til 6 p.m., and slowly walk back down. It is getting cooler and darker earlier now, especially within the mountains. We stop at Max I's Castle, what a view of the city. In town we walk around, and get a beer in restaurant, and then she sees me off at RR Station at 11 p.m., as I take the night train to Wien (Vienna), but I shall return to Innsbruck and Eva!

Monday, Oct. 11 arrive at 7:30 a.m., raining a bit, no sleep hardly on the train, so many people, I can imagine the trains in Yugoslavia (slow and crowded). I go immediately to an unlisted hostel, mostly Americans, Canadians, and Australian, for only 40 Schillings (17=$1.00). It's kind of beat, but friendly atmosphere, speaking of beat, I nap for 3 ½ hours. Then walk into the center of Town, very big City, but beautiful around the center. Check times @ RR Station (South Station) thru Yugoslavia, and on to Greece. I go to the Theatre tonight for "SYLVIA" a ballet at the Staatsopera (10 sch. to stand). It is excellent, the ballet and the orchestra, the crowd loved it, BRAVO, BRAVO!! The Ballet was about 2 hours or so, great value!! The Staatopera Theatre is Gigantic, and Beautiful, 5 Tiers high, and standing room is way up and back! I walk back and crash about 11p.m. after reading for a while.

Tomorrow, visit to the Belvedere Palace, and beautiful multi colored fountain nearby.

Tues. Oct. 12 sleep in, take a much needed shower (4 days) and sit around bull shitting, and eat my daily bread. Meet Jack (California) and Gregg (Lincoln, Nebraska), nice guys and walk thru town finally about 1 pm. Exchange money, and made about

$ 5 exchanging BF (Belgian Francs) into Dinar(Yugoslavia), and Drachma (Greece). Greg and I walk thru stables of the Lippazon Stallions for 5 Schillings and then through the Center of Town. We see the Church where Richard Wagner played organ, then to Burg Theatre, past Parliament Building (One of nicest buildings I think in Europe) around the Ring area which is very beautiful with many old and big buildings, monuments and churches.

Gregg and I almost see "FAUST" in German at the Burg Theatre, recommended. Instead we see "BARBER OF SEVILLE" at Staatopera for 15 Sch., standing at 1st level with a big queue. We see Jack there, and meet a girl who went to Alfred Tech, my first college (small world). The Opera was fantastic, it was very funny, great music, and singing from 7 p.m. 'til 9:45 and a 20 min. break, It was very hot and crowded. Also meet Jim Broce from Boston, but formerly of Syracuse, for 26 years he lived near Our Lady of Solace (my first school). His home was on Candy St., and he went to Nottingham High School, seemed like a nice guy! Jack, Gregg and I grabbed a beer and a snack before the show which came in handy, for cost and the crowd.

We all walk back together, and meet Barbara from London, who was previously married to an American, and now dead serviceman. He was roughed up in Vietnam and reported missing after climbing in Superstition Mountain, Arizona. I meet John from LA, who I might drive to Istanbul with tomorrow!

I might leave for Istanbul today by car with John and a fellow from Pakistan. In the meanwhile, walk with Jim and Jack @ 8:30 a.m. to see Lippazon Stallions working out at 10-12 a.m., for 5 Sch. (normal 25 Sch.) Meet 2 Aussie girls there at the Hofburg, Spanish Riding School. The horses are great, big crowd, they are so magnificent, strong, and graceful at the same time.

Grab some food to picnic in little park nearby, then Jack and I go to see the Biggest Ferris Wheel in Europe (world maybe?). We walk along the Danube Canal, filthy and construction going on, and we stop at St. Stephen's Cathedral, big, ornate.

Thinking I am going to Istanbul, I go back to hostel to catch ride at 4 p.m.- 4:30 and nothing. My train pass runs out this Saturday.... No ride @ 12 p.m. If not tomorrow, I am taking train @ 10:20 a.m. to Istanbul. John and Jim come back from horseshow, quite good, I was reading and finished Centennial, finally (over 900 pages). Hang around talking to nice folks, but wish I had seen the Lippazon Horse Show for 40 Sch.

Thurs. Oct. 14, Hopefully Istanbul today! I see Schönbrunn Palace, and they are filming a movie there with the actor Beau Bridges and actress Ursula Andress. The palace is very ornate and beautiful, as well as the grounds. A fellow in the hostel from New Zealand got a job as Bridge's double, outrageous!!!!

Well, I was sick the whole bloody night, stomach pains, side cramps, feverish, like Ireland in the Summer. No sleep all night, 'til morning until 12 a.m. I have to eat, been eating only once a day for last 4 days or so.

I let John O'Neil borrow 50 Sch., about $3.00, take shower, walk to Belvedeere Palace, beautiful garden and statues... went with Jack. I have to get back to hostel, still no word about ride to Istanbul with fellow from Pakistan and John (LA). We were supposed to leave yesterday at 4 pm, through Yugoslavia, Bulgaria and to Istanbul! The guy finally says tomorrow morning, I can't wait, I am going to Athens tonight @ 10:30 p.m. from Wien, to Zagreb at 7:05 am, to Belgrade at 1:34 p.m. to Thessaloniki and Athens.

At least I stayed at the hostel free the last 2 nights (save $4.80), and sneak on tram, save 10 Schillings

A final outrageous note to Vienna! As I was getting ready to leave the hostel, one of the guys heard I was from Syracuse, and said a girl named Terry was here until last night and was also from Syracuse. Wow....not just from my home town, but we went to grammar school together at St. Patrick's in Tipperary Hill, with Patti B. who I stayed in Dublin with. Talk about coincidence, or a missed moment....

(Photos) Me at Innsbruck Ski Jump-Winter Olympics here earlier this year, Innsbruck surrounded by mountains, Lippazon Stallion in Vienna, and Salzburg

ON TO ATHENS

Friday, Oct. 15 I arrive in Zagreb approx. 7 a.m., I meet a nice fellow on train, unfortunately he can't speak English and we smile a lot, and make hand gestures…. Train was almost empty leaving Wien, and 2 different times, I had to switch to get to the right compartment going to Zagreb. It was very confusing especially at 2 a.m. and 4 a.m., got a bit of sleep though. Zagreb seems very dirty, people looked dark and gloomy (men mostly,) and I get a lot of stares, from everyone when I got off to walk around during our stop. Take 8:30 a.m. train to Athens (Athine), arr. 14:34 pm. tomorrow, straight thru. I meet Donna and Nina from Toronto and they're also going to Athine (Athens), and they thought we arrived today instead of tomorrow.

Nice Yugoslavs in our compartment, train gets packed after Beograd (Belgrade), many people have to stand! I read a little of "On the Road", by Jack Kerouac, and a big man buys us all pastry with something like cottage cheese inside. We arrived in Beograd approx. 1:45 p.m. The part of Yugoslavia we went through was dull in scenery, flat like Oklahoma. Strangest train ride yet, filthy toilet, people selling junk, nap now and then.

GREECE

Oct. 16th- My train pass runs out today in Athens! Off and on a hassle with passport and tickets (train pass). At the border there's a long delay, Banana Smuggling, and check bags and luggage, get hardly any sleep, wake up for good at 6 a.m. It's a nice sunny day and warm, Greece looks beautiful, mountains, ravines, blue skies, and the sea up north.

We meet a girl on the train who is from Switzerland and lives and works in Athens during winters (Christina Gerber). We should look her up later in Athens, she said. We arrive at 3 p.m., meet a petite 30 year old American woman from San Francisco and we all get a room together for 40 Drachmas each, 36 Dr=$1.00 near Symtacqua Square, past Omonia Square!

We all go out to eat and walk around, and I call Christina and take a taxi up to her place. I meet Jannis, Christoph, Hanna (from Saarbrucken), we drink wine and then go to restaurant with music and dancing. Drinking, and eating-stuffed grape leaves, anchovies, goat cheese, onions, good bread, yogurt. We also had spinach cake and Greek salad for dinner earlier. Have a great time, they drive us around, (1 hour late for hotel curfew) 1 a.m. is the curfew, but we called ahead.

I wake up hard you might say at 9 a.m., and it takes a while to get out of bed (been on trains too much!) We plan on seeing the Acropolis today. No mail today, and or no money. We walk to flea market at foothills of the Acropolis, where they sell everything, and anything, like Morocco. It starts raining, and I do mean pouring, thunder and lightning, we duck into café. At café we meet 3 Egyptians from Cairo, Hassan, Ahmad and Sammy, and have Turkish coffee, we give up on Acropolis for now!

Hassan is quite a character, and we meet the "King of the Gypsies" Dr. Photius, from New York. Many characters in Athens so far...

We go back and relax, because we are going to Hanna's later (girl from Saarbrucken) we get lost in a taxi, no English, so we get there 1 ½ hours late. I drink Ouzo, which tastes like a rough Pernod licorice flavor. Hanna makes a salad and snacks, Jannis, Christos, and Stephan are there also. Charlotte, Donna, Rena and I have a great time, very nice people... feel at home, pretty buzzed, and Jannis and Christos drive us back again about 1 a.m.

My head is not with it today, thanks to the Ouzo, not used to it, very subtle then boom! I get a nice letter from home, very good to hear from mom. I eat spinach pies, cheese pies, honey cakes, Baklava (honey and pistachios) roasted chestnuts and ice cream.

YANKEES won the Pennant 3-2 games, and the last game was a 9th inning HR by Chris Chambliss 7-6 win!!!! I get in trouble with the vendor who thinks I am stealing the paper, the International Herald Tribune.

I lose the girls shortly, as we head in different directions. First, Charlotte gets her flight to Tel Aviv, tonight for $48.00 (student), Donna and Rena go to Brindisi on Wednesday, because they want to wait 'til I go to Crete tomorrow.

I go to Acropolis, rains a little, then sunny, "hell of a place," great view, nice museum, old statues-6th century B.C. I run into girls as we're all leaving Acropolis, to meet Egyptians at 4 p.m. We go to café and play Backgammon, then back to relax and write letters.

Some new travelers arrive, a Japanese, Italian, German, and Englishman, who lives in Australia, and some Canadians. The Italian arrived from Pakistan with hash, and we get stoned, he's got 300 grams. In Italy it is legal to be in possession of 2 grams on street, 30 grams ok for possession in a room, he says (but we are in Greece and he has 300 grams)!!!!

A nice guy from Frankfurt, Martin, just arrived from Crete, tells me of a good village called Paleohora. I crash about 1 a.m., off to Crete tomorrow…

I take a boat from Piraeus just south of Athens, to Chania on CRETE. I sent out 8 postcards at the International Center, but I forgot stamps, to Dumbo, Richie E., Eva B., Mieke in Bruges, Karoline and Karin, Bab's aunt in Bergen, Martha Kari in Oslo.

Take a cold shower at hotel, been 5 days, eat spinach pies, cheese pies, pizza pie and pastry while hanging in park, don't see much of girls today, and they leave tomorrow for Brindisi for 600 Drachmas ($8.00).

Meet Bob from Daytona, while waiting for the boat , he is studying in Florence, and in Greece for Archeology, study Minoan Ruins and Excavations. I arrive at 5 p.m. – boat leaves at 7 p.m., we talk, then I read "On the Road" about 70 pages, finish that, and maybe "Story of Daniel", before I leave Crete! On the boat they put the T.V. on very loud, and very GREEK, and it's storming out! Certainly not a luxury liner, ha ha…………

CRETE

Wed. Oct. 20 Arrive in CRETE to Souda, the port on the northwest side of the large island. I then take a local bus a short distance to Chania, 2nd biggest city after Iraklion, 8 Dr. for bus.

Bob and I get a Nescafe, then I get my bus to PALEOHORA for 98 Drachma ($2.75), 2 ½ hours of some of the toughest, mountainous, winding roads. Partly cloudy, but it's early as we approach the destination where it really looks hot and sunny….

I turn down the first offer of a room, and follow an older lady to a decent room on the sea, for 50 dr. with a hot shower? It might be a lot, but 5 dr. cheaper than the other place. I will ask around later, or look for the caves that I had heard of.

It could be interesting here, peaceful if I want, or people if I want them. There's an Englishman, Chris staying here, but leaving tomorrow by boat for 65 dr., to a gigantic gorge, east of here, then walk 5 hours to YH at Omalos. I take a nap then I shop for supplies, such as bread, peanuts, apples (I have cheese). I stay in tonight, and read more of "On the Road", as I did in the afternoon. I should finish it by Friday.

It is quite windy tonight, and I sack out about 10 p.m.

Chris takes off by boat at 8:30 a.m. (Monday & Thursday are the days of departure). I do some wash, 5 pairs of socks, pants, jacket, 3 shorts, 2 shirts, not bad. It's still very windy, with the waves crashing right up to the patio. The clothes dry fast in the heat and the wind.

I take a walk up the main street and up the hill overlooking the town, and the sea. It looks like an old fortress… It is calm on the other side of town, where the beach is, and tents pitched among the rocks with make shift shelters. Walk on the beach is nice, but a bit dirty. There is nude sun bathing, and a lot of young people. I meet a couple that are traveling by Land Rover to Iran, Afghanistan and Pakistan.

Back in town, I get a drink and a cake at an outdoor café, with a lot of young people, but it's very quiet. The Greeks are in the other cafes across the street, and everyone is spread out.

I eat when I go back to my room, and take a nap. I have no track of time. Later I go out to the same cafe, and have a bottle of Retsina (Peteina). The TV is on and people are playing backgammon, and chess. It is still very windy on the beach side, when the sun comes over. I am content with reading, but meet a German guy from Bremen, also just relaxing.

Back at the hostel, there are 2 French girls, and an American couple that have checked in. I have my room to myself since Chris left.

Friday, October 22, I wake up at 8:30 a.m., but up a lot during the night because of the wind, as the waves and sea are very high, and very turbulent. I took some photos, and I was almost blown away….

Storm perhaps, then I am stuck here, c'est la vie! What a day, rainstorm and gigantic waves reaching just up to my room almost! The dock is completely submerged. In a funny way, it's kind of nice having a very to myself day, thinking and reading, sometimes lonely, which is why I write, read, and eat a lot (huge sandwich).

Film is 183 Dr. for 36 exposures ($5.00), that's like Scandinavia prices!

I finished "On the Road" by Jack Kerouac in one week. I bought a pack of Greek cigarettes for 10 Dr. and a Herald Tribune, yes here! Yankees, lose 1st 2 games of the Series to the Cincinnati Reds, a lot of relaxing, naps, sleep, reading and storm!

Sat. Oct. 23 I wake up to the wind again, and who knows when, as my watch always stops during night. Read "Book of Daniel" by E.L. Doctorow, about Jews and the FBI that Donna and Rena gave to me. I stay in much of day again, except to buy bread and walk a bit, buy Herald Tribune, Yanks lost 3rd straight and the 4th rained out, paper always a day late here of course....But they have it, amazing!

It is still windy and rainy a bit, but not as bad as yesterday. I am eating the same thing the past 3-4 days, bread (long loaves) Feta cheese, tomatoes, cucumbers, onions, margarine and apples (I am on my backpacker's budget, ha ha).

I send a postcard to Eva in Innsbruck. I feel like a recluse, constantly staying in, not talking to anyone, the most out of character in nine months, as I think my money crunch is getting to me. I am doing a lot of reflecting and hope to regroup soon.

The American couple left today. I leave Monday by boat to Gorge hopefully, if not Chania (Xania, Gr.).

I decided to go out, went to same café, had 2 ½ litre bottles of RETSINA, watched Hawaii 5-0, everyone is glued to the television set, English, American, German, Canadian, Belgian and even Greek, especially.

A nice young Belgian couple from Ghent offered me a cigarette, then a seat with them. Had a very nice time with them, we closed 2 cafes in town down, as I dance with Greeks, and switch to beer. We then go to Maria's on the beach, all English music, rock, dancing and yelling, a big crowd, get a bit wasted. The Belgians have been buying me beer and a Greek too! Bad to mix, I stagger home about 2 a.m. in pitch dark, and surprised I made it back…

Sun. Oct. 24, almost 8 months exactly since I left NYC "What a hangover", Retsina, the main culprit, and didn't eat much. No more Retsina…. and the French people move out, not too bad a day, but cold. I try reading, but difficult, cold, damp, a weather change. Take a very cold shower, after 5 days too. I finally get out 3:30 p.m., take a long walk to Mts., and new road on other side of town. I sit and watch a beautiful SUNSET about 5:35 p.m., not dark 'til ½ hour later or so, very peaceful, good just to get out, rainy and cooler weather 'til the sun came out today… I didn't eat much today, only the bakery was open.

I sleep early tonight, no drinking and no cigarettes as I have to get up early for boat!

NO BOAT! Missed early morning bus too! Take the 2:30 p.m. bus which gets me to XANIA, about 5 p.m., dark an hour later. I stay here one more day, beautiful day it is too! Pretty windy, lie out on terrace in sun and read my book, might finish it today. I buy a lot of fruit, grapes, pears, apples, tomatoes and feta cheese, for my sandwiches. Mostly windy on beach side, but I go back later for beautiful glowing sunset, took a couple photos, see 2 Belgians at Watersport! They are such nice folks, I MUST GET A VAN and A BICYCLE, like they have!!

I finish my book "The Book of Daniel" in 3 days (318 pages) by E.L. DOCTOROW, author of "Ragtime".

I take early bus in morning, 7 a.m., I better get up and I go to sleep early.

Yankees, swept in 4 games, but at least they made it that far (only 2 teams do)!

Another very quiet, to myself day, I think of the past a lot, friends, family, and my future, as well as my present. I am very confused inside, but what else is new, like my solo in Outward Bound. After all, I haven't been at this stage in life before, and I am travelling still, and at this point without much money.

I write a postcard to Christine in Athens, thanking her for her hospitality and the great time with her and her friends.

Leave for Xania, then Rethymon, and to Iraklion, in a couple days. I wake up at 6:30 a.m., pay the woman her 50 Dr., too much, 35 or 40 plenty, as other places, still only $1.40 for 6 nights! I catch 7 a.m. bus for Xania, for 98 Dr. Rough ride in, Rough Ride out, but I know the trip now. I walk around Xania, for about 1 hour, then 10:30 a.m. bus to Rethymon for 85 Dr. I meet Ruben, from Argentina, Beunos Aires (he works in London).

Cute girls on bus, and I decide to go straight thru to Iraklion instead of Xania, free for 101 Dr savings. Meet one Australian guy, and I think an American girl on bus, and they are going to beach town before Iraklion. Maybe I'll see them on boat, Friday night. Meet a couple German girls from Köln from bus, noted one of them earlier on bus, cute! We go to hostel, for 35 Dr., dirty, and no shower. Ruben and I, walk to historical museum, shops, couple churches that are beautiful Greek Orthodox of course!

We continue thru the Market Place, eating cheese pies, (Tiropita), but no Spinach pies (Spanokopita). Later, the 2 German girls, Ruben, and I go out for a while… Ruben, got his own room 130 Dr., because no hostel card, and flies to London tomorrow from here!

Long day on bus today, 7 a.m.-2 p.m., with 1 hour break! The two German girls Ingrid and Maria, with Ruben and I, go out to outdoor café near the market. I had 2 beers and stuffed vine leaves (grape leaves, dolma) 80 Dr. (rip off). We meet the English couple from bus, also from Paleohora. Back to hostel before 11 p.m. closing, very nice time at café! Feels good to move on from Paleohora, I was in a rut, relaxed, read, but something about it…

Wed. Oct. 27-I go to Knossos today to see 3400 year old Minoan Archeological Ruins and King Midas, which were discovered in the late 1800's by Evans? Meet Ruben for breakfast by chance, as he's flying to London today.

I walk 5 km to Knossos, find out bus is only 4 ½ Dr., Fabulous ruins, rains quite a bit, and I end up writing a letter to Kevin for his birthday

Nov. 2. I ran into Australian and American girl from the bus yesterday, who both got off before Iraklion at a small village. They ended up in Iraklion 1 hour later, because village was "dead". I take the bus back, and see Aussie and American, who say the movie Lyztomania is not playing,…

Mail Kev's letter, and go to Archeological Museum for 5 Dr., regular 25 Dr., grab some cheese pies of course, and go back to hostel as it is raining. I see Chris, from my room in Paleohora, then check on buses to Lassithi (windmill) Plain, Cave of Zeus and then on to Ag. Nikolaus, which is just east of here.

I walk to exhibit of Icon Frescoes, near fountain up the street. I meet the 2 girls from Köln again, but they moved to hotel, 2 guys from Montreal, Austrian, guy from München, girl from Bristol, 3 Americans, a girl from Eugene, girl from Chicago, now Boston, and a guy from Buffalo, and we talk for quite a while 'til about 1 a.m.!

I am going to Lassithi in the morning to see the 10,000 windmills, but they are not pumping now I am told, but should be interesting and beautiful.

Meet 2 girls from Florida State, studying in Florence, Sue and Jane, bus leaves for Lassithi Plain at 8:30 a.m. It is 2 hours by bus mostly on rough mountainous roads inland. Fantastic view of Gohie, and another village from pass entering on to Lassithi.

The Lassithi Plain has many small quaint little towers, many men, women and children are out, as today is the National Holiday, OXI DAY or "NO" Day to Germans in 1940 when asked to surrender.

I take a bus to Psihron, it's about 80 km from Iraklion for 86 Dr. Along the way, some places were barely passable, a woman throws up, quite a ride! It's a 20 minute walk up to the Cave, then you pay for a guide thru Cave, 36 Dr., normally 50 Dr. It's a very slippery, dark, wet, 100 meters deep, ZEUS, was born here, as the legend goes! Kronos was his father and Reyon, his mother. There's Stalactites, and Stalagmites, with a 20 meters long water hole at the bottom. There were archeology remains found here, but are in Iraklion Museum now apparently.

I rip my jeans even more, and almost fall. The guide is a very nice woman who hikes like a mountain goat and she gives me water, apple, and a needle and thread... nice! Then 3 busloads of German tourists come, but they don't go down to Cave though, figures...

I think I will catch the 1 p.m. bus to Ag. Nicholaos, but first I grab a Feta, cucumber, bread and apple lunch. Guess what. I left my pack back in the café in the village, but no panic. 1 p.m. bus goes to Iraklion, the same way I came, so I head out walking and hitching to Ag. Nicholaos. I walk about 9 km, 1 ½ hours in the sun, and the German couple who stopped earlier, picked me up and take me right to the café for my pack which was still there, and then they buy me a couple Ouzo's at the café to celebrate.

They are from Frankfurt, and have been all over, S. America, Japan, S.W. Africa, and the States, not counting Europe. He's a big shot Architect, very nice couple, and ultimately take me right to the youth hostel!!!

It's a beautiful day, and Ag. Nikalaos is very nice, very touristy though, and the hostel is crowded. I walk around town and the harbor at sunset, come back, read Tribune, eat and write. Early night, but it's been a very good and long day. Plan on a (hot) shower tomorrow for sure, it's been 5 days, and I am filthy and itchy. The hostel costs 30 Dr., and the shower 10 Dr. for hot water. A lot to write for one day, and I am beat and dirty, go to Kritsa & Zato tomorrow...

Guess what, no shower 'til later the man says, I was so looking forward to it! I have to sew my pants up again!! Looks like a beautiful day, clear skies, sunny and hot, and I eat my standard meal, cheese, tomatoes, cucumbers, bread and some grapes. Catch a bus to Krista, town outside of here with 13th century monastery with Frescoes, but first out to Lato, 3 miles from here by foot. Meet 3 girls from Glasgow, they are all doctors.

We all walk to Lato together, 7th century B.C. Archaic Period ruins of city. There is a fabulous view back to Ag. Nikalaos from top of mountain (nice photo) and the ruins are interesting as well. We all walk back to Krista, eat yogurt with honey (great) and a couple pastries.

I run into fellow from München that I met on bus coming here, and we walk to monastery together. After, the girls and I take 5:30 p.m. bus to Nikolaos, and plan on meeting at MIX'S GRILL. Great, I have to take cold shower again, no hot water left, and in the dark, no less. Meet Bruce a Canadian and Johan a Swede, from my room. The 3 of us go to MIX GRILL, and meet the 3 doctors from Glasgow, Pediatrician, Obstetrician, and General Practice. We drink a lot of wine, MINOS-brand, for 48 Dr., then switch to beer 20 Dr. Girls head to Iraklion tomorrow for day, Bruce, Johan and I walk back to hostel and talk a while.

Sat. Oct. 30, wake up @ 8 a.m., absolutely beautiful and hot already, for 3rd day in a row. I realize that I left my bag, with passport, money, etc. at the taverna last night I go there, end up it's still there, thank goodness. I can be a bit lucky, absent minded, reckless, etc....

I decide to hitch to Sitia today, and walk out to road past bus station. I meet a fellow from Mexico City, hitching with his girl and a German guy. They are on their way to pick olives in Zakros, on the East Coast, it starts in 4 days. They get first ride, he says May and June, best time to go to his city is January he says, there is a 45 day Carnival, and now it is very touristy. I get a ride right after them to Ierapetra, so I was going there sooner or later (a van with 2 Dutch and 3 French). I only wait maybe 1 hour or more.

Beautiful day, there's a beach in town, I look for the YANNIE Hotel, but it's crowded and beat. I walk to hostel outside of town, and I meet Shirley from S. Africa, who runs it, and is very nice! I go to beach right behind hostel, 2 girls from Vancouver, and John from Portland here also (Nikalaos, too!) Meet Frenchman from Avignon, here picking fruit, olives and grapes, as the picking starts in France late August thru September, Marseille, Dijon and up, as it starts in South. Meet a fellow from Dublin, who flies to London tomorrow, and Russ and Charlotte, who are 2 of Shirley's friends from Australia. The 3 of them are going to Israel in 3 weeks.

John, the 2 girls and I go to the taverna across street, with Greek Music and Dancing, when in Crete don't be cheap, as it It costs 55 Dr. for white Domestica!

SUNDAY Oct. 31 "HALLOWEEN", The United States Presidential Election is in 2 days, and it's my brother Kevin's birthday, also on Nov. 2!

Yogurt and honey for breakfast for 10 Dr. I hit the beach about 10:30 a.m., and the sun is finally out for good. I have 40 days left after today!! It's a nice day so I lay out with Christine from Vancouver, and we are out most of the day, talking, and me reading Dr. Zhivago, which I just traded the Exorcist for (which I had no interest in reading, really....sorry)!

It's time to get ready to party, celebrate Halloween! Christine, John, Beth and I walk to town looking for Watermelon and vodka, but there is no vodka, so we get Banana Liqueur instead. It's a 12 kilo watermelon that we cut up after sticking bottle in, us 4, 3 Canadian guys, 2 Swedes, Australian, German, and another Swede girl (12 of us total)! Cut my finger carving up the watermelon, and the liqueur is not that strong.

We go out for cheese pancakes down the street, and in to town to MINOS TAVERNA. We order some Raki and wine, the Raki is like Tequila or Ouzo for 3 Dr., ½ litre of wine 12 Dr., then to we go to the DISCO, 30 Dr. for Ouzo, ridiculous, and back to MINOS to get more Raki and wine, then to different DISCO, dancing like a madman, and more Ouzo!!!!! HAPPY HALLOWEEN, as we crash about 2 a.m.

All Saints Day, what a head! John, Beth and Chris go on to Myrtos, 12 km from here. I meet a couple of Canadian girls, and 3 Canadian guys going on to Sitia, where I head next. First, I crash on beach for a couple hours, but not too sunny after 4 beautiful days in a row. I hang around talking with the Swede, English and German couple, I also meet 3 other girls, 2 from Massachusetts and one from Sydney. I have to sew my jeans again, wearing thin!

November 2: Presidential Election Day in the USA, and my brother Kevin's Birthday- he's 25 years old!

Wake up about 9 a.m., have my yougurt and honey, and probably go to Sitia today. A couple others are headed there as well, wash my clothes, it's cloudy and windy, sun is gone!!!

First I eat, then start hitching about 1 p.m., and walk for 1 ½ hours. I get a short ride to first village of Ferma, 2 ½ hours more walking to Koutsouras and wait for the 6 p.m. bus to Sitia for 44 Dr., (76 Dr. from Ierapetra as I covered almost 25 km walking and short ride) I make it to Sitia at 7 p.m. (1 1/2 hours from Ierapetra about 62 km) I don't find hostel very easily, run into 3 Canadians from Ierapetra who tell me directions to the hostel.

I meet all these people, like 20 of us: 2 Aussie girls, then a party around the corner with Corie (Calif. Girl) Aussie, Bob and Canadian, 2 South African Twins (very intense ex-soldiers), Andy (YH @ Ierapetra), small world "Island," Mark who runs Pension, couple girls from Vancouver, 2 guys from Canada. American from New Hampshire, and another Aussie! We play "Switch" (card game) and drink wine all night, good time! Meet an American girl from San Francisco, Charlene and Canadian girl, Claudia, who want to go to Istanbul and other parts of Turkey! I'm on board and going for 10 days approx., meet English girl from Iraklion and Nikolaos, and Aussie girl from there as well. Now, with German girl from Berlin, named Ulla, a great day for meeting people, I think I like it here!

Wed. Nov. 3 Beautiful, sunny day, wake up about 8:30 a.m., buy bread and apples with Ulla (Berlin). Eat bread, marmalade, margarine and tea, but can't seem to hold anything in, especially bad in the morning! Talk to Charlene, San Francisco and Claudia, Ontario about trip to Turkey, which sounds great! I would be back in Athens by Nov. 18, approximately 10 days in Istanbul and Turkey, and gives me still 3 weeks to go to Rome, Venice, Innsbruck, Wallau, hopefully Zurich and Corfu.

I go to the beach with Ulla, Lynne from Melbourne, and Pauline from Bristol England. See Charlene and Claudia, the boat doesn't leave here for Rhodes (Rodos), then Istanbul 'til Tuesday (in 6 days). Hitch to Iraklion Friday, catch ferry that night for Piraeus on the mainland. We crash on the beach a few hours and then we go through town eating ice cream, honey balls (Lukomavas), cheese pies and walk around harbor. Go back to the hotel about 5:30 p.m., read

Zhivago a bit, sit around and eat a small feta, cucumber, onion, and tomato sandwich.

Later go out with Pauline, Lynn, Ulla and Rita (Aussie, but parents are German). We go to outdoor café on Waterfront, I have potato omelet (17 Dr. which is cheap) ½ litre of Cretian Krassi (wine) for 13 Dr., then out for Chocolate Mousse Pastry (13 Drs). We meet up with Charlene, Claudia, 3 Canadian guys, Aussie girl and girl from Ontario. We all go back and rap a bit over coffee. I talk with Mark, one of the S. African twins about parachuting, as he and his brothers were in the army and had many intense experiences! Their demeanor was worn on their sleeves, like badges of honor! These guys are very hard, like the two from Northern Ireland guys I met earlier on. Both were from militarized backgrounds!

It's a sunny morning, and I don't feel well again, like the last few days… not holding much in. I read some of Zhivago, 35 pages then finally get up about 10:45 a.m. eat marmalade, margarine and bread with Oregano tea.

All 4 girls are still around today, nice! I wash my old Levi's which are barely hanging on. Lynn, Pauline, Ulla and I go to beach in late afternoon, about 2 p.m. (still hot and sunny) I go swimming for a change, nice with a mask, see little fishes. Meet Dave from Bristol down at beach (and also at the hostel). We all go for coffee at 4 p.m., then Pauline, Lynn and I go shopping for dinner. We share for 33 Dr. each or 5 ways, for 4 litres of wine (14 Dr. each) cabbage, to-matoes, onions, feta, cucumbers, margarine and bread. This will fill up about 6 people, with plenty for leftovers. We also meet Richard from England, and all go in to town later, everything is dead by 11 p.m.

I sit up talking with Ulla, all night. She was going to Egypt, but now to Turkey with me, Claudia and Charlene. We also seem to like each other which I already knew, very nice!

Fri. Nov. 5, We are leaving Crete today for the mainland, and then to Turkey!

Sunny and I'm up early but not much sleep. I pack, get book

"Kon Tiki" from Richard and eat breakfast with the girls, fried potatoes, salad, yougurt and honey with tea. Then Donna and Charlene head out 1st hitching to Iraklion at 9:30 a.m., quick ride and call to tell us Caroline (Aussie) and I go next, she's going to Ag. Nikolaos, and might be in States next year. Ulla and Claudia, with 2 Canadian guys are already on the road. Caroline takes bus after 1 ½ hour wait, don't see Claudia and Ulla, presume they got ride (92 Dr. to Nik). I wait by myself for 2 hours, no ride and take bus to Iraklion for 86 Dr.

I realize Iraklion Rd., where the boat is departing from is on the other side of town, as I arrive 1 hour before boat leaves! See Charlene and Donna, Donna going to Rome, 326 Dr. for boat (Couchette). Ulla and Claudia arrive as they are taking down gang plank, but they let them on, as we had been screaming for them to wait! We relax finally, get settled and go on deck.

Ulla and I meet an America Air Force guy stationed in Crete, Charlie, also stationed in Turkey 6 months, and a guy from Santa Cruz. We get a 2 litre bottle of wine, Charlie's got Budweiser and we talk and drink from 7 p.m. 'til 11. The other girls show up for a bit, meet other servicemen too who are decent guys, a bit tipsy. Ulla and I get a couchette together and hardly any sleep again today, especially since I met ulla. Very hot and noisy early in morning, and we arrive about 6:30 a.m. or so to Piraeus.

We take the subway to Omonia Square, I have a letter waiting for me at Poste Restante from Karen Burch in Texas, a very nice letter! No money from home, which I desperately need financially, since I'm going to Turkey further and further away, and a different type of place altogether!

We have spanakopita, which I longed for, and leave our rucksacks at Lotus Student Travel, at Niki's Street, Donna gets her ticket for Brindinsi at Filellinon St. off Symtagma (600 Dr.), The bus to Istanbul up to 700 Dr., was 600 Dr. and other Student Travel places here as well. We check out Jimmy's Student House, where Donna is staying tonight, and change more money.

I write another letter to ask for money to be wired to American

Express, if it hadn't been mailed already. We spot a sign for a ride to Istanbul, but no one is there. We take the subway from Plaka to Piraeus to get a boat for the Island of Samos for 286 Dr., then a boat to Turkey from there, very expensive, because of Greek-Turkish relations. We take boat at 2 p.m., bus was just too expensive 700 Dr. and too long at 36 hours.

This way we go to another Island, and stop at the Islands of Syros, Tinos, Hikeria, and then Samos in 14 hours total. About 5 hours to Syros, 6 hours to Tinos… meet 2 girls from Massachusetts, 2 Australian girls from Sydney on the boat. What a dump of a boat, and really crowded, at least at the beginning. We drink wine, and eat our bread, marmalade and apples. Ulla and I get cabin for a couple hours 1:30 a.m. to almost 4 a.m. when we arrive.

(Photo) Greece: Athens, Parthenon, view of Acropolis, Guide on donkey near Lassithi, Me at ancient Arcadian ruins overlooking Agios Nikalous on Crete, Paleohora storm

SAMOS ISLAND

Sun. Nov. 7- It's very dark upon arrival, and we're exhausted. We meet a Canadian, a French girl (Sylvie), another Canadian from Toronto, who'd been here before, an Australian named Roger and an Aussie girl, both from Sydney. Mel the Canadian, French girl and guy, and the 3 girls with me, and we all sleep on cement park near harbor. It's close, but noisy and the mosquitoes are bad. We maybe get 2 ½ hours of sleep, then we go out and get (cold) coffee and (cold) cheese pie at the harbor café, as I don't think they were ready for us.

We check on boat to Turkey, 400 Dr. + 140 Dr. for the port tax, or $15.00 to maybe go 1 ½ hours by boat. At hostel which we get for 30 Dr., which is run by an old French lady "The Warden", who had all these strict rules, we meet 4 Swedes, who found a boat for 300 Dr., leaving Tues. or Wednesday?

After getting settled in at 11 a.m., the 3 girls and I go to Kokarie, a small village with a beach about 10 km from here. We split up and hitch, Charlene and Claudia get a quick ride, Ulla and I walk a bit, a little later an older couple take us right there. We pass Sylvie and the Canadian guy walking it, 2 hours by foot. It's really nice little village and very nice day too, very hot and sunny.

SAMOS town is also very nice, but bigger. Very quiet in Kokarie, it is Sunday, and has one big beach, but Ulla and I find a small one, with an old man on a little island in a small house, it was so quaint or fairy tale like, I don't know.

We find the other girls after a while, we swim, lay in the sun (stony beach), I took a couple pics of Ulla. Later we walk all the way back, as the sun was going down. It was getting chilly after 3:30 p.m., and it took 3 hours, picking oranges and goofing around.

There's a beautiful FULL MOON tonight over Samos, shining across the harbor. We are all really beat, relax, I talk with 4 Swedes, Ulla, Charlene and Claudia. The Swedes are also going to Turkey, 3 girls and 1 guy, all very blonde, and then on to India.

Later, Ulla and I go out for pastry and hot chocolate (Kacao) with cognac, and a chocolate mousse. Many soldiers in town, and we get back barely on time, after 10 p.m., we find out Hostel closes at 10 p.m. after October.

Mon. Nov. 8, I have only 32 days left in Europe!

Not much time, but for some people it's a whole holiday or a year's worth of Vacation, so I might as well live it up still, especially with the 3 girls. Ulla and I are really getting along great, and we are definitely a couple at this point.

I catch up on some writing in my journal, walk around town, shop for food, check on a boat to Turkey, one leaving Wenesday at 10 a.m. for 350 Dr. maybe. Get some postcards, check on bus to Pythagorin. Ulla and I are now sharing costs, as she knows how broke I am getting. We bought our food staples of feta, tomatoes, cucumbers, onions, peppers, bread, marmalade and margarine for 42 Dr. each.

We catch the 12:30 bus to Pythagorin for 13 Dr., a 14 km trip with Charlene and Claudia too! We met a nice woman on the bus and she spoke very good english. Pytahagorin is a beautiful town and no tourists now, very quiet, windy but sunny now, as it was cloudy earlier. We walk around some old ruins on the sea, and then up to a beautiful church.

We help get a cat out of a well with some of the villagers, after we see the commotion ahead of us. They were so thankful and happy...a festival almost broke out!

Then Ulla and I walk to next town called Hora, couple hours away, we stop and eat berries and cactus fruit (like melon...) very plentiful. Hora is a very nice town, a village off the Sea, with very friendly people and I take a couple pictures of Ulla and a Greek family. Nice villager buys Ulla and I a drink, we then walk back to Pythagorin.

Turkey is in plain sight across the Sea, swimming distance (not me). A lot of military in Samos, especially in Hora! Catch bus back to Samos at 6:30 p.m., bus also stopped at Hora, who knew, then Mitillini for 18.5 Dr. When we get back, Ulla and I share our cactus fruit we picked earlier, and the others at the hostel appreciated the treat.

Later we go to see the movie "Lucky Lady," with Gene Hackman, Lisa Minelli and Burt Reynolds. It was almost all men in the theatre except 2 other women, a lot of military, Navy and Army! Greek news reel, plus previews, and the film was very scratchy, and sound not that good, but for 20 Dr.

Get back late again 10:05 p.m., just past curfew and everyone is talking politics, the US Presidential election not that long ago, and here the Turkish and Greek bad blood.

The next morning, we are still very tired, from walking so much yesterday. Ulla and I make our sandwiches, do some wash. We check on the boat to Turkey, and about leaving our passport, but he's not there across from the wharf. We stop at the Post Office, and I send some post cards to Marty back home, and Grethe in Denmark.

Ulla and I take a walk up the mountain side behind the village. It's beautiful, but we walk like 80 year olds, and we lay down and fall asleep on terrace on the Mt. later walk back, take "Ice Cold" showers, which was bad news, but after 5 dirty days, with 2 on overnight boats, good to be clean. We read and talk about Turkey. Reni from Toulouse we talk with, he had just come from Turkey, also Afghanistan, Pakistan, Iran, and India for 6 months. He's a very nice guy!

Ulla and I go to get some Retsina, a 1 ½ litre bottle for 20 Dr., and meet Janne, Anna, Lissen, and Bödil from Stockholm. Janne also gets wine, and we sit in café outside and drink and eat Souvlaki, mine no meat and good! John from Iowa joins us, he's writing a book about Samos. Dave (Canada), Roger (Australian), Charlene and Claudia, also join us. It's getting near hostel closing time, Janne and I refill bottles, and girls go to get Brandy and Kacao at other restaurant.

We're late again at the hostel, that's all 3 nights now, very tipsy, have a very nice time, and drink back at the Hostel.

Janne, Anna, Ulla, and I exchange addresses, and they will write me from India, when they make it, "SAFELY." The Swedes are very nice, Janne falls asleep on table, and we were 1 hour late and stayed up another hour easily.

TURKEY-ASIA

We leave today at 10 a.m., Wednesday-November 10th to Kusadasi in TURKEY. It's a 3 hour trip by small motorboat from Samos, which cost 350 Dr., Regular 540 Dr. and we're all still a little tipsy in the morning. Dave the Canadian brings our passports over as he is the first one up.

Janne is still drunk, not tipsy, as the Swedes, Ulla and I go to the boat together! There are 11 of us total from the hostel from a number of different countries. The boat is small, old and slow, 17 of us altogether on the boat. "Coincidence", a fellow born in Syracuse is also on it, now living in NYC, older fellow, he had BS from Yale, MS in Business from Harvard, quite smart! He works for Texaco, on a 3 week holiday to see Ancient Ruins!!

BOAT TO TURKEY-The 17 of us:
1) Australia- 2, a girl and a guy (Roger)
2) Canada- 3, Dave , Charlene, and Mel
3) France- 1, Sylvie
4) Norway- 1, guy from Oslo
5) Sweden- 4, Janne, Anna, Lissen and Bodil
6) Argentina- 1, guy from Buenos Aires
7) Germany- 1, Ulla
8) England- 1, Keith from Leeds
9) USA- 3, myself, Charlene and NYC guy from Syracuse

We are from 9 countries +the boat captain makes 10, as he is from Greece!

We all meet at the dock and then we get on the small motor boat as we head out in very rough seas, and of course with no life jackets..... There is definitely some nervousness, anxiety and a lot of excitement, for what we are going through and where we are heading! It was probably the roughest ride I'd been on after a lot of different boats, ferries, and or ships this year, mostly because of the boat size....

After landing, there are 13 of us that get bus to Selcuk (Ruins of Ephesus), old city, and maybe tomorrow on to the City of Ismir? Later the other 4 people come as well, as we were contagious, because we were fun and excited "Refreshing".

13 of us go to Hotel Selcuk for 20 Turkish Lira (16.50=$1.00) for each. There's a hot shower, nice place! Ulla, Keith and I share room from Marmat, Turk who works here, and others are sharing rooms too.

We meet Ali when the 4 Swedes, Ulla, Keith, and I walk thru town, eat at restaurant, have eggs in some sauce (good), and beans and rice, and bread which is very filling, with a Turkish Tuborg beer for 20L.

Then we go to a small local Mosque, see them praying, 5 times per day and on Friday 6 times, for about 20 minutes. It's very, very interesting, one takes shoes off before entering, Ali explains much, speaks many languages. The girls must have something on their head, men on the ground floor, women above in balcony, or chair, no furniture, carpets to kneel on, and facing Mecca (Saudi Arabia). Many countries, non-Islamic people can't enter mosque or Mecca, "HOLY CITY", a man says prayers from Minaret (tower). It is really all fabulously Interesting!!!

We then go to have flower tea in shoe repair shop with Ali and 2 of his friends. He speaks German with Ulla, as many Turks live and work in Germany and Austria, as Ali was in Ludwigshafen at a time! We visit another shop that has live snakes, I play with one because of my experiences with them at the North Carolina Outward Bound program. Go back to relax with Ulla, after long day, boat ride, new town, country and continent, crazy day, wine from boat, beer, I am in Asia now, outrageous!!!

Meet Danish couple staying in the next room, he works for UNESCO, and spent the last 2 years in Jordan! Come to find out, there's beer all over Asia and Africa, as compared to the lecture on the boat, how the Muslim world is, and no alcohol, etc., we see those folks at café later…

See the Argentine and Norwegian, they got a room for 15 Lira each, down the road, but our place is a bit nicer…

Mara Haba – Hello!

Very nice people the Turks we've met so far, friendly, and I like very much so far. Some people went to Ephesus today, Dave, Sylvie, Roger, Charlene, Claudia, Norwegian and Argentine are leaving in the morning, some for Ismir, others for Pamukale (hot water springs).

Thurs. Nov. 11th The Swedes, Keith, Ulla, and I, have breakfast, then with Ali, we go to the Ruins here in Selcuk. 1st we all took pictures and exchanged addresses. Aussie and Canadian girl in town are going on to Africa, Dave, Sylvie and Swedes are going to India.

Breakfast was great, an omelet and rice pudding with cinnamon. My stomach is still very bad. We see Basilica of St. John, supposedly the Virgin Mary died here, and Muslims say Jesus is buried here! Then we go to Artemis's Temple, which Nero destroyed, and on to Ephesus (Smyrna in Bible) where 250,000 people once lived. St. Paul said it was the greatest city in the world, once capital of Asia Province during Roman Empire, 3-4 km from Selcuk (pop. 12,500). We walk, it's a beautiful day with a nice breeze, but Ali is upset that we are ready so late, and then because we don't eat at his friend's restaurant for breakfast, and he wants Ulla's address and this, and that is another side of the Turks.

The Amphitheatre at Ephesus is tremendous, it once held up to 25,000 people, with tremendous acoustics, and restored now very nicely. Celsius's Library is great, under restoration on Harbor

Blvd. and the great fountains and homes. We spend a few hours, and then walk back to Selcuk, and take a walk to an impressive Fortess in Selcuk., where we meet some older American Tourists at the ruins.

Later we are off to get the bus to Ismir, we miss 1st one, but get the next for 10 TL, and we get there about 6:45 p.m. Turks all over, helping us too much. We take a bus from Terminal into town for 1 ½ TL, student price.

Turkish boy shows us to Hotels for 40, 35, 80 TL each, no way! Meet Frenchman, named Mark, from Marseilles and Chris from Toronto. We try a place for 15 TL, but full up, we go to their hotel for 30 TL each, 3 in one room, 4 in another, pretty good! We go out to eat, but my stomach is bad, probably from cheese pies and onion pies in Selcuk. For 20 TL each, we get RAKI and wine with many different plates, yogurt and cheese, fried octopus, etc. Then we go to little outdoor café and smoke water pipes, 2 feet or more high, and drink tea and beer, very nice, beautiful pipes. We wander streets, get rice pudding, and get back about 1 a.m. to hotel.

Mark paid for the smoking and beer, etc. There was a mishap, when a big Turk grabs Anna, but little Turkish guy steps in!! The very young and blonde Swedes really draw a lot of attention, not always favorably.

Still have an upset stomach, my diet, drinking the water, or all of the above?

Fri. Nov. 12- Janne went out to check on a guitar to buy, because he had his stolen in Athens! I write a bit, Ulla goes to Tourist Police. We don't know whether to stay another day or go to Bodrum, one of 7 wonders of Ancient World, Mausoleum of Halicarnassus, but now little more than ruins possibly. Swedes are moving on to Ankara? Mark and Chris are going to Selcuk, to see Ephesus.

We stay today in Ismir. Anna, Lissen, Bödil, Ulla, Keith and I go to café that we drank and smoked at last night, for tea. We run into Roger the Aussie, and the 3 Swedes go on to RR Station to check on tickets to Ankara for Sunday night. Roger, Ulla, Keith and I go on to Bazaar, Agora and Fortress, but 1st to the Post Office and buy beautiful post cards. There we meet a Finn, named Seppa, who takes us to an old Swedish Sailing Ship. There are 2 young Swedes aboard, Magnus and Pennula, and they Charter out for 2 weeks to paying passengers (usually Swedes, for 1700 crowns, about $425.00), learn to sail along Turkish Coast! Finn sailed with them this past summer, and he might have party tonight at his flat.

Ulla, Keith, Roger, and I go to the Bazaar, it's big, sells everything, not for tourists, a commercial district! We then go to the Roman Agora, Market but for Government, a Turk shows us around, he wanted to go to America! Up to mountain to the Fortress, overlooking city, hazy, cloudy day, about 5 p.m., early for sunset, Fortress is dirty, and many steps up Mt. We go back to Hotel to get the Swedes, Janne bought a guitar for 1600 TL, which was not too bad, as he was happy.

8 of us, plus Chris (Can.) and Mark (Fr.), go to dinner. It's expensive, and not that great for 367 TL Mark doesn't have to pay, because he bought last night. It cost 10 TL for one beer, 45 TL for ½ litre of "shut up" Table wine. Meet Turkish friend of Mark's, then we all go to Swedish Boat, because there is no party at the Finn's flat, so we start a party on the boat. Dan, an Englishman there as well, we get 16 bottles of beer 4.75 TL each, 3 bottles of wine, 1 ½ litre for 14 TL each, 2 juices, total 145 TL (I pay)!

The boat is beautiful and was used in the Swedish movies "The Emigrants", with Llv Ullman and "Pippy Longstocking"! What a cool boat, certainly unique in the harbor, as it was an older style, wood clad vessel.

We all get a buzz and go to a DISCO at a big park in town, and dance from midnight 'til 3 a.m. Crazy, rip my jeans again, all of us dancing at once. We forgot about attention to Anna as Ulla and I are really having fun, Keith got sick earlier on the boat, and I end up carrying him around over my shoulder. Keith is totally pissed, Ulla in a daze, Roger and Pennila took off, and Janne had gone back to the hotel from the boat.

We get a ride back with 5 Turkish guys, but they start grabbing at Lissen in front seat, they took us out of our way, and tried to make us pay, NO WAY I Shouted! And we get out, Lissen crying, what Assholes those Turks were!

Ulla, Keith, Anna, Lissen and Bödil and I are all in the car with the 5 Turks, me, 4 women, and a small guy (Keith) that I was carrying around, he was so messed .I felt so bad for Lissen, they were fondling her and none of us knew 'til we heard her crying , 11 of us in the car @ 3 a.m. They left us pretty far from our hotel, about 30 min. walk. I felt this overwhelming big brother protective feeling, and that I could take them all on!!

Sat. Nov. 13 Wake up about 10 a.m., more like 11 a.m., eat breakfast about noon. The end of last night was pretty traumatic, but it could have been a lot worse though!

Roger came over, he leaves with Ulla, Keith, and I to Bodrum! It's on the S.E. Coast, near the Greek Island of Kos, 268 km away, 35 TL by bus. Ulla and I are as tight as ever with each other, Keith had made advances to her, and that upset her when he was drunk!

We hate to leave the Swedes, they are such great kids and we quickly bonded. They are staying on the Swedish Boat tonight, then on to India gradually. We are off, 3 TL Dolmus (Van) to Bus Station, and a 5 ½ hour ride to Bodrum, Free bottled water on bus, with a rest stop along the way in a small village.

Bodrum is a very nice harbor town, and we get a hotel for 25 TL each for 2 double rooms. I didn't eat much all day, my stomach bothering me again, and my money is really low, down to $61.00 for 26 days. It is 8:15 p.m. when we arrive, got hotel, then to a restaurant. Bodrum is a beautiful place at night, quiet now in late Fall, but it looks touristy.

We meet a British couple, and an Aussie guy with a Dutch girl who are sailing around the Mediterranean (very nice people). A Turkish guy asks us to sail to Antalya on Monday and it would take about 40 hours, but 3 days with stops at a few places. We think about it, perhaps we'll have dinner on his boat tomorrow.

Take "ice cold" shower like Samos after 5 days, clean at least. Today do we stay on boat, and miss seeing the Pamukale Hot Springs? Do we take the boat, or stay at hotel?? Go out to bakery and store to get bread, cheese, and vegetables to make HUGE HOAGIES, as usual for Ulla and myself! Out of hotel at 12:30, see Roger and Keith on the pier, decide not to take boat with rich Turk, something didn't feel right.

Ulla and I then go to St. Peter's Castle, overlooking the harbor, the bay and the town. We go to a couple of museums, then up to the amphitheater, with 3 little puppies there, then to the Rock Tombs at top of mountain with a beautiful view of Bodrum. And a BEAUTIFUL SUNSET! At King Mausolo's Tomb "Mausoleum," 4th century B.C., one of the 7 wonders of Ancient World, only the foundation is left!

We get wine 14 TL- 1 ½ litres with our hoagies, Roger and Keith join us, and we have a little party. We go out later, try 3 different restaurants, but all are too expensive, and go back to the one from last night, 60 TL big bottle of RAKI, like Greek Ouzo! We are always up for some mischief within reason, ha ha. Get a bit buzzed, then go for pudding and try to steal Turkish Flag at Castle, but it's closed. We're not that pissed, and head back to hotel about 11:15 p.m. We do have our share of escapades I've noticed!

Thanks to Roger we were hung over, and did not get much sleep (like he twisted our arm last night). We pay our bill 25 TL each for two nights, with an ice cold shower,but it was an ok place though.

We catch the 8:15 a.m. bus to OKAR LAR for 30 TL in 4 hours, then 20 TL and 2 hours to Denizli. We made our huge hoagies for the ride, and arrive in Denizli by 2 p.m., take Dolmus to Pamukale for 5 TL each, 20 km ride. We meet English speaking young doctor Stephan, get a bungalow for 25 TL each, 2 people to a place, and we can swim in the hot pool. We go along white, hot water cliffs, down to the town below to buy food and beer, and come back up and get wine, combination cherry and grape wine in doctor's office. We eat and drink 5 bottles of wine then we go to motel restaurant, with beer for 8 TL.

A bus load of American, Dutch, and Australians of all ages, but mostly older, stop by on their way to India (5 week trip).

Tues. Nov. 16, I did not sleep very well, go to the leu, and up then to see the ruins, especially the amphitheatre in very good shape, 2nd cent. B.C., city destroyed in the 13th century by Earthquake. The Tauras Mts. are across the plain, in the background of Denizli (pop. 106,000).

Roger and I take swim in naturally heated pool, 35°C, beautiful day also, at least early!

Off to Denizli, and then on to Antayla today, 5 hours by bus, earlier one full. Bus 40 TL, we hang around town 'til 3:30 p.m. bus. Ulla and I walk around town, small bazaar, very dirty and not much to see.

Exchange $40 into Lira, with only $20 left after, plus I owe Ulla 240 TL ($14.40). So I have approx. $46.00 for 24 days unless money in Athens.

We see the man who had the little restaurant in the little village last night at Pamukale, also the Doctor, all at the station. Meet a soldier who gives us cigs and buys beer and cola. Beautiful sunset over Mts. Ulla, very tired, not feeling so good, have one stop for ½ hour in Burdur, about 120 km from Antayla, have herb tea (dolechi pronounced) Arrive in town about 9 p.m., 5 hours later, down dark, winding, Mt. roads, which were CRAZY! 80,000poulation here, meet a Peruvian, from Lima, named Alex, who shows us to his hotel for 25 TL for Dbl. Ulla, stays in and we go to a nice restaurant to talk from about 9:45 to midnight, about Mt. Athos in Northern Greece (monasteries) 4 day pass only to visit!

Alex, has been travelling for 3 years, speaks English, Italian, French, German, and Spanish quite well, and is an Interior Decorator and Artist, and on his way to work for the Shah of Iran!

Wed. Nov. 17 Ulla feels better this morning, last night tired, cold, chills and sore throat. She hangs with Roger and Keith, while I get info at Tourist Office, then the Antayla Archeological and Ethnographic Museum, which is pretty good, only 1 hour inside. We get tea in Park, either Attachi, dolechi or herb tea.

We decide to leave here and go to Side, ruins of the amphitheatre on the sea, and see Aspendos, the best preserved theatre in Turkey, and Manavgat Waterfalls, which is 10 km north of Side. 2 nights and a day here, we'll then head to Konya, want to see Alanya, too!

Get back about 2 p.m., but Ulla not around, no Ulla at 4 p.m., she shows up about 6 p.m. Good time to relax, write to Karen Burch, Sue McGrath, Madame and Bart, Mieke Lingier in Bruges. Read some of Zhivago, 20 pages, eat huge hoagie, when she returns, we take a Dolmus to Serik, the 5 of us! Half way to the town of Side, and I see my first cock fight, not to the death, at least. 5 TL Dolmus to Serik, then 20 TL more to go to Side, because no more Dolmus, it's after 8 p.m. we pay it, it's a good deal, we enjoy the people, tea and cockfight! By the way, a fighting cock is worth about 1000 TL's, or $60.00 they told us...

In the village of Side, there are many ruins and the theatre is located between 2 bays of sand! It seems like a very touristy village, but not so much now! Meet a man who runs Pensione, before we even stop Dolmus back in Serik, it's crazy how a whole village will crowd around you, like you're a freak, same everywhere in Turkey, especially in the small towns. But the people are so nice, helpful, great help when you speak German (Ulla), many Turks having worked in Germany (Arbitten). Learn a few more German and Turk words tonight, things happen at night in Turkey, and I like it here very much!

We get the room down from 20 TL to 15 TL, dbl. room and one single, GREAT! Cheapest yet @ $.90, then we go to restaurant with landlord. Roger and I just drink, others eat, yogurt and carrots, lentils like an omelet or paste, shiskabob, wine, salad w/ cheese, 6 TL a beer, 25 TL almost a litre of wine, with 10% service charge, but only in Tourist spots. There are other tourists here, like a rowdy American, 2 Canadians, and others in town. We meet a loud drunk Turk, who gets down on America "Punishment isn't hard enough, for example, for a rape in Detroit, punishment was one week in jail" says Seuliman.... What was he talking about?????

We go to the Pensione with the landlord, decent place, hot shower thrown in, nice guy, we all sit around talking for a couple hours 'til 1 a.m. or so. We even have a balcony, landlord brought out some wine. Talk about a lot of things, in many languages and learn more Turk and German, Sickish-Fucking, Sickeez-8 eggs, Boke- shit.

Thurs. Nov. 18 Beautiful out when I wake up 30°C in morning. Roger goes to museum, Alex, Keith, Ulla and I, go for Tchai on waterfront, then to museum, it's small in an ancient Roman Bath. Across the street is the biggest theatre in Southern Turkey, held 20,000 people originally. There's a beautiful view of both sandy beaches, bays, and the town in back. Walk down to beach thru old ruins, black goats all over one ruin, with statue on it. Go back to pensione to eat, after a quick swim in sea, beautiful and so hot out, like summer back home. Obviously it is warm in winter in Southern Turkey...

For some strange reason I quit smoking today, rip up the packs! Was it the cost, the unhealthy feeling I get with the nagging colds that I've had, whatever the reason.

I wait for Ulla as she took a swim elsewhere, later we all eat our hoagies, with garlic! Then we walk to Manavgat to see the waterfalls, along the beach for 4 km, or so, then up into the bush another 3 or 4 km... getting dark by then, and waterfalls 5 km more. There were houses on stilts along the beach that weren't typical of housing we've seen. A Farmer picks us up hitching, 4 of us on his tractor at the nice little village between the sea, Main Rd. and Manavgat.

We meet a Turk, who takes us to the bus station, and we buy 5 tickets to KONYA, for Saturday @ 8:30 a.m., he also drives us all the way back to Side, nice of him. The bus tickets were 45 TL each to KONYA.

We get wine when we return, 1 litre for 9 TL and one for 11 TL, pretty good deal, and 36 TL for a big bottle of Durvek (Raki), and Ulla rests for a bit.

We meet Hussein the Landlord's son, who speaks pretty good English. He studied and lived in Belgium for a while, France, Holland, and Germany as well. He has a cassette player and plays the Temptations, Pink Floyd, Deep Purple, and later on we all go to the restaurant from last night, all 6 of us, and Hussein too! Get auborgine and yogurt, spinach and yogurt. Ulla's and my plate of hot peppers, auborgine, potatoes and whatever' bread, beer... 7.50 TL for each plate and 6.00 TL a beer... my bill was 16 TL, ha ha. Then we go for Tea, Ata Thai-Island Tea from Cypress.

Friday Nov.19ᵗʰ- 3 weeks from today I am back in the USA, I look forward, but I'd love to stay a lot longer. I would love to go to Israel for Kibbutz, overland to India, down to Egypt and thru Africa. It's going to be cold when I get home, and in Australia and Peru, the summer is beginning now, 'til March or April.

Alex, who I was talking with, has a wife and son, and knows Stevie Wonder. He worked for the Shah of Iran before, has a lot of class, and he speaks 5 languages... He's a good guy as well, half Austrian and half Spanish...

It's our 10ᵗʰ day in Turkey today, I realized last night, I will be in Turkey on Thanksgiving, dig it! Ha, ha... It will also be Ulla's birthday, that day...

Leave Pensione finally about 11:15 a.m., dolmus to Manavgat immediately for 2 ½ TL each, then Dolmus to Alanya as soon as we get there at noon. More people today, all over the place, I think it's the 50ᵗʰ Anniversary of the Turkish War of Independence...

The Marketplace is hopping all day. Get Ata Tchai first thing for .75 TL each (cheapest yet) then walk over to famous Red Tower(Alanya) near shipyard, leads up mountain to 13ᵗʰ Century Castle. A Turk, who speaks German gives us a ride to Dalmatas Cave, very touristy place, no one there now. It is all lit up, the chairs, benches, and tables down in the cave it's 25°C in cave, 99° humidity... supposed curing purpose of Asthma, but really beat! Beautiful white pebbly beach outside of it, really hot again today water is so nice! I really wanted a swim, Turkish Riviera it's called...

We then walk up to Castle, quite a walk, even along the road, 1 hour to top almost, with a couple breaks... haven't had this heat since August (3 months ago). It is a beautiful view, some really old buildings, there are little kids trying to sell woven goods. We have to hustle to bottom to find out no dolmus 'til tomorrow, after a 20 minute fast paced walk to bottom Autobus not 'til 8:30 p.m., 3 ½ hour wait, and Alanya, is not so hot, except weather and beach near cave, and beautiful Mts. very close to town and in the background.

We go for a meal at 6:30 p.m. at a restaurant that a man at the station recommends. It costs 65 TL for dish of beans and sauce, with bread and water, and potatoes with the same sauce (Good)! Man comes in, who is a bus driver, and buys us Pomegranets, then a bottle of RAKI, bananas and apples, more RAKI, and gives as a taste of his omelette. Toasting for 1 ½ hour, serefe (cheers, sounds like "Sher i feh"), get a bit tipsy and they want us to stay. The man pays for our meal as well. They drive us to bus station, and wanted to drive us all the way to Side, we take 8:30 p.m. bus though. In Manavgat we get taxi with a Turk, who pays half the fare to go to SIDE.

Run into Roger and Alex at shop, and we get some wine and with them and with Hussein's cassette, and himself we go off drinking and dancing in the Amphitheatre. There are fantastic acoustics, and "What a Riot", dancing on the top steps of the amphitheatre to the cassette player below!!

It is very dark, and we are so buzzed, Keith can't even walk (he easily gets pissed)! We go back to the pensione finally, and I take a shower after 5 ½ days… Ulla and Alex got more wine "Free", when they said they were on their Honeymoon, ha, ha, ha! Alex and Roger had gone to the Waterfall and Appendos today…

What a time today!!

Wake up @ 6:30 a.m. that's right! Beautiful Sunrise over beach and sea… we have to get bus at Manavgat at 8:30 a.m., and we have to get there 1st, after not much sleep last night. Make a hoagie, and eat one for breakfast, and make another for bus ride.

We get a dolmus in the village, and say goodbye to the landlord, Mr. Erol and son Hussein. We get to Manavgat, just in time, and it is 8 ½ hours to KONYA we find out! It's a beautiful ride, the scenery of the Tauras Mts., lake, small villages… we stop at 3 different places for breaks. Meet a young man studying English, knows of a hotel in Konya for us, 22.50 TL for a dbl. room (each), not bad!

We need a ride, end up with 8 people and luggage in an old American car taxi, 10 TL for ride, charges 25 TL though! There are Volcanic Mts. all around, city looks big and filthy (250,000 pop.). Get our ticket for Goreme in the Cappedocia region at 3 p.m. tomorrow, after arriving here in Konya at 5 p.m. The road was not very good most of the way, fall asleep a few times on the bus... eat hoagie and drink many liquids.

In Konya now and we go out to eat immediately. I get spinach, yogurt, and bread and water for 8 TL (48¢). Then go to Post Office, get Whirling Dervish Envelopes and Paper. We meet a young Turk studying English, and we go for tchai, talk of Cypress. I write home, and in my journal. The Turk wants to go to the Museum with us tomorrow.

Sun. Nov. 21-Go to Mevlana Mosque (Monastery) and mausoleum at about 9:30 a.m., our bus to Goreme in Cappadocia is at 3 p.m., to Urgup, actually. The Turk doesn't show up, so Ulla and I eat our hoagies, of course. We all go to Mevlana's Monastery and Mausoleum, then to Mosque...which is very impressive. Many Turks come as tourists, and to make Pilgrimage, there's an exhibit on Dervish's, who were banned in 1925 by Ataturk. Mevlana is from (207 AD), and we have to take our shoes off before we go in, women put scarf on. We go to Karataty Mosque and Museum at other end of town (Ceramics).

We have to check out of the hotel in the morning, and they tried to charge for 2 nights, because we check out at 2:15p.m., but we didn't see it posted!

We are heading to the Cappadocia Region with a lot of volcanic formations, located in Central Turkey. Our bus to Urgup is at 3 p.m., and we take a 3 wheel Dolmus to Otogar (main bus station). Alex, is taking a bus to Ankara, but will try to come to Urgup tomorrow. By bus it is 2 hours to town near Nevisehir, then take a Dolmus to Nevsehir, a guy was playing with Ulla's hand, funny (to me, not her), seeing how much he could get away with. It's the same Dolmus for 12.50TL to Urgup, 20 km away, but regular Dolmus stopped running. Arrive in Urgup about 7 p.m., a small town in Cappadocia, with a population of 6,750. We get a hotel for 20 TL, down from 25. They speak English

OK here, and other places in town, very touristy in summer. I just eat nuts and mandarins with wine when we go out to dinner. The man who brought us here, will drive us all over Cappadocia on Tuesday, to Goreme, and the underground cities (that's right!!!!), etc. for 200 TL, 50 each unless Alex comes.

We drink 5 bottles of white wine, a big glass of raki, and the Turk pays for everything, and everybody is very nice. Roger walks back as Ulla, Keith, Turk, and his younger brother, and I go to the Disco. It is all men except for the female singer, and Ulla, the only female customer. Ulla and I dance, but overall a bit odd, but OK!

Mon. Nov. 22 Wake @ 11 a.m., Leave hotel at 12:30, run into Osmond, the youngest of Turk brothers after going to Tourist Office. We see Roger and Keith eating breakfast (Lunch), Ulla and I get lunch then, I have Turk beans (peas) w/red sauce, and rice and beans with bread, and Osmond buys us a Gurkin (Pickle) 16.5 TL for everything.

We walk up towards homes built into the mountain which are all over the place, some quite ancient, and the Fairy Chimneys! Ulla went off on her own for some reason. We go to eat and a few beers (The government owned Teckel Beer), meet Osmond, and he drives us back to the hotel. When I get back, Ulla was lying down in bed, very upset, she had walked to the next town Orthisar, 7 km there and back again. She wasn't happy we walked off on her, it was just a misunderstanding, not a great vibe. There is an underlying friction because of things the Turks say to her in German!

Wake 8 a.m., Izmet is over by 9 a.m. to take us for our ride all over Cappedocia.

1st stop ORTAHISAR, "Rock Chateau", 2nd to KAMAKI, underground city of 20,000 people, 8 stories underground. Christians hid for 2-3 years from the Muslims, without coming up, we are told. 3rd DERINKUYU Biggest of underground cities (lights out), we get lost with just flashlights. There are very low ceilings, narrow passages. There were animals, stored food, it was a whole city…AMAZING! (Come to find out, there was an earthquake in central Turkey around the time we were here, and my mother receiving my postcard, would reach out to the Red Cross for news about the casualties, etc. She was of course freaked out, but I had no way of knowing her concern, as we were far enough away, and unaffected.)

Lunch Break, then the 4th on to UCHISAR and more coned like mushroom hills; people used to live in volcanic rock, like the moon landscape, meet 2 girls from Vancouver there. Women shaking up raisins that goes in to making RAKI, then on to AVCILAR, in little valley near UCHISAR, then to Göreme with all these churches with Frescoes built into the rock. Zelve, an old deserted Mt. city in ZELVE Valley, has best fairy tale chimneys. Go to AVANOS, and buy little onyx vase for 25 TL, Izmet buys food and we go back to Zelve, to eat where his father works. We eat and drink, as Izmet sings and dances (drunk), it was crazy trying to understand him. Osmond speaks with Ulla in German, but I'm not sure about what, but seemed sly and underhanded possibly?

Some drunks come in, and Izmet makes one go crazy, breaking glasses, there's blood, I don't know what they were saying. We split for Urgup and the Disco, and there are all men again. We are all a bit drunk, everyone wants Ulla to dance, I dance with Izmet, the way they do it here, Ulla gets offended and leaves (she's very tired). I take off late, and I thought Osmond was with her, then Roger.

Wed. Nov. 24, Ulla, tells me she is leaving for Ankara, not Istanbul, because she is upset, about last night and days before. She was upset with some of the things they say to her, and in German I did not understand and thought she was overreacting. But, they were a bit devious in their attention, which I didn't pick up on at first!

I take the coldest shower in my life, plus it's freezing in the hotel. I repack and straighten out my rucksack, make a hoagie with many hot peppers. Pay for taxi yesterday, and hotel for 3 nights 110 T. Ulla loans me $40.00 in TL, more that I owe her now!

After pleading with Ulla to stay with us (me), and continue on to Istanbul, at the bus station she decides, ISTANBUL, Great! I need to stay around her more, so the men and their intentions would be screened.

We get the bus at 3 p.m. we thought, but at 4 p.m. a dolmus takes us to Nevishir, and we wait until 5 p.m. for bus to Istanbul. It's a 12 hour ride maybe. Meet a friendly Turk family, buys our dinner gives us candy, nuts, soda, cognac, etc.

THANKSGIVING

Thurs. Nov. 25- Ulla's Birthday and Thanksgiving back home, and here I am in "Turkey" ☺!! And we are on our way to Istanbul, yeh!!! Snowing at midnight, no snow tires or chains, so the bus can't go 'til 7 a.m. in morning. Got a bit of sleep on the bus, had to ignore pushy Turk, I couldn't understand him anyways. My legs are really cramped, snows very hard, funny saw my first snow in Norway back in late September. Well, we still have a long way to go, in fact we arrive 22 ½ hours later at 3 p.m.!

We walk all the way to the PUDDING SHOP, a cornerstone hangout for travelers going east or west, near TOPKAPI PALACE, HAGIA SOFIA, SULTAN AHMET, which are all located across the street. We stay at Hotel Güngör for 30 TL each per double, next door to the PUDDING SHOP… catch up on journal and relax for a bit. Later take off walking towards the GALATA BRIDGE, it's a pretty good walk, and it's freezing outside.

Keith, wants to find a fresh fish restaurant, he and Ulla are a bit tipsy from the wine back at our hotel. Roger is starving, but not much around, but in a sleazy area nearby, we find a cheap restaurant. I have a plate of sardines with salad, 6 TL for Dolma (rice and meat stuffed in cabbage leaves, mine without meat), 3.5 TL for salad. I just drink TEKEL, government issued beer 16 oz. for 5 TL, good deal, as I had eaten earlier at hotel. We eat and drink 'til 10 p.m. or so, then walk back a long way! Everything seems to be closed, or closing, and people going home.

PUDDING SHOP is packed, doesn't look like Turkey, London or any international place, all young people, travelers, hippie types.

Meet a Swede, driving to India in a 1963 beat old Saab, he lived 2 years in Boston, he sounded like an American, and was looking for a passenger.

I have a beer with Keith and Ulla, Roger a coffee… Sack out early about midnight!

Fri. Nov. 26- I HAVE EXACTLY 2 WEEKS left in EUROPE, 16th day in Turkey, looks like I won't be leaving 'til Monday, cheap bus every Friday and Monday at 10 a.m. , and no way I'm leaving this morning. Bus would get me in Athens Tuesday morning 6 a.m. or so, bus for London at noon for 1800 Dr. I would probably take the bus to Salzburg or Frankfurt. If I miss that, I'll take ferry to Brindisi next morning, and train to Innsbruck or Frankfurt, I shall see!

There's a lot to see here in Istanbul, it is such a unique big city. Part Europe, part Asia, but really feels Eastern.

Only 2 days in last 17 or so, we haven't been drinking, wine, beer, RAKI, brandy (Cognac), the Turks too helpful for me, but not bad people, constant staring, I will be happy to exit!

Noon or so, Ulla, Roger, and I go down near Galata Bridge, looking for the Spice Bazaar (Egyptian), don't find it and end up in Grand Bazaar (Biggest in the World). There are hundreds of shops, they sell everything, and Ulla buys some jewelry. It's a completely covered Bazaar, and we get split up, but what else is new, and unintentional! I check on buses to Salzburg, and decide I don't want to go back to Athens, even to check on my money or mail. I'll contact Poste Restante, and have them mail it to Belgium or USA. Bus to Salzburg on Monday night 6 p.m. for 500 TL + 100 TL for Bulgarian Visa, also have to change $5.00 into Bulgarian money at border.

I check around at many different bus agencies, all the same price almost! No buses to Athens this week because of Festival, normally $20.00, train 410 TL or $24.60. Roger will take that and fly to London from there on Sunday or Monday. Ulla is going to Graz, Austria, just before Salzburg. We take the same bus for 36 hours and arrive approx. 6 a.m. Wednesday.

I go down to the Pier at Galata, get pizza sandwich for 4 TL 24¢, filling and good, get a couple of them. Run into Roger, and he gets fresh fish sandwich for 5 TL. We walk to Post Office, and I write to Poste Restante in Athens to have them forward my mail. Then back to hotel, Ulla, Roger, and I go to eat at café. Then to PUDDING SHOP to drink Tuborg draught for 6 TL per ½ litre, good drinking from 8-12 p.m. and decent music! There are a lot of Turk guys tonight, just hanging around, hustling girls, talking to anyone who will listen, selling hash or student cards, and we meet a guy who is on his way to Sweden to work and maybe marry a blonde Swedish girl, SURE.....!

Finally, Keith flew to Athens today and flies to London on Sunday a.m. He had a good, but up and down run with us. How would he have survived on his own in these places?

Sat. Nov, 27- We go on a boat up the Bosphorous today towards the Black Sea, we grab a snack on the pier first. The ferry is at 10:20a.m. and it costs 7 TL return for a 2 hours up and 3 hour 15 min. return. We stop and stay in village of Andolou K...., old fort and Navy Station there. The trip was very nice going up as there are many old Palaces, Forts and Castles on both the European and the Asian sides. Many tourists are on the ferry, and most get off on the way to the Black Sea.

We stop in many little docks and ports along the way. It's really a cold and windy day and the sea is real choppy.

Ulla and Roger get a nice fresh fish dinner in village we finally dock at. We then walk up mountain to castle fortress looking out to Black Sea, and you can see quite a distance, looking towards Russia (nice photo)! We meet a very young Turkish Shepherd on the Asia side that we dock at, funny picture with Roger!

We catch boat back at 2:30 p.m. 'til 5:45 return, this time along the Asia side, with beautiful old Black Sea type wooden homes, some were very beat though! We meet 3 couples from London, 2 older, one young coming from India, very nice folks. We dock and we all of course get pizza sandwich, which are really good, especially for the price. Ingredients are onions, peppers, and tomatoes inside rolled up pizza like patties.

Then we buy our tickets to Salzburg 600 TL, altogether Ulla buys my ticket, and my bill with her is up to 1344 TL or $80.66 so far. Then we watch as Ulla eats rice pudding in café, a lot of attention, 3 people one rice pudding, too funny, or too desperate! The Pudding Shop is loaded with too many "Cool" Turk guys, and one is looking for a fight! There's a lot of resentment, antagonism, I've noticed the last couple days.

At the end we go back to our room, Ulla sews my pants again, and I do some writing.

Sunday Nov. 28- I only have 12 days left in Europe, as Ulla so kindly reminds me. Roger came up to wake us up because he has all his gear up here (he stays in dorm for 20 TL). It looks like a beautiful day, but we'll be inside museums all day.

Guess who we meet downstairs? Raphael, the Argentine who was with Claudia, Charlene, and the Norwegian, Irvine! He's been in Istanbul for 11 days, teaches English to a Turk 1 ½ hours a day for 50 TL. Claudia, is also here because got her purse ripped off in the PUDDING SHOP, with money, passport and plane ticket in it. Everything is replaced though now, and she leaves Tuesday, 12 days after she planned. We check at her hotel, but she's out.

Roger, Ulla and I go to pier to eat, fish sandwich for Roger, rolled pizza for me and Ulla. Funny, the man at the food stand remembers me again, and shakes my hand. Then we go to see Hagia Sophia, gigantic former Byzantine Church, converted to a Mosque, then a museum by Ataturk, cost 5 TL, ½ price on Sunday.

Then we go to Topkapi Sarvayi (TOPKAPI PALACE) 7 ½ TL (1/2 price), it has a beautiful collection of Chinese Porcelains, Japanese and Turkish also. There are jewels, the Topkapi Dagger, thrones, clocks, etc. Then to Archeology Museum 5 TL (1/2), with a great abundance of statues and artifacts, poorly presented. Finally, see Harem of Sultans for 6 TL, extra in English, German and Turk translation. It has 400 different rooms, Sultan's mother had 40 rooms, always 300-500 girls, Eunuchs (black slaves) interesting.

Finally, catch 5 p.m. prayers at Sultan Ahmet Mosque, "Blue

Mosque" Beautiful and enormous with 6 Minarets.

Back at Hotel, see Roger, Raphael, meet American girl named Jill from Calif., on her way to India. She spent 2 years in Japan, and speaks Chinese, Japanese, and Hindi. There are 2 Dutch, from Groenigen which is north of Amsterdam. We call Claudia, but she is still out. We all go out to eat and drink, 1st to café to eat, and a few beers, then to PUDDING SHOP, for a few more. It was a fun evening, our last night here in Turkey! Tomorrow we leave at 6 p.m. for Salzburg, and a 36 hour bus ride!

Mon. Nov. 29- Hazy out, take it easy, and lay around 'til 10 a.m., and take a shower. 19th Day in Turkey, it went by fast, only 11 days 'til I fly home, as well. We have to be at bus office at 5 p.m., they drive us to bus.

Ulla, Roger, and I walk to Sulelymane Mosque, which is beautiful and huge, for noon prayers.

Rules at the Mosque:
1. Women wear scarves
2. No shoes
3. Don't walk around during prayers
4. Sit in back like Turks during prayers
5. No pictures during prayers
6. No loud talk

We walk down to the spice market on the Waterfront, thru really old section and very poor area! Spice market is great, where they bring in goods from ships, horses and wagons, porters, and mud. Only men working here, like turn of the 20th century, only us walking around, nice photo of men shoeing draught horse. We walk along Galata Bridge, really busy. We had a real good meal at the Spice Market, brown rice, auborgine, stuffed bread, and a beer for 14.50 TL (88¢), and I'm stuffed. Nice photo at Galata Bridge... then we walk back towards Hotel.

(Photo) Turkey: Galatta Bridge-Istanbul ,boat on the Bosphorous, View to opening of the Black Sea from Bosphorous, Volcanic town in Central Turkey –Cappadocia Region, Ismir Harbor-famous Swedish sailing ship, Mevlana's Tomb in Konya Pammukale Hot Springs, Side, Bodrum

CHAPTER 8

Homeward

I PICK UP passports on way at the Bus Agent's Office, we wait around 'til 5 p.m. Raphael and Roger there, Roger leaves at 7:20 p.m. by train for Athens, we exchange addresses. Then off to Bus Agency, they walk us down to Main Bus Agency, then, we take a taxi to Bus Station. We meet Robert, an Australian, who shares a cab with us.

At the Bus Station, we meet many people, we are all waiting for bus to München, Roland and Bobbie, an American couple on their way to Berlin, girl's father is in the Air Force, 2 English guys from Yorkshire, Peter a Dutchman from Tilburg, on way home or to hospital, as he has Venereal Disease, An Englishman from London, spent the last 5 years in India, another Amer. Couple from Philly, and Boston (might visit me in Bruges) 2 guys from Saskatchewan, on their last leg around the World trip. There's a German, from Frankfurt, who had his passport and money ripped off in Tehran, Iran, another German from Bamberg, who drives cars back and forth to Middle East (Bernhardt), a Frenchman from Paris, 2 quiet Englishmen, English couple on way home from India, a big German girl, from Northern Germany, who has had nothing but problems, 3 Afghans, and the rest seem to be Turks!

We have to wait around for bus, and we go next door to café for beer, tea, whatever. We talk and bullshit, then we find out BUS IS NOT COMING, it Broke Down they say, wait now 'til tomorrow at 1 p.m., we will leave ...SURE!! They are half assed here, but they pay for our hotel tonight (time is important now, and it's also extra meals here). Some of the other people have to find their own room and pay for it, as it was a different bus agency (agencies are like brokers). We go to sleep early in a nice room behind station.

Tues. Nov. 30-Wake up late 11:30 a.m., go to station with Ulla, no bus, everyone waiting. We go next door for pudding and tea, but first Ulla, Peter, and I, buy fruit, vegetables, bread, cheese, and cheese pie, then back to station café where everyone seems restless, no wonder, no Bus. Today's 6 p.m. bus will probably come first, that goes to Amsterdam. Yesterday's bus broken down, they are putting finishing touches on it, new tires etc. It finally arrives at 6:30 p.m., over 24 hours late... We spent extra TL here, 100 TL each for Ulla and I! I made big hoagies while sitting in café, the patron even helped, ha ha!

MAD RUSH to get on the Bus, as they sold 51 tickets, but only 43 seats... It's also, muddy and rainy, I put luggage in, as Ulla stakes out our seats. They try to change us around, NO WAY, someone has our seats, and we have someone else's. One American couple they try to kick off bus and catch next bus in ½ hour, but we stand up for them, because who trusts these Turks now? They hustle everyone but the other Turks, but we finally leave, about 7:30 p.m., and we are at the Bulgarian Border by midnight. Ulla and I sit over wheel, very cramped... BUT WE'RE ON THE BUS, and MOVING!

Wed. Dec. 1- We are still at the Bulgarian border at 3:30 a.m. (here since midnight). They go thru the backpacks, luggage, and throw my backpack off the bus from the top, very difficult and rough. They could have smashed it, but it is sturdy and tough (like me ...ha ha), with only small rip of material at the frame. My backpack, boots, and sleeping bag(slug proof...ha ha) were the best investment!!!!

The other Bus from Istanbul passes us, they have 8 extra seats, and it's a nicer bus. It's really freezing on the bus, but after the border, we sleep finally. We're driving thru Sofia at about 10 a.m., it looks nice, modern, clean, parks. We are at Yugoslavian Border at

11:30 a.m. or so, and another 3-4 hours here. When we first crossed into Bulgaria, we had to exchange $5.00, 100TL, or 15 DM into Bulgarian Levs ($5.00 cheapest, the others about $6.00) You can't change back at the other Border. We have to buy souvenirs or eat a lot, so we eat a lot!! ! Very expensive $21.00 for 6 of us, I have $4.50 left in Levs, save a bit of it! Thru Belgrade, about 7 p.m., we stop 1 hour, and eat last of 2 hoagies I made, and we drink wine we bought in Istanbul. It's a lot warmer on Bus tonight, get better sleep, still very uncomfortable.

Thurs. Dec. 2. I have only 8 days left, I already decided to skip Innsbruck, and not getting off at Salzburg. We arrive in Graz at 7 a.m., hit Austrian Border 1 ½ hours earlier. Ulla and Peter get out here, it's very dark and wet and everyone is going to work, and I definitely won't be in München 'til dark.

I think it will be strange without Ulla, after over 3 weeks together in Greece and Turkey! She will be back in Berlin in a week or so, and me in the States. I will miss her as she has been the closet person to me for these past 4 months, if not my whole time abroad.

(Photos) My dear travel companion Ulla in Greek Island of Samos then in Turkey, ancient tombs in Bodrum, Istanbul on Bosphorus....etc.

I think I'll still head for Frankfurt tonight, I am very dirty, and tired now as I write, and a bit hungry for hot food. I will wait for a ride to Frankfurt, and I hope to be in Wallau tonight hitching. Everybody is heading the same way, mostly towards England, I go to Nurnberg, and then Frankfurt, some others go Stuttgart way.

I'll miss Ulla, but I don't have much time left anyways over here.

It is so slow always at these borders, now at the German/ Austrian Border, what a hassle, have to get out of bus take out our backpacks and or luggage, as a dog and man searches bus and baggage. They then take us inside the building, and do it again thoroughly. They give us a German bus to go to München., and the Turkish Bus stays at the Border…

We arrive at München HBF @ 6:30 p.m., 47 hours later after Istanbul, plus leaving a day late. Bobbie takes train to Berlin, Rowland hitches there tomorrow. Everyone else and including me, are hitching towards England!!!

Get on road by 10 p.m., rainy and cold, take S. Bahn to Autobahn. I ask truck driver parked there for a ride, and gets us on our way at 11 p.m. It's a small truck he's Swiss, with a big German Shepherd inside. The Englishman with me speaks French to him, pretty good lift, he's on way to Basel, and we're let off @ 2:30 a.m. at a Resthaus near Stuttgart, on the wrong side of the Autobahn though!

We go inside for coffee, ask around for rides, no luck at 5:30 a.m. German truck driver, who spent 8 years in Niagara Falls, promises us ride to Koln, few hours later he doesn't show up. We get out hitching at 7:45 a.m., POLICE tells us to move back 200 meters but we move 2m. Meet a South African, who starts hitching as well. POLICE come by again, and are pissed off. It's really cold out, my feet and hands are frozen. We head back to Resthaus, for him to eat, and I get coffee to warm up.

There are two big buses filled with American Army families on weekend holiday, and the English guy wants me to ask them for a lift, but no way as the people from the bus are acting like jerks. We go back out where we were, S. African still there, and so are the police. By the time we walk up to him, a car stops and takes all three of us to Heidelberg. From there, we all get rides separately, and it's very rainy. There are so many Amer. Military around here. I get the last ride, after English, then S. African, a ride right to Frankfurt HBF at 2 p.m. I catch train to Hoffheim and bus to Wallau by 4 p.m.

ALWAYS SO NICE TO SEE THE SCOT FAMILY! We have a Luigi's style pizza tonight, and I talk with Pat as usual, then Scotty and I go out about 6 p.m., first to Jim's house to move a T.V. set, then to Gasthaus to get pissed! Scotty is playing cards, loser buys drinks, for me too! I have a great time, see a bunch of familiar faces. Meet a couple English men, and 2 Turks working here, get back about 1 a.m. (7 hours).

Sat. Dec. 4- Wake up @ 11:30 a.m., hitching to Bruges today. I got my plane ticket, books, and things, eat lunch and take a hot shower, after 5 day average, and SAY GOODBYE. I am leaving the Scots for the last time, what a great family they have been to me...

I walk up to Köln turnoff on the Autobahn, a few kilometers thru "muddy fields." I get a pretty quick ride to Linburg, then 1 ½ hour later, a TRUCK from ENGLAND stops, he's going right to Zeebrugge, then London GREAT! Great Guy, Chris, married a girl from Long Island 5 years ago in NYC, they met in Spain! He might run out of gas, he has no money, only personal checks, but they let him cash on Belgian side of border. He buys a beer, and it cost £70 to fill 80 gallon tanks, because it only gets 4 miles to a gallon.

I decide to go to England with Chris, after we get stoned on hash oil from Syria. It was stashed in the center module, in a jar inside a mechanic's container for degreasing. I dip a cigarette into the oil, and without totally saturating it, lit and it burned great...we were "IN LIKE FLYNN"!!!!!

We stop in Bruges @ 12:15 a.m., and we are pretty high, go to the Cactus of course! Chris drove the huge LORY right thru most of town, very narrow, cobblestoned, and brick paved streets. "NARROW AT TIMES" to say the least, but what a trip!

See Johan from Ghent, and the girl working at the bar I had met at the Lotus Bar party. We get a couple of Trappist beers, sandwiches and leave. First, I check our old residence/hotel at Riddersstraat for mail, but it is LOCKED!

It's 2 a.m. now, and I'm supposed to cross on the boat to Dover for free, because Trucks (TIR) can take 2 drivers for free. They (customs) say I'm not a driver, but a student and I have to pay a full fare £6.60, not even half prices like Chris's wife, because we weren't honest. REAL JERKY FLAMS, and I am ready to scream because I am so frustrated (and broke). It was hilarious and scarey at the same time, as I probably could have been arrested. We pay, I owe it to Chris, but I only have 50 DM, and I have to pay for the boat back!!

We miss the 4 a.m. ferry, late, take a nap, and just make the 7 a.m. ferry. Chris gave me his bunk, and he goes to eat, take shower and find a cabin. The cabins were full, the meal was terrible, and the shower just trickles he said! After all that we just make the 7 a.m. ferry!

England, is one hour earlier, on Winter Time again, begins October-April. It takes 6 hours to cross, including customs. Beautiful Day, but cold, everything is frosted. It's about 80 miles to London, nice drive but slow, see castle again that I took pictures of last March.

We arrive in RICHMOND about 2:30 p.m., meet Wendy (Chris's wife), 2 neighbors, Rose and her roommate, then John and Kathy who were former neighbors. We sit around drinking strong home-made beer and Glen Fiddich Scotch Whiskey, get stoned and have a few crackers to eat, only thing since last night. We all go to a pub, which is crowded but nice, and they all buy me beers, as I have no £'s, Pretty stoned and pissed, come back to Rose's for a meal, finally. Kathy and John split, we drink and smoke more.....

Monday Dec. 6, I only have 4 more days in Europe- I get the nice warm living room to crash in, but my stomach is off the last couple days. "I WAKE UP" to a knock at the door, and there are 2 policemen there!!!! A Motorcyclist ran into Chris's parked Trailer and DIED during the night. WOW…we are shaken in disbelief, half awake but quickly in shock mode….The police were very cordial and business-like as they explain the situation. It was tragic, he had parked in that place many time before he said…Chris gets a ticket for not having parking lights on, but was parked legally overall. What a fucking nightmare, guy dies, a ticket from the police was nothing in comparison, and everyone feels bad!

After all that has just happened, I still have to buy my ticket to Bruges, and call Margie Mason Cox. Most of my things are still on the truck, and I have to change DM to £. Take a walk in town with Chris and Wendy, call Margie again, she's not in England yet. The fare across went up from £5.80-£7.15, grab a pint, walk along the Thames. Nice town RICHMOND, it is 8 miles from the center of London!

Wendy and Chris have Kathy and John over tonight for Dinner, and Rose as well, to watch the movie Bananas with Woody Allen!!! Wendy made Brownies, which are so strong, they hit me very hard. I end up crashing in the middle of Living Room in front of everyone… oh well.! Like everything hit me, travel, time, exhaustion, what was in the Brownies???

Tues. Dec. 7, I am leaving England today!! It's like a delayed reaction as I am stoned as I wake up! I have to catch the bus to the tube, tube to train station, train to ferry and ferry over to Europe. I am serious, I was really stoned, and Chris and Wendy split early, and I still had to actually get my ticket at Trans Alpino (student travel agency). I have a couple hours 'til 1:44 p.m. train to Dover and ferry to Oostende, will arrive at Oostende at 8:20 p.m. perhaps?

While waiting for the train, I meet a lovely young Portuguese girl, Christina Lopez Diaz from Lisbon. We get on the train and she has some 7 year old Port from Portugal that we share. Who can refuse such an offer?? She shares chocolate and crackers, and we are getting along quite well. Christina was so nice, and there is an instant attraction. If I had more time in Europe, I was welcome to visit her. Who would have thought parts of 12 different months was not long enough!!!!

BACK TO BRUGES....LAST TIME

When I get in Bruges, I go directly to Hotel St. George at Riddersstraat 12, and Bart and Madame are home, or should I say up! They give me Reenie's old room, and they are very happy to see me, and me them... but it's freezing in the room.!!!!

I'm still hazy and go out to CACTUS immediately, Mieke is sitting there, no food, and music not right, go to De Goezeput (no food) then Loch a Dizzy, cheese sandwich, and stuffed chairs and promptly passed out, after visiting with Rita and her friends. Somehow I got home about 1 a.m.!

Wed. Dec. 8- Up about noon... the bank not open 'til noon, then Cactus for a beer. Have to get my last $50.00 out of bank... say good bye to the girl there. I walk to RR station, and call Brussels, about flight on Friday the 10th. I leave Friday at noon, my flight is a charter, check in @ 10 a.m. and I will leave Bruges at 8:06 a.m.

I meet 2 secretaries at the Europa College, at a new building now, and Jeremy C. is not in. I go back to Hotel, read and fall asleep 'til midnight (4 p.m.-12) and Mieke comes to Hotel looking for me, I was supposed to meet her for lunch at LOTUS, but was too hazy the night before. Mieke thought I was mad at her, we go out to Cactus 'til 3 a.m., 4 Trappists, and we see Brigitte. Mieke, and I go back to the Hotel, which is my home away from home!

Thurs. Dec. 9, I'm really cold and sick, like when I was in Vienna, and Donegal, with stomach pain and headaches! Mieke goes to the drug store for me, I can't eat, but I think that's why. I feel bad, no eating and just drinking lately. I take a nap, and pack up finally for the trip home. Mieke, and I go out for a bit, nice to have a nurse...

Didn't do some final things, like see Jeremy, buy the wood shoes, or write Ulla and Eva P. Only had a very short time left, and did I still really miss some things, places, people and deeper relationships of course!!!!!

Fri. Dec. 10- I leave for USA, probably a good thing. For I've run out of just about everything…I was a little slow yesterday but I could gather myself better today, train to Brussels and then Airport to fly home.

WHY IS THIS LAST DAY an AFTER THOUGHT, like a mechanical action? Could it be, because I was still sick, broke, worn down, but for all the right reasons… What a year, almost the full year in fact!

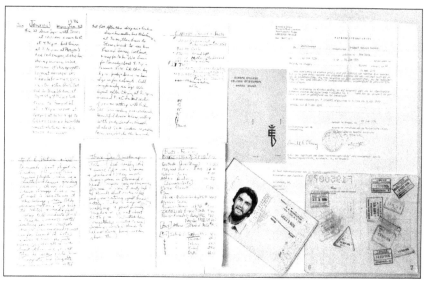

(Photos) Journal, Passport, College ID & Visa

Met a great guy going home, who needed to borrow my last $1.80 to help get out to Long Island. I was done traveling and I didn't need it, just a flight to Syracuse and I'm HOME!

Currency

BACK IN THE USA, MISSED ALMOST ALL OF 1976, "THE BICENTENNIAL"!

CHAPTER 9

The Future

1978- I WILL have taken off from Syracuse again that March, for 5 months starting in the south to Daytona, Florida, then on to Texas (Houston, San Antonio, Austin, and Dallas), Arizona (Phoenix area), Mexico, Guatemala, and up the coast of California slowly, after stops in San Diego/La Jolla, Newport Beach, San Simeon, Sonoma, Lake Tahoe, Yosemite National Park, and end up in San Francisco. I ended up living out west for almost four years, and those four years would be an adventure within itself, in one of the most exciting cities in the world (San Francisco). There was a major stretch that whole last year. where I averaged being out 6 1/2 nights per week...MIGHT AS WELL GO TRAVEL AGAIN!!!!

I had many friends and or acquaintances from all over the world while living in San Francisco, and knew many people who had been to many different parts of the world. Remembering Ulla for instance from earlier Greek and Turkish adventures....She lived with me for a while in San Francisco.

I also would have many side adventures out of town, out of state, and out of the country, such as Alaska, British Columbia, back to Mexico a couple more times, and back East to NYC and of course Syracuse.

1982-I would start an entirely new nine month adventure further west, or east depending on which way you were coming from, ha ha ha. That trip would commence from San Francisco to HK, or Hong Kong, Philippines(gambling scam), Thailand(Golden Triangle-TREK from north of Chiang Mai, Phuket-mushroom boy...), Malaysia (Penang, KL or Kuala Lumpur), Singapore(camera), and I find out my niece Shannon was born back in Syracuse, Java(batik), Bali (sarongs,jac paks), on to Europe via, Bombay ,Moscow, to Milan, and on to Austria, Germany (East & West-with Holger & Klaus), Switzerland (job offer Zermatt)and France (Paris Apartment), in Europe.

1983-1987 -One thing I can say, I got inspired in a new way, to start over or back up again. Hell, going back to college for architecture at 29 years old, and spending the next four and a half years as a student again in Syracuse and Buffalo. It was both a continuation of the adventure, as the architecture which inspired my thoughts of studying was a mixture of what I saw while traveling around the world. Also, the idea to be creative, and a new incubation of one's self, and how I saw things. At that rate, and because of such, I will be working until I drop, to make up for all the offbeat and magnificent years of glorious travel, years of studies, life experiences, and a world full of memories and acquaintances, from a lifetime ago.

1988- Europe and get engaged in Venice (brought our rings just in case), tried to get married in Innsbruck, Austria while visiting friend Eva P. from 1976 and 1982 trips, but the local bureaucrat says "THIS IS NOT LAS VEGAS, YOU HAVE TO WRITE TO VIENNA 6 MONTHS IN ADVANCE..."

1990-2019 - Starting a family was a whole new adventure! Between 1995 -2016 there were approximately 1,200 basketball, baseball, soccer, lacrosse, volleyball, track, crew(rowing) games and competitions, Irish dance offs , dance performances, chorus, band, plays/musicals, drug quiz, talent shows. etc. It was all worth it, and is worth it, in mind, body and soul!

TO BE CONTINUED ☺

Thanks to my family and friends who supported me in many ways in this endeavor, especially Zoe O', Tess O', Kevin O', Dan O', Deacon F. Tommy G., Danny D., Vince E., Tim P., Sue M., Julie S., Sam V., Greg H., John S. and Nancy R. ☺

CPSIA information can be obtained
at www.ICGtesting.com
Printed in the USA
BVHW060354151222
654221BV00022B/1128